"'Tricia Williams's probing, patient study has brought real insight and empathy to a neglected aspect of Christian spirituality and discipleship. Her findings provide new understanding of the faith of people living with dementia and a rich resource for those of us who would like to accompany them on their way. Academics, clinicians, caregivers, and pastors will all benefit from reading this book."

—**PETER KEVERN**
Staffordshire University

"Attentiveness, integrity, rigor, and wisdom are key features of this book. Its carefully and meticulously organized chapters open up the life and faith of those living with memory change. It is written within the framework of practical theology and models good practice in qualitative research. Williams has made an important contribution to the field of dementia, faith, and pastoral care. I hope that it will be both read and acted on."

—**JAMES WOODWARD**
Sarum College

"There is a great beauty in listening to people whose voices are often silenced or overlooked. When we come close to people living with dementia, we discover surprising things and open up new and vital possibilities. In this thoughtful and compassionate book 'Tricia Williams helps to bring to the fore the voices of people with dementia as people reflect on and work through vital issues of faith and the impact that dementia has on this aspect of people's lives. As we are enabled to listen carefully, so we are allowed to share in deep insights which will lead to new theological and practical possibilities."

—**JOHN SWINTON**
University of Aberdeen

"Dr. Williams's invaluable, pioneering study opens up the experience of evangelical Christians with dementia by listening with care and thought to these people, and thereby opens windows into their lives which were previously closed. This well-constructed project collects valuable experiential data and provides thoughtful and engaging reflection on the experiences of evangelical Christians with dementia, in conversation with theology and Scripture. It will inform, stimulate, and challenge churches to be better stewards of their members with dementia by advocating on their behalf. Highly recommended!"

—STEVE WALTON
Trinity College, Bristol

What Happens to Faith When Christians Get Dementia?

What Happens to Faith When Christians Get Dementia?

The Faith Experience and Practice of Evangelical Christians Living with Mild to Moderate Dementia

'Tricia Williams

☞PICKWICK *Publications* · Eugene, Oregon

WHAT HAPPENS TO FAITH WHEN CHRISTIANS GET DEMENTIA?
The Faith Experience and Practice of Evangelical Christians Living with Mild to Moderate
Dementia

Pickwick Publications
An Imprint of Wipf and Stock Publishers
199 W. 8th Ave., Suite 3
Eugene, OR 97401

www.wipfandstock.com

PAPERBACK ISBN: 978-1-7252-7213-2
HARDCOVER ISBN: 978-1-7252-7214-9
EBOOK ISBN: 978-1-7252-7215-6

Cataloguing-in-Publication data:

Names: Williams, 'Tricia, author.

Title: What happens to faith when Christians get dementia? : the faith experience and practice of evangelical Christians living with mild to moderate dementia / 'Tricia Williams.

Description: Eugene, OR: Pickwick Publications, 2021 | Includes bibliographical references and index.

Identifiers: ISBN 978-1-7252-7213-2 (paperback) | ISBN 978-1-7252-7214-9 (hardcover) | ISBN 978-1-7252-7215-6 (ebook)

Subjects: LCSH: Dementia—Religious aspects—Christianity | Memory—Religious aspects—Christianity | Dementia—Patients—Religious life | Pastoral care

Classification: BT732.4 W55 2021 (print) | BT732.4 (ebook)

01/21/21

For disciples of Jesus
who are walking through
the shadows of dementia.

Contents

List of Figures

Acknowledgments

I AM INDEBTED TO Professor John Swinton, my PhD supervisor, whose wisdom, thoughtfulness, rigorous questioning, patient support (and good humor) enabled me to complete my research and thesis.[1] I am deeply grateful for his profound thinking in the area of faith and dementia which has contributed greatly to my own curiosity and search for understanding. I am also grateful to the University of Aberdeen for enabling me to carry out this research, and to the Bible Society,[2] who part-funded my PhD study. I am thankful to James Gordon and Margaret Goodall, the examiners of the thesis, for their careful work and reflection on this. I am also very grateful for the skillful support of the Pickwick publishing team who have brought this work to publication. I am especially thankful to the participants in the research project, who were living with dementia during the time of the study, and to their families and friends, who made this research possible. Thank you for your grace and courage in being willing to take part. My thanks also to my dear family (including "my cat Jeoffrey"!) and friends, whose loving support has upheld me in this work. Especial thanks to my husband for his patience, critical faithfulness, and willing endurance throughout the writing of the thesis and

1. This book arises from my PhD thesis, lightly edited for this publication. For the original thesis, see Williams, "What Happens to Faith When Christians Get Dementia?"

2. Bible Society, Stonehill Green, Westlea, Swindon, SN5 7DG. For more information, see www.biblesociety.org.uk.

this book. Above all, I am thankful to God who brought me to this work. His love sustains me and particularly those disciples of Jesus I have met who were living with dementia.

Scripture Abbreviations

·

ALL SCRIPTURE QUOTATIONS ARE taken from the New Revised Standard Version, Anglicised Edition, unless another version indicated, as follows:

ESV   English Standard Version

NASB   New American Standard Bible

NIVUK   New International Version

NLT   New Living Translation

1

Introduction

THIS CHAPTER PRESENTS THE issue for investigation and begins to indicate its significance for evangelical Christians living with dementia, for the community of Christian faith and for theology. The discussion outlines the goals and outcomes for the research and its rationale. I describe my own situated-ness in the evangelical faith tradition and how my interest in this subject arose, and discuss the terms used in the book title. Recognizing that there are a range of views, I also explore my understanding of the word "evangelical" as used in this research. I will consider this further in chapter 2, discussing how this understanding relates to the field of Practical Theology, the location of this research. In the final section of this introductory chapter, there is a brief overview of the book, which outlines the structure I have used to fulfil the goals of this study.

The Problem

Recent research suggests that dementia is one of today's most feared diseases.[1] At this time, there are around 850,000 people living with dementia in the UK. By 2050, that figure is projected to rise to over two million.[2] The term "Dementia" covers a range of illnesses, for example Alzheimer's Disease or Lewy Bodies Disease.[3] Each one affects a different

1. Saga, "Dementia More Feared Than Cancer."
2. Alzheimer's Research UK, "Facts and Stats."
3. Alzheimer's Society, "Types of Dementia."

part of the brain and consequently has impact on different capacities, although bringing a range of characteristic symptoms. In the early stages, many types of dementia begin with memory loss. Cognitive function is progressively severely affected, eventually bringing loss of ability to think rationally, and loss of a sense of time and place. To the observer, the person in advanced dementia may appear to have lost both rational and relational capacities, and with these, some would suggest, their personhood.[4] Stephen Post comments:

> The most urgent bioethical problem of our time may not be death but dementia and the hypercognitive idea that forgetful persons are already in the house of the dead.[5]

For the Christian from the evangelical tradition, the questions raised by dementia, are especially pertinent to the presuppositions involved in having such faith. These particularly concern the emphases on cognitive assent to propositional truths, and on personal, responsive relationship with God, which seem dependent on the notion of personhood. Keck has aptly described dementia as the "theological disease"[6] which, as Swinton summarizes, "erodes the very essence of the self and raises profound existential questions about personhood, love, sin and salvation."[7] If evangelical faith is presumed to be dependent on the cognitive aspects of belief and relationality, then it would seem that such faith is threatened by the advent of dementia. For those who are in the early stages of living with dementia, the prognoses are frightening, bringing threat to self and faith. MacKinlay discusses this in her work with Bryden who is in the early stages of her dementia:

> As she struggled with these factors that went to the core of who she was, this question of "would she lose God?" became a crucial one for her. From the Christian perspective, God would still be there, but the other question, "would she still have a sense of God being there?" was a different matter.[8]

---

4. Keck, *Forgetting Whose We Are*, 22–24.

5. Post, *Moral Challenge of Alzheimer Disease*, 136.

6. Keck, *Forgetting Whose We Are*, 14–15.

7. Swinton, *Dementia*, 9.

8. MacKinlay, "Walking with a Person," 43.

Where such faith is core to identity, it is a most significant area for well-being as the disease develops.[9] As Sabat's concept of malignant social positioning suggests, acceleration of decline and damage occur when this important aspect of the self-narrative is neglected.[10]

A recent government paper stressed that, in caring for those with dementia: "The whole person needs to be considered" and this includes their spiritual well-being.[11] Kevern, discussing the Department of Health's paper, "Living Well with Dementia,"[12] asserts the importance of learning about and addressing the spiritual needs of those with dementia, suggesting that: "The theological implications of a dementia diagnosis may be as important as early engagement with its financial or practical consequences."[13] Shamy concurs:

> Neglect of the spiritual dimension of care seriously impoverishes the quality of life for people just as surely as neglect of the physical dimension—though the latter may be more apparent.[14]

This book therefore seeks to discover deeper understanding of the faith experience and practice of Christians with dementia from the evangelical tradition.

A hermeneutic phenomenological approach is used for the qualitative research with Christians in the early to moderate stages of their illness. The qualitative research, and the theological reflections which follow, are conducted in order to bring insight to the spiritual lives of those who are living with this illness. It also aims to resource communities of faith with increased understanding to enable their support of those who live with dementia. Addressing the spiritual needs of Christians with dementia may be, I propose, more important than other aspects of care for the individual person's life.

9. MacKinlay and Trevitt, *Finding Meaning*, 22–24.

10. Sabat, "Mind, Meaning, and Personhood in Dementia," 287–302; Kitwood, *Dementia Reconsidered*, 48.

11. DHSC, "Joint Declaration."

12. See DHSC, "Living Well with Dementia."

13. Kevern, "I Pray that I Will Not Fall," 293.

14. Shamy, *Guide to the Spiritual Dimension of Care*, 60.

The Research Situation

There has been a growing body of writing and research in the area of dementia and Christian spirituality in recent years, for example, demonstrated in the works of Jewell, and the work and research of Snyder, Dalby, Katsuno and Stuckey.[15] There are also an increasing number of studies which have focused on spiritual well-being and spirituality as a "coping mechanism," for example in the research of Beuscher and Grando and of Jolley, Benbow, Grizzell, Willmott, Bawn, and Kingston.[16] Scholars such as Kevern and Hudson have focused more specifically on dementia and Christian faith.[17] There is also a growing response to this issue in pastoral literature, for example, Crowther's work on pastoral approaches for those on the dementia journey.[18] Keck and Swinton have written significant theological accounts of dementia.[19]

However, there has hitherto been a paucity of writing and research which has explored the faith experience of Christians of the evangelical tradition, apart from the notable autobiographical accounts of Bryden and Davis.[20] Whereas the research of scholars such as Snyder, Stuckey and Katsuno have looked at the broad area of religiosity and religious practice, this has not focused specifically on the subjective faith experience of Christians. In particular, there is little research which has considered the significant questions which the disease and its prognoses raise for evangelical faith, or, how indeed, the experience of dementia illuminates understanding of that faith.

In addition, there has been little investigation where, as Karen MacKinlay notes, "researchers actually converse with the person with dementia," yet this is clearly an important area of understanding.[21] Snyder comments:

---

15. Jewell, *Spirituality and Personhood in Dementia*; Snyder, "Satisfactions and Challenges," 299–313; Dalby et al., "Lived Experience," 75–94; Katsuno, "Personal Spirituality," 315–35; Stuckey, "Blessed Assurance," 69–84.

16. Beuscher and Grando, "Using Spirituality to Cope," 583–98; Jolley et al., "Spirituality and Faith in Dementia," 311–25.

17. Hudson, "God's Faithfulness and Dementia," 50–67.

18. Crowther, *Sustaining Persons*.

19. Keck, *Forgetting Whose We Are*; Swinton, *Dementia*.

20. Bryden, *Dancing with Dementia*; Davis, *My Journey into Alzheimer's Disease*.

21. MacKinlay, "Listening to People with Dementia," 91–106.

Although much of the literature speaks sensitively to the perceived spiritual needs of persons with dementia, there is a relative absence of commentary from the individuals to whom these services are directed. Rarely do we hear the direct testimonies of those diagnosed or learn of their experiences or needs.[22]

Whilst those living with advanced dementia may find it difficult to participate in conversation, those in the earlier stages may be willing and able to contribute to research. This stage of their illness provides, therefore, a valuable opportunity to learn and understand more about their experience. Bryden writes:

> All of us travelling this journey have a right to be heard, to be listened to, and to be regarded with respect. There is no time to lose to hear our voice as we struggle to communicate.[23]

However, such commentary can be difficult to obtain. For example, the person with dementia may be experiencing increasing difficulties with spoken communication and concentration. Another issue is the sensitivity of the person themselves about their illness or the anxiety of their loved-ones who are frequently the gate-keepers for such research.[24] However, in recognizing the importance of such lived experience, the qualitative research in this study set out to hear the voices of those with dementia, believing that not to do so is to miss a huge opportunity to gain insight from those who live with this illness.[25]

Whilst many studies have focused on later stages of dementia, there is increasing recognition of the importance of the spiritual lives of persons of faith in the early to moderate stages of the disease.[26] There are different definitions of the "stages" of these progressive illnesses and the course of a dementia illness varies from person to person,[27] but in this book I use the terms "early" to describe the symptoms of those who are recently diagnosed and are beginning to notice cognitive difficulties, and "moderate" to describe those who have lived with dementia for a number of years and for whom conversation is possible, but is becoming more

22. Snyder, "Satisfactions and Challenges," 300.

23. Bryden, *Dancing with Dementia*, 48.

24. MacKinlay and Trevitt, *Finding Meaning*, 38–39.

25. Robinson, "Should People with Alzheimer's," 104.

26. Kevern, "I Pray that I Will Not Fall," 293.

27. Shamy, *Guide to the Spiritual Dimension of Care*, 50.

challenging. Research into the earlier stages is significant for the person's ongoing and later well-being. Post comments:

> The person with a diagnosis of AD [Alzheimer's disease] must deal with a terrible sense of loss, at least until he or she no longer has insight into that loss. These persons usually want a great deal of pastoral care if religion and spirituality are important in their coping strategies.[28]

Hattam has highlighted the gap which sometimes exists between diagnosis and provision of services to support the person with dementia.[29] This is true as much for the spiritual well-being of the person as for financial and practical arrangements. This study aims to make a contribution towards the repair of this gap, allowing the voices of evangelical Christians with early to moderate dementia to be heard as participants in the transformative conversation of practical theology.

Summary of the Goals and Outcomes for the Research

The goals:

(i) To gain new understanding of how Christians from an evangelical tradition with mild to moderate symptoms of dementia experience faith and faith practice;

(ii) To gain fresh insights into theological understanding of evangelical faith through the lens of dementia.

This will result in:

(i) Deeper understandings of the nature of evangelical faith experience of Christians living with dementia;

(ii) New understanding for the community of faith, enabling more effective spiritual care of evangelical Christians living with dementia;

(iii) Fresh theological insights into evangelical Christian faith in the light of dementia;

(iv) New insights that will be helpful in providing faith sustaining resources for Christians who live with dementia.[30]

28. Post, *Moral Challenge of Alzheimer Disease*, 11.
29. Hattam, "Mind the Gap."
30. See also description of initial motivation for the research in the "Context of the

The Research Rationale

The book will contribute new insights and understanding in this area through the following means.

- Qualitative research. A hermeneutical phenomenological approach is used to explore the lived faith experience of Christians from the evangelical tradition who are living with early to moderate symptoms of dementia. I propose that, as others have discovered,[31] this is a particularly appropriate approach to understanding experience of this stage of dementia, "as a qualitative interpretive methodology lends itself well to the research purpose of understanding the phenomenon of early stage AD."[32] The hermeneutic phenomenological research will be an important participant in the overall conversation of the book.

- Reflection on key theological issues arising from the lived experience and from the literature will contribute to the response to the book's core question and the pastoral implications which emerge.

Dementia brings profound questions, particularly for those of evangelical faith, such as what it means to be a person and what is the meaning of faith if cognitive capacities are under threat. For those recently diagnosed with dementia and their loved-ones, such questions are matters of great concern.

The research will draw especially on a phenomenological study with eight individuals who are in the early to moderate stages of dementia. The small number of participants[33] is consistent with methodologies in the field of Practical Theology which look for thick, rich descriptions of unique experiences in order to deepen understanding and bring new insights to the subject.[34] Research participants were selected from these stages of the illness because at this point in their experience of dementia, all had understanding of the purposes of the research, capacity for use of language, a sense of linear time, and imaginative awareness of the

---

Research" section below.

31. See, for example, MacQuarrie, "Experiences in Early Alzheimer's Disease," 430–41; Dalby et al., "Lived Experience."

32. MacQuarrie, "Experiences in Early Alzheimer's Disease," 430.

33. Clarke and Keady, "Getting Down to Brass Tacks," 34. Clarke and Keady draw here on Cotrell and Schulz, "Perspective of the Patient," 205–11.

34. Swinton and Mowat, *Practical Theology*, 122–23.

future.[35] The gap between diagnosis and the development of advanced symptoms provides an opportunity to hear from the people who are best placed to help us to gain a fuller understanding of the experience of their disease, both in the present and in their anticipation of the future.[36]

The research has sought to listen carefully to those living with this disease, then brings their experience into mutual dialogue with reflection on theological questions which have emerged from the qualitative research. The analysis of this and the theological reflections bring implications which, it is hoped, will contribute to important changes towards transforming pastoral practice.

The Context of the Research

This book is written within the context of my field of Practical Theology which I consider in the following chapter. My own faith has been formed within the evangelical tradition, and has placed a high value on Scripture. My research has, in part, been funded by the Bible Society who aim to make the Scriptures accessible to all.

Orienting to the Experience of Faith and Dementia

My interest in this area of faith and dementia has arisen out my personal context and experience. In my publishing role as creative developer of Bible resources with an evangelical Christian organization, I was concerned with faith nurture and discipleship through the means of Bible engagement and prayer. My interest in the faith support of those living with dementia was initially prompted by a friend seeking appropriate devotional resources for his wife who was living with dementia. She was finding regular Bible-reading difficult due to diminishing cognitive capacities. This led to conversations with experts, engagement with apposite literature, and, in due course, the publication of resources.[37] In turn, this has resulted in my involvement with workshops and conferences concerning faith and dementia. It was this publishing project and the associated workshops which led me to want to investigate further the

---

35. Alzheimer's Society, "Progression of Alzheimer's Disease."
36. Robinson, "Should People with Alzheimer's," 104.
37. Williams, *Words of Faith*; *Words of Hope*; *Words of Peace*.

faith experience of those who were living with dementia, and to begin the work of this book.

My involvement in a volunteer chaplaincy team at a home for those living with dementia has also contributed to my learning about the experience of faith and dementia. A further factor in shaping my own understanding is that I live with a chronic illness myself. My primary progressive Multiple Sclerosis is, of course, a different condition from that under investigation here. Yet, some of its symptoms and effects mean that I can identify imaginatively with some of the issues which confront Christians who are beginning to live with dementia.

In my publishing role, I was aiming to serve those of an evangelical faith tradition, and it is the faith experience of Christians such as these, who live with dementia, that this book sets out to explore. In the following, I consider a key aspect of this research: the nature of faith identity and understanding of evangelicalism as used in this study.

Understanding of Evangelical Faith

The term "evangelical" in contemporary society has, as Greggs describes, "a rainbow-like variety of meanings."[38] It transcends denominational boundaries, including a spectrum of emphases from protestant reformed, through to open evangelicalism in the Church of England and free churches, to the charismatic emphases found, for example, in today's network of New Wine churches.[39] The participants in the qualitative study reflect this range. All were deeply committed to their faith. This was not the "extrinsic religiousness" dependent on church-going and religious practices.[40] Rather it is the "intrinsic faith," where a sense of relationship with God has been internalized, shapes values and moment-by-moment living. Rowan Williams, writes of this from the perspective of being a disciple of Jesus: "Discipleship is about how we live; not just the decisions we make, not just the things we believe, but a state of being."[41]

My purpose in the following is not to embark on an in-depth theological discussion of evangelicalism, but rather to provide a contextual

---

38. Greggs, *New Perspectives for Evangelical Theology*, 5.

39. Bebbington, "Evangelical Trends, 1959–2009," 93–106; New Wine (www.newwine.org).

40. Swinton, *Spirituality and Mental Health Care*, 31.

41. Williams, *Being Disciples*, 1.

description for the research. I highlight aspects which are of particular significance for this study and the theological reflections.

"Always on the Way"

A key definition of evangelicalism is found in Bebbington's historical account of evangelicalism, often referred to as the "Bebbington Quadrilateral."[42] He describes four attributes (conversionism, activism, biblicism, crucicentrism) which have been seen as static, transcending cultural and historical context. Today, however, whilst these aspects are still important, many evangelical theologians recognize that theology and practice are inevitably integrated and shaped by social context.[43] This is giving rise to changing expressions of contemporary evangelicalism in the western post-modern context.[44] As Congdon and McMaken write in *Christianity Today*: "There is no single right way to be an evangelical. In truth, evangelicalism is always *in via*, always 'on the way.'"[45]

Ongoing diversification and realignments are seen in the different groupings of evangelicals from the conservatives, through the "open," to the charismatics.[46] Whilst Bebbington's more recent discussion concludes that "the former unity of evangelicalism had been broken," Stanley, in his account of evangelicalism, points out that the movement has always been fluid and diverse.[47] In this book, I assume this dynamic understanding of a developing evangelicalism as considered, for example, by Greggs.[48] Despite the different perspectives and understandings, there seems to be agreement in the following areas which are all envisaged as being Christ-centered and "in the light of the Word."[49]

---

42. Bebbington, *Evangelicalism in Modern Britain*, 2–3.

43. Harris, "Beyond Bebbington," 201–19.

44. Seen, for example, in movements such as "Fresh Expressions" and "Emerging Church."

45. Congdon and McMaken, "Ten Reasons Why Theology Matters"; Greggs, "Introduction," 1–13.

46. Stanley, *Global Diffusion of Evangelicalism*, 236.

47. Bebbington, "Evangelical Trends," 93–106; Stanley, *Global Diffusion of Evangelicalism*, 27.

48. Greggs, "Introduction," 1–13.

49. Gutiérrez, *Theology of Liberation*, 13.

Relationship with Christ

A sense of transcendent relationship with God through Christ is a key aspect, understood to be brought about by Spirit-mediated re-birth into God's family.[50] The starting point of this relationship has often been understood as indicating a crisis, life-changing event akin to St. Paul's conversion experience on the road to Damascus when he met the risen Jesus (see Acts 9:1–19). Today, there is "a greater openness to conversion as a journey towards the cross and an embrace of its message."[51] Such Spirit-mediated faith is dependent on the death of Christ on the cross and his resurrection, and its appropriation, bringing forgiveness of sin and eschatological hope for the future.

In spite of a more open and relational understanding of what it means to come to faith, biblical understanding of the "new birth" still eventually seems to be dependent on the individual's rational capacity to affirm faith and commitment in intentional, responsive relationship with God.[52] For Christians in the earlier stages of living with developing dementia and declining cognitive capacity this brings crucial questions such as "Who will I be?"[53] and "What will happen to my faith when I can no longer remember?"[54]

This relationship with God is not static but, following the New Testament model (see, e.g., Acts 2:42–47), is dynamic and grows through attention to Bible reflection (God's Word), individual and corporate prayer, and participation in communal worship and teaching. As concentration and cognitive understanding decline in dementia, important questions arise about how the growing spiritual life of those with dementia can be recognized and supported.

---

50. Zahl, "Reformation Pessimism," 80–81. See John 3:1–8: "You must be born again" (John 3:7); Rom 8:15–17: "You received the Spirit of sonship. And by him we cry, 'Abba, Father.' The Spirit himself testifies with our spirit that we are God's children."

51. Harris, "Beyond Bebbington," 205; Peace, *Conversion in the New Testament,* 4–5. Peace considers the Pauline conversion alongside "the unfolding conversion of the Twelve" in the Gospel of Mark, as their understanding of Christ and his mission grew.

52. This has arisen from some evangelical interpretations of Rom 10:9: "If you confess with your mouth, 'Jesus is Lord,' and believe in your heart that God raised him from the dead, you will be saved"; Gaventa, "Which Human? What Response?" 50–64.

53. MacKinlay, "Walking with a Person into Dementia," 46.

54. Shamy, *Guide to the Spiritual Dimension of Care,* 21.

Relationship with Others

The individualistic emphasis of evangelicalism arising from its view of personal encounter and relationship with Christ, is being challenged by a more holistic vision of "missional communities of invitation, welcome and embrace."[55] Christ's challenge to Nicodemus of "You must be born again" (see John 3:1–8) remains a central notion in the faith of evangelicals, bringing together the salvific work of God the Father, Jesus the Son and the Holy Spirit, and for the believer a sense of a transcendent, personal relationship with God.[56] However, this is increasingly balanced with more attention being focused on belonging to the believing community as the body of Christ. New Testament biblical faith is inherently relational with the church being typified in Paul's writing as "the body of Christ," in which both the whole and every part is significant (1 Cor 12). Harris writes: "While in modernity, evangelical apologetics could deal in certainties and sure proofs, in a postmodern era, a relational apologetic has been birthed."[57] This mutuality of faith in relationship with others in the body of Christ is profoundly significant for those living with developing dementia. This perspective on faith is both challenging and motivating in the quest for understanding about how the belonging-ness of those with dementia can be expressed and affirmed within their communities of faith.

Mission

Spreading the Good News of Jesus Christ has been a priority for evangelicals in response to the injunctions of scripture such as that in Matthew 28:19: "Go and make disciples of all nations." The word "mission" has often been used to refer principally to the church's role in preaching the gospel with the goal of making converts.[58] Perhaps missing, in the past, has been an emphasis on the ongoing nature of discipling followers of Jesus. However, in recent years a broader understanding of the term "mission" has emerged. Bosch's seminal work *Transforming Mission* changes the perspective, reminding the reader that the mission of God (*missio*

---

55. Harris, "Beyond Bebbington," 213.

56. Zahl, "Reformation Pessimism," 80–81.

57. Harris, "Beyond Bebbington," 212.

58. Harris, "Beyond Bebbington," 204; McGrath, *Evangelicalism*, 55–56.

Dei) provides the narrative for God's action in the world, supremely demonstrated through the embodied life of Jesus, in his ministry and redemptive work through the cross and resurrection.[59] The transforming mission of God, therefore, impacts every aspect of human life and community. So, whilst personal encounter with Christ is significant, for some, a more holistic vision is emerging of "missional communities."[60] Dementia prompts questions about how this transforming *missio Dei* is embodied and expressed in the faith community in ways which embrace and "disciple" those who live with this disease.

The Bible

Belief in the central role of the Bible and its authority is a defining hallmark of evangelicalism. There is however great diversity amongst evangelical scholars in the way scripture is understood and interpreted.[61] My own evangelical tradition has emphasized commitment to the whole Bible, with awareness of the contextual (as it was written, as it is read and as it is lived out) and to a christological understanding, with Scripture ultimately relating to Jesus Christ. The devotional practice of regular, prayerful Bible reading, both corporate and personal, is perceived as a way of meeting with God, undertaken in humility and dependence on the Holy Spirit.[62] Many evangelicals have followed this practice as a key element in their relationship with God, and this has been a significant part of their faith lives. The experience of Christians living with dementia raises questions about how their illness affects their understanding of the Bible and the ways in which its importance is expressed in their lives.

Harris summarizes the essential characteristics of evangelicalism in the post-modern era in this way. A community of people who are

> gathered around a deeper and more expansive understanding of the cross, . . . committed to a holistic view of salvation (including but moving beyond mere conversionism), and shaped by the transforming narrative of the acts of the God and Father

---

59. Bosch, *Transforming Mission*, xv.
60. For example, "Seeker Sensitive" churches and the Willow Creek movement.
61. Briggs, "Bible Before Us," 15.
62. Hoggarth, *Seed and the Soil*, 145–47.

of our Lord Jesus Christ, as illuminated in the Spirit inspired
Scriptures (more than mere biblicism).[63]

This book seeks to explore how this faith can be expressed authentically
both by Christians living with dementia, and by implication, the communities of faith to which they belong.

Whilst using the term "evangelical" in this book to mean a movement which is dynamic and fluid, I recognize that some members of the
tradition may not agree with the open definitions of evangelicalism described above.[64] Greggs's approach invites evangelicals to strive with the
reality of God and the truth of Scripture in "the contexts and situations"
of today's world.[65] For this study, that means wrestling with the questions
and challenges that dementia brings to biblical understanding of faith.

In the conversation of Practical Theology, this will mean not de-
limiting in advance where the Word of God leads, but allowing the Bible
to be a "genuine partner in the conversation."[66] This is discussed further
in the following chapter in consideration of the relationship between
evangelicalism and the research field of Practical Theology.

Book Overview

This study sets out to bring deeper understanding and new insights into the
faith of evangelical Christians living with the early to moderate stages of
dementia. In doing so, it aims to contribute to the church's and para-church
organizations' ability to provide appropriate spiritual care for those who
are living with dementia, and, in doing this, to facilitate their continuing
spiritual growth and their contribution to the community of faith.

Chapter 1 has introduced the topic, proposing the need for the research, discussing its rationale and providing a summary of goals and
outcomes. It provides context for the book's question with discussion of
how the key term "evangelical" is understood.

Chapter 2 considers the research field of Practical Theology in
which this study is located. It discusses the ways in which its methodology and methods are especially suited to this research with its particular focus on evangelicalism.

63. Harris, *Beyond Bebbington*, 213.

64. Greggs, "Introduction," 1–13.

65. Greggs, "Introduction," 3.

66. Briggs, "Bible Before Us," 19.

Chapter 3 explores writing and research pertinent to the core question and, in particular, to the experience of the lived experience of early to moderate dementia. This literature review, arising out of the methodological foundations, will take a hermeneutical approach which aims, as Smythe and Spence discuss, "to provide context and provoke thinking on the phenomenon" of interest.[67] In doing so, it becomes a partner in the conversation of the book.

Chapter 4 describes the methodology used for the qualitative research. Drawing on the philosophies of Heidegger and Gadamer, it uses a hermeneutical phenomenological approach in order to gain deeper understanding of the lived experience of evangelical Christians living with early-moderate symptoms of dementia. The chapter describes the methodology used in this study, and the philosophical basis underlying the approach.

Chapter 5 describes the design of the research, introduces the participants, and describes how the research was conducted.

Chapter 6, following a hermeneutical phenomenological approach to the qualitative study, presents the data in the form of thematic analysis,[68] highlighting themes which emerged from the conversations with the study's participants. These include: transforming faith: responding to dementia; memory funding faith; knowing God in dementia; faith in practice; finding meaning in dementia.

Chapters 7–9 reflect on the experience of walking through the shadow of dementia as a person of faith. Using a model of orientation, disorientation and reorientation,[69] it reflects on key theological themes in response to the book title, and to the insights which emerge from the lived experience.

- *"Orientation"* considers what it means for those living with dementia to be created in the image of God and to find their identity in Christ.

- *"Disorientation"* reflects on the experience of walking through times of adversity and struggle as a person of faith living with dementia.

67. Smythe and Spence, "Re-Viewing Literature in Hermeneutic Research," 12.

68. Manen, *Researching Lived Experience*, 90–92.

69. Used by Brueggemann in his exploration of the Psalms. See Brueggemann, *Praying the Psalms*, 3; *Spirituality of the Psalms*, viii.

- *"Reorienation"* seeks theological understanding of faith response to the advent of dementia. It focuses particularly on the relationship between memory and faith and then, in the light of the lived experience of participants in the research, reflects on a New Testament model of response to suffering.

In keeping with both the hermeneutical circle of hermeneutic phenomenology and the dialectic approach of practical theology, these reflections will draw other voices into the conversation too. This conversation of faith takes place "in the light of the Word." In line with Swinton's method of re-description from a biblical perspective of the Bible,[70] it will seek to uncover new insights into the faith experience of those living with dementia, and to reflect on how these illuminate an evangelical theological understanding of faith.

Chapter 10 presents a summary of findings and considers the implications which emerge, seeking resonance with other research and writing in this area. I then make recommendations towards the desired outcomes of this research as described in chapter 1. Limitations of the research are also considered, leading to questions and issues which arise for further research, towards faithful practice.

70. Swinton, *Dementia*, 19–21.

2

The Research Field

Practical Theology

IN THIS CHAPTER I describe and discuss the research field of Practical Theology in which this study is located. My aim is to show how the methodology and methods of Practical Theology provide a hospitable location for this study, and in particular, its focus of evangelicalism. In the last section, I describe Osmer's four tasks of Practical Theology which are used to provide a structure for the book.

The Work of Practical Theology

The discipline of Practical Theology developed from its early concerns with the working out of theology in the context of church ministry, and how theology might be applied in practical contexts.[1] Today, practical theology is, as Osmer discusses, no longer "solely concerned with application with helpful techniques and skills applied to the life of the church."[2] Rather, it is based on an understanding of the synchronicity of theology and practice, where theological understanding might arise *from* the lived experience of people in today's context.

Contemporary practical theology, therefore, situates its work in a range of situations, both lay and clerical, in the community of faith and public arenas, wherever practitioners (for example, ministers, health care workers, teachers, editors) envision their work as theological enterprise.

1. Schleiermacher, *Christian Caring.*
2. Osmer, *Practical Theology*, 9.

My own work, as developer and editor of faith resources, prompted my early thinking about the meaning of faith for people living with dementia, and how their spiritual lives might be supported in their journey with this disease (for example, through Bible reading and prayer).

Increasingly, leading practical theologians argue that there has been a false dichotomy between the theory of faith and its practice.[3] In Scripture, Jesus the Word (*Logos*) came into the world in embodied form: "The Word became flesh and made his dwelling among us" (John 1:14).[4] It is in the embodied action of the incarnation that God the Father is revealed. Swinton points to God's love, with its consequent embodied love of neighbor, as the central tenet of Christian faith: "Love the Lord your God. . . . Love your neighbor" (Matt 22:37, 39). Hence, he concludes, "Intellectual knowledge requires embodiment if it is faithfully to participate in the practices of love."[5] Root extends this idea of the mutuality of theology and practice in his concept of "Christopraxis," arguing that "theology . . . can *only* be practical" as theologically demonstrated in the practical act of God in Jesus "ministering to creation."[6] Reflection on encounter with God in lived experience and the transformative implications of this for individuals and their communities underlie the goals of practical theology.

Practical Theology concludes that lived experience precedes cognitive knowledge of theory, but also that theory and practice have a reciprocal relationship in which both have a role in the faithful practice of God's purposes. It is this "critical faithfulness"[7] which shapes the vision for this book as I consider the experience of faith for those in the early to moderate stages of living with dementia. This reciprocity is worked out in the methods of practical theology which I consider below.

3. See, for example, Swinton and Mowat, *Practical Theology*; Root, *Christopraxis*; Swinton, *Becoming Friends of Time*, 5–6.

4. See McFadyen, "Embodied Christianity," 127.

5. Swinton, *Becoming Friends of Time*, 5–6.

6. Root, *Christopraxis*, 94–95.

7. Swinton and Mowat, *Practical Theology*, 93.

Tasks, Methods, and Models

Four Core Tasks

At the heart of Practical Theology is the activity of theological reflection on lived experience. Osmer elucidates four core tasks which are involved in this.[8] Although his work mainly assumes a congregational context, these tasks function as helpful markers for the exploration and reflection in this book. These are:

- The descriptive-empirical task, which considers the question: What is going on?
- The interpretive task, which asks: Why is this going on?
- The normative task, responding to the question: What ought to be going on?
- The pragmatic task, in conversation with others, asks: How might we respond?

These tasks don't indicate a linear structure, and may be weighted differently in a particular project, but nevertheless, are defining, integral tasks in the work of practical theology and in this book. These are represented in this book in the Introduction, in the discussion of the literature and methodology, in the accounts of lived experience, in the theological reflection and in the consideration of the implications for pastoral practice (see Fig.1).

8. Osmer, *Practical Theology*, 4.

The Four Tasks of Practical Theology

1)	The descriptive-empirical task	What is going on?	Chapters 1–6. The task begins to be addressed through the Introduction and literature review, then in the hermeneutical phenomenological chapters (chapters 4–6).
2)	The interpretive task	Why is this going on?	Chapters 6–9. The lived experience and the theological reflections begin to reveal insight in response to the research question.
3)	The normative task	What ought to be going on?	Chapters 7–9. Theological reflections seek answers in the light of theology, Scripture, tradition and lived experience.
4)	The pragmatic task	How might we respond?	Chapter 10. Reflection on findings, resonance with other research and consideration of implications lead to suggestions for renewed, faithful practice.

Fig. 1. Outline of Book, Based on Osmer's Core Tasks of Practical Theological Interpretation[9]

The Pastoral Cycle

This approach for the book resonates with Practical Theology's pastoral cycle. Taking a hermeneutical phenomenological approach, the cycle begins with human experience, seeking "to be close to people's real experience of life."[10] It proceeds through reflection, drawing on the perspectives of theology, scripture, tradition and writing from other disciplines (for example, sociology and psychology), and then as different insights emerge and merge, new understandings come to light in ways which can transform our understanding and the situation. In a dynamic cycle, there is movement back and forth between the different stages, and the circle is

9. See Osmer, *Practical Theology*, 4.

10. Lartey, "Practical Theology as a Theological Form," 132.

ongoing as the context changes. It is Practical Theology's transformative task and goal, as Swinton and Mowat envision, to participate faithfully in God's mission, through "critical, theological reflection" on the lived experience of our contemporary world.[11]

Various models for facilitating this have been proposed. In this study I will draw on a mutually critical correlational approach. Whereas the Tillichian correlational approach sought to bring answers from theology to questions arising from different circumstances in life, the mutual critical correlational approach brings a dialectic perspective consonant with the pastoral cycle of Practical Theology.[12] As later discussion of the hermeneutical phenomenological approach to the qualitative research demonstrates, this cycle is set within the interpretative/hermeneutical paradigm, recognizing the situated-ness of all participants in the conversation.[13]

Pattison's critical conversation model provides another helpful way of imagining the mutually critical correlational approach.[14] Contributors to the discussion (for example, lived experience, scripture, tradition, writing from other disciplines, my own perceptions) are seen as participants in a conversation. The conversation model suggests a willingness to listen, allows discovery and disagreement, and expects change. This image has been held in view as the research has listened to the voices of those living with dementia in the light of scripture, the evangelical tradition and my own understandings.

Practical Theology and Evangelicalism

The nature of Practical Theology provides a hospitable location for learning and ministry in the evangelical faith tradition.[15] It has the capacity to honor significant characteristics of dynamic evangelicalism and, as such, is an authentic and effective vehicle for ministry in the chosen topic of this book. These are seen in its valuing of transcendent experience, its Christocentric focus, its social and relational dependence, its missiological and ministerial impetus, and its biblical perspective.

---

11. Swinton and Mowat, *Practical Theology*, 27, 6.

12. Hiltner, "Meaning and Importance of Pastoral Theology," 44–46; Browning, "Pastoral Theology in a Pluralistic Age," 93.

13. Swinton and Mowat, *Practical Theology*, 75.

14. Pattison, "Some Straw for the Bricks," 139–40.

15. See Root's discussion in his *Christopraxis*, ix–xv, 10.

Transcendent Experience of Relationship with God

A sense of personal relationship with God enabled through the work of Christ and the Holy Spirit is affirmed and assumed by evangelical Christians. However, such transcendent experience of God, whilst life-changing, is difficult to capture through some conventional social science methodologies. Practical Theology, on the other hand, is committed to understanding "unique, non-replicable experiences" which have unique potential, as Swinton and Mowat argue, to disclose meaningful knowledge.[16] Such ideographic knowledge is significant because the experience of faith brings profound changes to people's lives. This is demonstrated in scripture and in the lives of present-day Christians.[17] Root, citing his own personal experience, argues that whilst experience of God is transcendent, it is nevertheless for evangelical Christians "real . . . in the most practical way."[18] Of particular importance for this study, it allows the researcher to take seriously this "evangelical experience"[19] as it hears the voices of Christians living with dementia talk about their own experiences of faith and how this is enabling their response to their illness. This ability to access lived experience also resonates with the methodology of hermeneutic phenomenology which will provide the methodological approach for the qualitative study.

A Christocentric Focus

Fundamental to the transcendent spiritual experience of relationship with God is the centrality of Christ.[20] The evangelical sense of present relationship with God depends on the work of the cross bringing justification and the hope of resurrection. Root's *Christopraxis,* focusing on the divine/human encounter, provides rich exploration of this theme.[21] He envisages justification as a "significant framework" for Practical Theology, as the place where the divine meets human experience:

16. Swinton and Mowat, *Practical Theology,* 43.

17. For example, Moses' experience of the burning bush (Exod 3); the disciples' experience of the Resurrection (Matt 28).

18. Root, *Christopraxis,* x.

19. Root, *Christopraxis,* xi.

20. Hunsinger, *How to Read Karl Barth,* 229.

21. Root, *Christopraxis,* 90.

I turn to justification as a way to embrace and explore human experience as the location for the encounter with God's own ministry of being in becoming.[22]

Root uses this perspective to connect the lived experience of Christians with the theology of the intervening action of God at moments of hopelessness. The qualitative research in this study sets out to hear from Christians living with dementia about their experience of this encounter with Christ as they live with dementia.

Social and Relational Dependence

Practical Theology's pastoral cycle and conversational methods depend on listening carefully to different voices in order to deepen understanding in a particular area of faith. This activity reflects the theological model of community where accountability is provided in the body of Christ. Relational dependence, as an aspect of this, is profoundly relevant to the lives of people with dementia as their disease develops. Practical Theology is in itself a relational ministry which in this project aims to bring fresh insights into how the church can support Christians with dementia.

A Missiological and Ministerial Impetus

Seen as participant in the *missio Dei*, practical theology's methods reflect the missiological impetus and ministerial focus of evangelicalism, which bring together the lived-out encounter of divine and human action.[23] Its dynamic and transformative goals, represented in various models of circles and cycles, enable Christian ministry to pursue its missiological goals of change and growth in the light of experience (and of the Word).[24] Swinton and Mowat identify Practical Theology as a fundamentally missiological discipline which:

22. Root, *Christopraxis*, 123.

23. Root, *Christopraxis*, ix–xiii.

24. See for example, Lartey, "Practical Theology," 128–34; Green, *Let's Do Theology*, 24–32.

receives its purpose, its motivation and its dynamic from acknowledging and working out what it means to participate faithfully in God's mission.[25]

This brings impetus to this study of Christians living with dementia, not only seeking to discover new insights, but also to bring transformation through those new insights and understanding. This study itself is missiological in purpose.

A Biblical Perspective

As discussed earlier, an important question for the evangelical practical theologian concerns the way in which the Bible is understood as the authoritative Word of God.[26] For Pattison, the voice of Scripture is important: "A lengthy conversation with the text . . . stands at the heart of the worshipping community," but it remains one participant along with others.[27] Yet, for the evangelical, recognition that changing context inevitably shapes our understanding and interpretation—"prompting fresh perspectives for understanding of the Bible"—brings questions to their understanding of biblical authority.[28] The issue of dementia helps to bring this issue into sharper relief. With the changes that the illness brings to cognition and communication, the Bible is likely to be, and eventually, must be accessed in new ways and understood from fresh perspectives. Volpe brings insight for considering this in the context of dementia:

> The Church is constantly involved in meditation on the Scriptures in the light of past interpretation and in the face of new questions to which Jesus is the answer, and new situations in which the Spirit's power is desperately needed.[29]

Deusen-Hunsinger carefully defends the priority of theology and biblical revelation over any other dialogue partner.[30] But her argument raises the question: What *is* the definitive interpretation of Scripture? Within the limits of our context, interpretations differ and are incomplete.

---

25. Swinton and Mowat, *Practical Theology,* 27.

26. Root, *Christopraxis,* 99–100n33.

27. Pattison, *Critique of Pastoral Care,* 130; "Some Straw for the Bricks,"139.

28. Vanhoozer, *Is There a Meaning in This Text?* 460–61.

29. Volpe, "Living the Mystery," 98–99.

30. See Deusen-Hunsinger, *Theology and Pastoral Counselling.*

Yet, as Swinton and Mowat consider in their response, the difficulty of a mutually critical conversational approach for the authoritative voice of Scripture is that it might bring "unfettered interpretative dimensions."[31] Swinton and Mowat suggest a solution to this tension. Whilst holding onto "critical faithfulness" which "acknowledges the divine givenness of scripture and the . . . working of the Holy Spirit," the researcher takes seriously "the interpretative dimensions of the process of understanding revelation," with the understanding that all human beings are contextually limited.[32]

> Doing theology is an interpretative enterprise within which divine revelation is interpreted by human beings who are fallen, contextually bound and have a variety of different personal and denominational agendas.[33]

Faithful practice must involve a humble open-ness to new understandings of the Kingdom which are being revealed, and this requires constant reflexivity on the part of the practical theologian and this researcher. Hauerwas helpfully proposes that it is the Bible that "sets the agenda and boundaries" for the conversation.[34]

Further help with this tension of Scripture as conversation partner comes from Brueggemann, who offers help in how we imaginatively interpret scripture in the post-modern situation.[35] He talks of the artistry of reading Scripture as "redescribing the world."[36] Swinton picks up this motif of redescription and develops it as a practical theological method seeking redescription from the perspective of the Bible:

> The deeper task is to see what current understandings of dementia and the practices that emerge from them look like when they are viewed and redescribed from the perspective of the strange biblical world. . . . The task is to redescribe the world in the light of Scripture and tradition and to look carefully at what dementia really looks like within this strange new world.[37]

31. Swinton and Mowat, *Practical Theology*, 88.

32. Swinton and Mowat, *Practical Theology*, 93.

33. Swinton and Mowat, *Practical Theology*, 89.

34. Hauerwas, *Peaceable Kingdom*, 98.

35. Brueggemann, *Redescribing Reality*, 26–29.

36. Brueggemann, *Redescribing Reality*, 4–6.

37. Swinton, *Dementia*, 19–21.

His resulting practical theological method aims to offer, "in the light of Scripture and Christian tradition . . . a fuller and more accurate description that highlights alternative understandings and previously inconceivable options for theory and action."[38]

This book embraces this method, seeking to explore, describe and look for alternative understandings to furnish theory and action from within, as Barth coins, the "new world" of the Bible.[39] Here are seeds for exciting approaches to practical theological method which enable the evangelical to enter into its conversation about dementia and faith whilst listening to the "disruptive and complex" voices of Scripture, expecting new discoveries.[40]

In this chapter I have discussed Practical Theology in relation to evangelicalism. In particular, I have argued that the field provides a hospitable location for this study whose participants are Christians from an evangelical tradition. Its methodology, sets out to bring practice and theology together, allows the participants' voices to be heard in conversation with theology, the tradition and Scripture. Recognizing the deeply personal nature of evangelical faith, it allows, as Root has argued, the honoring of the evangelical experience.[41] In this study, that experience is within the context of living with dementia.

In the following chapter I consider literature and research which explore this area of faith and dementia in order to provide further context, prompt questions and disclose gaps in the existing research.

38. Swinton, *Dementia*, 21.

39. Barth, "New World in the Bible," 15–30.

40. Greggs, "Introduction," 4.

41. Root, *Christopraxis*, xiv.

3

Literature Review

Attuning to the Phenomenon

⁕

Introduction

THIS LITERATURE REVIEW, ALONG with other voices, is one of the dialogical partners in the conversation of Practical Theology's pastoral cycle. It is also part of the iterative[1] journey of the hermeneutic phenomenological approach which I have used for the qualitative study. Its role is to provide context and provoke questions as it begins to attune the conversation of the book to the experience under investigation. In this field, initial questions arise from the experience which is being studied, in this case, living with dementia as a committed Christian. In the wider context of the book, it is this experience which is the starting point in Practical Theology's pastoral cycle. In this way, this chapter begins to respond to Osmer's four tasks of Practical Theology as outlined in chapter 2.

Recognizing my own situated-ness,[2] I begin with a description of theological perspectives which have been significant in shaping my own approach to and understanding of the experience. I will consider questions which have particularly engaged my interest in this area, arising from the experience of those who are beginning to live with dementia. These find focus in the issues of identity, the experience of faith and its interweaving with memory. This literature conversation also includes the voices of those who speak out of their own experience of faith and

1. Boell and Cecez-Kecmanovic, "Hermeneutic Approach," 257.
2. Smythe and Spence, "Re-Viewing Literature," 13.

dementia. In this area, I consider the research which has listened to people with dementia, then the autobiographical accounts of Christians who are living with dementia.

The review seeks to provide context for the analysis of the lived experience which is presented in chapter 6, and to reveal gaps in the conversation so far. Inevitably, because of my own situated-ness, the choice of literature and the organization of the review begin to suggest an argument. However, these are intended to prompt further thinking and invite the engagement of the reader in critical conversation arising from the literature, with the purpose of growing understanding of the phenomenon.[3]

In the following I seek to present a discussion of the literature and other sources which present a range of perspectives from philosophy, psychology, sociology, theology, biography, pastoral care and other sources which have been shaping others and my own understandings of dementia. These provoke new questions and insights, all of which are discussed in the light of dementia.

Experience Prompting Theological Reflection

Keck names dementia "the theological disease" because it asks questions about human identity and faith.[4] As an editor of devotional resources, whose approach to her task has been challenged by the specific needs of evangelical Christians living with dementia, asking such questions has been a natural and necessary response. As an evangelical, a question to emerge was whether "saving faith" is certain when you can no longer remember God. If so, how can the case for this be made biblically and theologically?

Theological writing has been a major part of developing my understanding of the experience of dementia. Whilst I will use the theological lens later in the reflections following the analysis of the data, here I will discuss briefly some of the important writing which has brought me to new understanding, not only of the experience of dementia but also my own understanding of faith.

---

3. Smythe and Spence, "Re-Viewing Literature," 14.

4. Keck, *Forgetting Whose We Are*, 14–15.

Theological Writing

There has been little writing which looks closely and specifically at the theology of dementia. One of the earlier works investigating this was Keck's *Forgetting Whose We Are*. His phrase "deconstruction incarnate" provoked questions for me and further biblical consideration.[5] These words, unreasonably, initially deterred me from looking at his work more closely. Yet, I have discovered that he wrestles compassionately with the questions of identity and personal faith, especially as relevant in later dementia. His work includes provocative and insightful discussion of the issue of memory. Whilst he is sure in his encouragement to carers that their loved-ones' faith is secure, he seems less sure about their ongoing lived experience of faith in later stages of the illness.

More recently, Swinton's ongoing work in the theology of dementia presents a major contribution in this area.[6] I have drawn on his work significantly as I began and continue my investigations and reflections. His insistence on the continuing personhood of people living with dementia and their soteriological security drew my attention to questions which were piquing my interest. The issues he raises also include: the issues of memory and time, the importance of the embodied self, relationships and participation in the body of Christ, the sacred-ness of people living with dementia and the importance of recognizing being "in the moment" and the value of "being with" others, the importance of love—all continued to resonate with my early investigations and emerging understandings, and with my pastoral responses to those whose cognition was beginning to wane. Swinton's practical theological approach was important for me, not only because of my own previous work in this field, but because my work in Christian ministry had given me the deep conviction that theology must connect to lived experience, and that the Bible provides fresh perspectives from which to understand our present situation.[7]

There are also a number of shorter works which have contributed to my thinking about and reflection on this issue from theological perspectives. Saunders has written a brief introduction to some of the main theological questions about the nature of dementia, and how that

---

5. Keck, *Forgetting Whose We Are*, 32.

6. See, for example, Swinton, *Dementia*.

7. See Root, *Christopraxis*; Swinton, *Dementia*, 5–6, 17–21; Brueggemann, *Redescribing Reality*, 1–11.

informs pastoral care.[8] He discusses issues such as personhood and how theological tradition informs understanding. More recently, Hudson, a contextual theologian has contributed theological understanding in the area of personhood and the faithfulness of God.[9] Kevern has written several articles as he continues the conversation about identity and the nature of faith in dementia.[10] There are, of course, other articles which begin to bring into focus the theological questions which inform understanding and practice, and I will draw on these in more depth in the later theological reflections. First I consider the writing which has begun to give glimpses of the context of my research.

Perceptions of Context

Dementia and Faith: Glimpses from the Current Context

In recent decades there has been a growing awareness of dementia in the Western world. Popular books such as *Iris* and its subsequent film version and, more recently, the biography *Still Alice* and the film which followed are amongst several books and films which have contributed to the increasing public profile and understanding of dementia and the experience of those who live with this condition.[11] Magnusson's moving account of her mother's journey with dementia gives glimpses of the losses, and the self which endures.[12] Increasingly, the voices of people living with dementia are being heard and published.[13]

As awareness of dementia has grown in recent decades, the importance of spirituality and religion have also increasingly been recognized in academic and research literature as being significant factors in the well-being of those living with dementia. This has been explored in the writing and research of scholars such as Goldsmith, MacKinlay and Trevitt, Snyder, Stuckey and Gwyther, Katsuno, Dalby and Kontos. Aspects of their work will be discussed within this literature review. Post has drawn attention to the hypercognitive bias of western society's valuing of what

---

8. Saunders, *Dementia*.

9. Hudson, "God's Faithfulness," 50–67.

10. For example, Kevern, "Sharing the Mind of Christ," 408–22.

11. Bayley, *Iris*; Genova, *Still Alice*.

12. Magnusson, *Where Memories*.

13. For example, Whitman, *People with Dementia*.

it means to be a person.[14] Significant theological accounts of the nature of faith in dementia, as mentioned above, have been contributed by Keck and Swinton's *Dementia: Living in the Memories of God*.[15] The notable autobiographical writing of Bryden and Davis have given important insights into the faith experience of dementia, especially of the early to moderate stages of living with this illness.[16]

MacKinlay and Trevitt, in their writing about finding meaning in dementia, have written of the centrality of human spirituality.[17] Attention to the spiritual dimension is increasingly mentioned as an important aspect of care in policy and strategy documents, for example, Alzheimer's Society "End of Life Care" statement says: "The person's spiritual needs . . . should be addressed and respected as much as the medical aspects of care."[18] However, Higgins, writing about the importance of the spiritual dimension as an essential component of holistic care, found that it is still frequently overlooked.[19] For example, in the Department of Health's "Living Well with Dementia: A National Dementia Strategy," the words "spirituality," "religion" or "faith" did not appear.[20] Kevern also notes that in this paper, the goal of "'comprehensive care' . . . does not offer resources in personal spiritual or theological reappraisal."[21] In the "Equality, Impact Assessment" for "Living Well with Dementia" there is some scant recognition of religious needs: "Although there is no obvious religious dimension to dementia, feedback from the consultation told us that religion may play an important part in the lives of people with dementia."[22] In public arenas, "all-knowing medical science" often seems to have pre-eminence.[23] McFadden, Ingram and Baldauf write that in "favoring a strictly biomedical approach to Alzheimer's and other dementing illnesses, the research community has produced a limited view of persons who have these illnesses and of ways to offer care."[24]

14. Post, *Moral Challenge of Alzheimer Disease*, 5.

15. Keck, *Forgetting Whose We Are*; Swinton, *Living in the Memories of God*.

16. Bryden, *Dancing with Dementia*; Davis, *My Journey into Alzheimer's Disease*.

17. MacKinlay and Trevitt, *Finding Meaning*, 22.

18. Alzheimer's Society, "End of Life Care."

19. Higgins, "Spiritual and Religious Needs of People with Dementia," 24–29.

20. DHSC, "Living Well with Dementia."

21. Kevern, "I Pray that I will not Fall," 292.

22. DHSC, "Equality Impact Assessment," 12.

23. Saunders, *Dementia*, 7.

24. McFadden et al., "Actions, Feelings, and Values," 69.

In the understanding of spiritual experience of those with dementia and its importance for well-being, there is still work to be done.

A Changing Paradigm: Bio-Medical to Holistic Emphases

The question of how people with dementia are sometimes perceived and treated by medical and social care facilities prompted the person-centered thinking of Kitwood.[25] In his seminal work, *Dementia Re-considered: The Person Comes First*, he argued that when the medical-scientific perspective dominates, the person can come to be treated merely as a biological object needing "physical care . . . but little else."[26] He challenged this medical model, calling it "the standard paradigm," warning of the danger of allowing diagnosis to define the person and consequently influencing the way we treat certain people. Kitwood's work on dementia and personhood, together with Sabat's work on the self, have done much to focus the attention of caring professionals on the whole person rather than just the disease, including the spiritual, relational and social dimensions.[27] Sabat highlights the harm caused to individuals through his notion of "malignant social positioning."[28]

Swinton also challenges a dependence on medical definitions to describe the person, especially those who live with dementia: "Medical definitions are helpful for medical purposes, but they may be considerably less helpful for working through the contribution of theology and pastoral care to the process of defining and responding to dementia."[29] Drawing on Tallis, he points to the danger in medical understanding of the tendency to see the brain as the only path to understanding.[30] Lange has argued that Swinton is sometimes over-combative in his interdisciplinary dialogue with neurobiology.[31] However, Swinton is not denying the importance of neuroscience, but rather asserts that theology is the necessary lens when seeking understanding of the *whole* of being human. In the case of this book, such holistic thinking is highly pertinent to the

25. Kitwood, *Dementia Reconsidered*, 1, 37–38.

26. Saunders, *Dementia*, 7.

27. See Sabat, *Experience of Alzheimer's Disease*.

28. Sabat, "Mind, Meaning, and Personhood in Dementia," 287–302.

29. Swinton, *Dementia*, 47.

30. Tallis, *Aping Mankind*, 15, 5; Swinton, *Becoming Friends of Time*, 13.

31. Lange, "Deterritoralizing Dementia," 168–79.

nature of being a person of faith who lives with dementia. As practitioner Shamy asserts, we are "more than body, brain and breath."[32] The spiritual dimension of human life is a significant part of what it means to be human, and it requires nurture especially amidst the challenges of living with dementia.

However, whereas theologians, chaplains and other practitioners working with people who live with dementia generally concur with the importance of this holistic view, it is important to acknowledge, as Goldsmith has suggested, that this is not the case in all expressions of Christian faith.[33] He refers to those for whom theological structure or doctrinal "soundness" are principal concerns and who are, consequently, in danger of excluding and de-humanizing those with cognitive loss. He compares this with a strict and authoritative biomedical approach to dementia, which at its worst, is similarly de-humanizing. My own awareness of extreme conservative elements of evangelicalism has made me aware of its potential exclusiveness of those living with dementia. The lens of theology is necessary in order to stimulate questions which lead to effective, whole-person caring of those who are living with this illness.

Understandings of Spirituality, Religion, and Faith

Spirituality

There is, as noted earlier, an increasing awareness of the spiritual needs of persons with dementia in recent years, both in public documents and in research and scholarly writing.[34] However, whilst there are some broad commonalities, there are different understandings of the terms spirituality, religion and faith. This is significant for the nature of the faith of the phenomenon I am exploring. These different perceptions provide context for understanding the faith of Christians living with dementia, and begin to point to why these are important for their well-being and the nature of care that is offered.

---

32. Shamy, *Guide to the Spiritual Dimension of Care*, 60–63.

33. Goldsmith, "Through a Glass Darkly," 124.

34. See, for example, DHSC, "Living Well with Dementia"; Williamson, *My Name Is Not Dementia*.

There is wide agreement that "spirituality" is difficult to define, "an intangible multi-dimensional concept," dependent on subjective experience.[35] Allen and Coleman write that, in addition to this, it is

> closely associated with a sense of meaning and purpose. It is particular to each person and yet, by virtue of its essential nature to all human beings, is shared with others. Some would say that spirituality is intuitive or even innate and, therefore, not easily susceptible to rational explication.[36]

Spirituality is recognized as being about the intangible and immaterial aspects of life. Sapp and MacKinlay and Trevitt explore the notion of transcendence.[37] Hughes draws on this idea to point to the dual aspect of spirituality which is both immanent (for example, caught in a smile exchanged) and transcendent, a "going beyond."[38] Spirituality involves in some way a sense of being connected to a divine or transcendent sense of purpose,[39] and it requires an openness to mystery.

However, the notion of spirituality being part of the essential nature of human being is widely recognized in the literature. Kevern writes: "What these definitions have in common is an attendant claim that spirituality is an integral, even fundamental, element of what it is to be a human being."[40] Resonant with Heidegger's concept of care (*sorge*) as an aspect of our being-in-the world with others, Kevern concludes that "'spiritual care' is close to the very heart of caring for another human being" and, in this, he directs attention to the importance of holistic care.[41] This recognition also begins to raise questions about what it means to be human, and the meaning of spirituality for those who are living with dementia.[42]

---

35. Beuscher and Grando, "Using Spirituality to Cope," 584–85; Higgins, "Spiritual and Religious Needs of People with Dementia," 24.

36. Allen and Coleman, "Spiritual Perspectives," 205.

37. Sapp, "Spiritual Care of People with Dementia," 200; MacKinlay and Trevitt, *Finding Meaning*, 85.

38. Hughes, "Situated Embodied View," 200–201.

39. Stuckey and Gwyther, "Dementia, Religion, and Spirituality," 291–97.

40. Kevern, "Spirituality of People with Late-Stage Dementia," 765–66.

41. Heidegger, *Being and Time*, 235–41. Heideggerian concepts are discussed further in the description of the methodology used for the qualitative research in chapter 4.

42. Hughes, "Situated Embodied View," 198–206.

Religion and Faith

The terms religion and spirituality are sometimes used together or interchangeably,[43] but spirituality does not necessarily include religion. The discussion, in general, seems to concur that religion involves structures, provides shared practices, rituals, understandings and language for "the working out of human spirituality."[44] Faith is mentioned less in the literature, but is a further category within the ambit of human spirituality. Again, whilst often situated within religion, it has distinct characteristics. As I have discussed elsewhere, Hull has depicted spirituality, religion and faith as three concentric circles, with faith at the center.[45] Spirituality, he contends, does not necessarily include religion, which places human life under, and in relation to, the infinite. Faith, a further category within the religious, Hull describes as a "trustful response to the object of religious worship."[46] The model suggests that whilst spirituality is common to human experience, it does not necessarily include religion, and being of a particular religion does not necessarily include faith.

Goldsmith envisions a similar picture to Hull's model, narrowing his discussion from the broad term of spirituality, through religion and then to faith.[47] Whilst acknowledging that people of other faiths will have different ways of expressing a living commitment to their religion, in the Christian context, he considers this faith commitment being expressed as "a follower of Jesus," bringing the understanding of being in personal relationship with God.

Swinton brings different perspectives to the ideas of being religious or having faith with his discussion of intrinsic and extrinsic religion.[48] Whilst extrinsic religion is "detachable from their essential sense of self," essentially self-serving and utilitarian, intrinsic religiousness is a meaning endowing framework which extends beyond religious activities into every aspect of life, determining "who and what they understand themselves to be."

---

43. MacKinlay and Trevitt, *Finding Meaning*, 17.

44. Goldsmith, *In a Strange Land*, 145; MacKinlay and Trevitt, *Finding Meaning*, 20.

45. See Williams, "Bible and Developing Faith."

46. Hull, "Spiritual Development," 171–73.

47. Goldsmith, *In a Strange Land*, 147.

48. Swinton, *Spirituality and Mental Health Care*, 30–32.

These ideas of faith, suggesting trustful relationship, obedient following of God in Christ, meanings and values which are deeply engrained in the sense of identity, are present in the experience of evangelical faith investigated in this study. I have been able to find little in the literature which relates to the experience of this particular kind of faith for those beginning to live with dementia, apart from the significant autobiographical accounts of Bryden and Davis. More recently Mast has written, particularly for carers, a compassionate account of dementia and faith from the biblical perspective of the evangelical tradition.[49]

Spirituality in Dementia

The literature widely acknowledges that a major function of spirituality, whether or not expressed in religiousness or through faith, is that it brings meaning. MacKinlay defines it as including:

> the need for ultimate meaning in each person, whether this is fulfilled through relationship with God or some sense of another, or whether some other sense of meaning becomes the guiding force within the individual's life.[50]

If, as the literature suggests, spirituality is part of what it is to be human, then that quality is inherent in those who are living with dementia. MacKinlay developed a generic model for the spiritual tasks of ageing and then realized that this could be used in her research with those living with early to moderate stage dementia aided by the practice of spiritual reminiscence.[51] Drawing on Frankl,[52] she places the finding of meaning at the center of her model which leads to, and is interactive with, relationship with God, transcending loss and disabilities and finding hope. This prompts me to notice the sense of and quest for meaning in the experience of dementia.

Mackinlay and Trevitt's model suggests that spirituality can bring a transcendence of loss in the experience of living with dementia. This has been considered to some extent in the literature and the research as a tool

---

49. Mast, *Second Forgetting*.
50. MacKinlay, *Spiritual Dimension of Ageing*, 42.
51. MacKinlay and Trevitt, *Finding Meaning*, 23.
52. Frankl, *Man's Search for Meaning*.

for coping with dementia.[53] Katsuno considers this function of religion and spirituality but questions whether this can also be true for those who live with dementia, and urges further research into this question.[54]

Such questioning asks whether the concept of spirituality is relevant for those with dementia. Hughes argues that if spirituality is part of what it is to be human, "our models of dementia . . . must be broad enough to encompass spirituality, not as an add-on, but as a fundamental feature."[55] He further notes that if spirituality is part of who we are, then we can support those with dementia in maintaining their personhood by paying attention to their spiritual needs, even into advanced stages of dementia. As Kevern has done, he also draws on Heideggerian philosophy to make the point that our human being-in-the-world together with others implies an intrinsic attitude of care (*sorge*) towards others, even those living with dementia.[56] However, if it is considered, as I discuss later, that personhood is under threat as a result of dementia, so also is spirituality in the experience of those living with dementia, including those of Christian faith. Kevern posits that, in response to this difficulty, there is a need to "reframe" spirituality "in ways that challenge some of the commonly-held assumptions about its very nature. . . . If we hold to the assumption that people with dementia retain a spirituality into the late stage of the condition, in what ways will our understanding both of spirituality and of dementia need to be revised?"[57]

Whilst Kevern is thinking particularly of those living in late-stage dementia, the challenges which earlier dementia bring to those who are still able to express themselves are distinctive. The work of scholars such as Dalby, Sperlinger and Boddington, Katsuno, Stuckey, Snyder, MacKinlay and Trevitt reveal the particular spiritual and religious experience of those living with early to moderate dementia. As Goldsmith has emphasized, there is a need to address the spiritual needs of those with dementia, "finding ways to ensure that they can continue to experience this."[58] Katsuno's work suggests that a person's spiritual resources will be

---

53. See, for example, Katsuno, "Personal Spirituality"; Beuscher and Grando, "Using Spirituality to Cope"; Beuscher and Beck, "Literature Review."

54. Katsuno, "Personal Spirituality," 315–16.

55. Hughes, "Situated Embodied View," 205.

56. Hughes, "Situated Embodied View," 205–6.

57. Kevern, "Spirituality of People with Late-Stage Dementia," 771.

58. Goldsmith, *In a Strange Land*, 144.

increasingly significant as their dementia develops.[59] Kevern agrees that there is a case to be made for developing a person's spiritual and religious resources as they come to terms with the early stages of dementia in preparation for the future.[60] Swinton brings a theological perspective:

> In those who are experiencing dementia, spirituality may take a different form than it had before, but it does not disappear along with their vanishing neurons. Our inherent holiness is not affected by the neurological decline, even if our previous modes of articulating it change or become unavailable. The challenge is for those around persons with dementia to explore how best this holiness can be sustained in the midst of profound changes.[61]

Across the growing number of studies of spirituality and religion of those with dementia there seem to be consistent findings that the spiritual and religious dimensions of their lives help both in the present, enabling coping with the impact of the disease, in finding meaning, and in developing spiritual resources for the future. The findings seem to suggest that increasing support for the spiritual lives of people with dementia is important for their well-being. As noted in chapter 1, early engagement with the theological implications of a dementia diagnosis are as important as other aspects of caring.[62] This study aims to make a contribution to the understanding of one dimension of this in order that, as a society and in the Christian church, we can learn how to care better for Christians from an evangelical tradition with dementia.

The issue of spirituality and the questions it implies for personhood are deeply theological as Keck's work has highlighted. These are questions which arise from the experience of Christians who find themselves living with dementia, and are therefore fundamental in thinking about the nature of faith in dementia.

Spiritual Growth in Dementia

When people hear the word "dementia," they may think only of decline and loss.[63] It might be assumed that spiritual growth in dementia is not of

59. Katsuno "Personal Spirituality," 332.

60. Kevern, "I Pray that I Will Not Fall," 293.

61. Swinton, *Dementia*, 174.

62. Kevern, "I Pray that I Will not Fall," 293.

63. Brockmeier, "Questions of Meaning," 86.

major concern. But for those living with dementia and whose identity is deeply embedded in their faith, continuing to grow spiritually is crucial for the present, and also in preparation for the future. It was my own conviction of this which inspired the development of Bible and prayer guides for people with dementia. The work of Bryden and Bute, Christians living with dementia, also assume that spiritual growth is a continuing part of their lives.[64]

There are several significant models for depicting spiritual growth through human life such as those of Fowler and Erikson.[65] In such models there is the underlying assumption that spiritual (or psychological) growth as part of human life. Heidegger's work on being-in-time has emphasized the temporal, suggesting that approaching mortality is itself increasingly a stimulus for personal growth as life is reassessed in its light.[66] In MacKinlay and Trevitt's own model for spiritual growth they have been concerned to show how human, spiritual growth continues even into the experience of living with dementia.[67] In fact, they suggest that difficult events in life, such as increasing frailty and chronic illness, may even be "the starting point for spiritual growth."[68] Important terms for their discussion are self-transcendence where the person moves "beyond self-centeredness to other-centeredness" which is enabled by discovering and ultimate response to new meaning.[69] They draw on the concept of gerotranscendence, suggesting that this "may provide a valuable new lens for viewing the person with dementia."[70] They note that this aspect of growth in older people living with dementia has hitherto been little studied.[71] "Struggle is part of life, and is not to be regarded as being negative. It is often through struggle that transcendence and subsequent spiritual growth occurs."[72] I was interested to discover how this question of spiritual growth would be evident in the lives of the participants in this study.

64. See, for example, Bryden, *Dancing with Dementia*; Bute, "My Glorious Opportunity," 15–23.

65. Fowler, *Stages of Faith*; Erikson, *Life Cycle Completed*.

66. Heidegger, *Being and Time*, 296–304.

67. MacKinlay and Trevitt, *Finding Meaning*, 87.

68. MacKinlay and Trevitt, *Finding Meaning*, 86.

69. MacKinlay and Trevitt, *Finding Meaning*, 86.

70. Tornstam, *Gerotranscendence*.

71. MacKinlay and Trevitt, *Finding Meaning*, 92.

72. MacKinlay and Trevitt, *Finding Meaning*, 166.

Questions Arising from the Experience of Dementia

For the Christian who is still able to contemplate their experience of living with dementia, profound and, for some, troubling questions of self-identity and the nature of faith arise. In response to these fundamental concerns, I look first at the question of personhood drawing on perspectives brought to these through biographical accounts, philosophy and psychology. Then, in the following section, the experience of those living with dementia responds to questions about their faith experience.

Perspectives on Personhood

Writing about her own journey with dementia, Christian psychiatrist, Wallace writes of her sense of grief and bereavement as she adjusted to the changes that her illness was bringing.[73] She felt that it raised basic questions: "Who am I? What is at the heart of who I am? . . . Is my personhood fixed or is it continuously evolving?" Bryden asked similar questions of herself, and spoke of the fears of dementia:

> Our main fear is the "loss of self" associated with dementia. We face an identity crisis. We all believed the toxic lie of dementia that the mind is absent and the body is an empty shell. Our sense of self is shattered with this new label of dementia. Who am I, if I can no longer be a valued member of society? What if I don't know my family, if I don't know who I am and who I was, if I don't even know God?[74]

Bryden concludes: "Suddenly we have become a non-person." At the beginning of this exploration of dementia and faith, I noticed that the perspective of loss of the person in dementia, was imposed by others, resulting in a sense of stigma, rather than by the person themselves.

This sense of stigma is recognized in Kitwood's work and by Sabat who write of the "malignant social psychology"[75] of dementia and "malignant social positioning"[76] observed in the way others treat those who are living with dementia. Kitwood emphasized the importance of

73. Wallace, "Maintaining a Sense of Personhood," 27.
74. Bryden, *Dancing with Dementia*, 156.
75. Kitwood, *Dementia Reconsidered*, 45.
76. Sabat, "Mind, Meaning, and Personhood," 288–95.

recognizing the full humanity of those who have dementia; they are not "person-with-DEMENTIA," but "PERSON-with-dementia."[77]

The expression "loss of self" is sometimes used when speaking of a person living in the later stages of dementia. But these questions of personhood and their threats to selfhood are present for the person from the beginning of their dementia journey: "Who am I becoming?"[78] Wallace and Bryden were professionals who, at first, continued their work and writing whilst aware of the developing changes brought by their illness. Both retained a strong sense of "me."[79] Keck's description of dementia as "deconstruction incarnate" brought robust protest from Bryden:

> David Keck's views shock me as a person with dementia in the early stages. Can I truly regard dementia as "deconstruction incarnate," "disintegrative, non-redemptive . . . amoral . . . challenging theologically" (Keck 1996)? Certainly, I challenge the view of Alzheimer's Disease International . . . that the "mind is absent and body an empty shell." The question is, where does this journey begin, and at what stage can you deny me my selfhood and my spirituality?[80]

From the beginning of knowing that they live with dementia, the troubling questions of personhood and identity are present. The voices of people with dementia change the perspectives on the nature of these. Philosophy, church tradition, psychology and theology offer a range of different responses. Some of these are outlined in the following because they describe the context in which people with early to moderate symptoms of dementia are living.

Bryden's question about disappearing personhood highlights the difficulty of what is meant by this always-shifting concept. Thinking about the nature of dementia, Swinton has pointed out, "you can be a person one day and not the next depending on whether or not you meet the criteria."[81]

Cartesian thought's *cogito ergo sum* and Lockean rationalist criteria do not bring solution to the questions around personhood for those who are living with dementia but know they are beginning to

---

77. Kitwood, *Dementia Reconsidered*, 7.

78. Bryden, *Dancing with Dementia*, 158.

79. Bryden, *Dancing with Dementia*, 159.

80. Bryden and MacKinlay, "Dementia: A Spiritual Journey," 71.

81. Swinton, "What's in a Name?"

lose cognitive capacity: "A thinking, intelligent being, that has reason and reflection, and can consider itself as itself, the same thinking thing, in different times and places; which it does only by that consciousness which is inseparable from thinking."[82]

Moreland and Wallace understand the Cartesian and Lockean views as making personhood dependent upon humanness.[83] Wennberg's understanding echoes this with his understanding that to be human is purely a biological notion.[84] When the attributes of personhood, such as thinking, feeling, intention and agency, are no longer present the person has gone. He considers therefore that being human is neither necessary nor sufficient for personhood.

The views of Singer compound such perspectives.[85] He has argued that the status of personhood rests on the possession of rational capacities alone. Warnock has also suggested that someone with such losses no longer has the attributes of a person, and, being no longer able to contribute to society, death is perhaps preferable.[86] Such views are deeply troubling for those who are beginning their journey of living with dementia. Post commented on the "hypercognitive snobbery" in which "the category of 'need' is arrogantly displaced as the dominant source of moral obligation by the category of 'personhood.'"[87]

Psychologist Kitwood's contrasting perspective with his argument for person-centered care argues that the characteristics of personhood are not primarily about autonomy and rationality, but about being in relationship with others: "It is a standing or status that is bestowed upon one human being by others, in the context of relationship and social being."[88] He argues that cognitive capacity has erroneously been given supremacy over relationship, which may be expressed through the embodied life of emotions and feelings. For Kitwood, it is not simply a matter of asserting the unique special-ness of each human being, but that this is discovered in relationship.

---

82. Locke, *Essay Concerning Human Understanding* 2.27.9 (115).

83. Moreland and Wallace, "Aquinas versus Locke and Descartes," 139.

84. Wennberg, *Terminal Choices*, 159.

85. Kuhse and Singer, *Should the Baby Live?* 132; Singer, *Practical Ethics*, 86.

86. Macadam, "Interview with Mary Warnock," 23–25.

87. Post, *Moral Challenge of Alzheimer Disease*, 79.

88. Kitwood, *Dementia Reconsidered*, 8,9.

However, the literature uncovers some deficiencies in Kitwood's notion of personhood. Kitwood's work with its emphasis on respect for the person is underpinned with Buber's[89] relational "I-Thou" philosophy.[90] The I-Thou relationship is deeply tied to the necessity of the reality and presence of God: God is the ultimate Thou." With this missing God-element, Kitwood's answers to the question of personhood may seem flawed.[91]

There are other difficulties with the relational criteria for personhood. If relationality is a key criterion for personhood, this doesn't answer the question of the status of those who are isolated, or for whom in later stages of dementia there are no detectable clues to response in relationship. Kontos and Naglie also address this problem.[92] Drawing on Merleau-Ponty's[93] discussion of embodiment, they argue that Kitwood's social interactionist concept is insufficient, proposing instead that recognition of the embodied self is an important component of personhood: "Bodily habits, gestures, and actions support and convey humanness and individuality."[94]

Others have built helpfully on the foundations of Kitwood's work. Notably, Sabat's social constructionist perspective, with its three models of self, moves from the outwardly expressed social interactionist criteria to empathy with the inner life of individuals with dementia.[95] He demonstrates how, in the later stages of disease, the "self" continues but may be increasingly dependent for its expression on the co-operation of caring others.[96] The importance of this understanding is highlighted by the development of his idea of "malignant social positioning" with its demonstrable effect of accelerated deterioration in the expressions of self.[97] Post's work resonates with that of Sabat.[98] He refutes the impact of western rationalist criteria for personhood which exclude "the deeply forgetful . . . by neglecting the emotional, relational, aesthetic, and

89. Buber, *I and Thou.*

90. Swinton, *Dementia,* 149–50.

91. Williams, "Knowing God in Dementia," 1–16.

92. Kontos and Naglie, "Expressions of Personhood."

93. See Merleau-Ponty, *Phenomenology of Perception.*

94. Kontos and Naglie, "Expressions of Personhood," 801.

95. Sabat, *Experience of Alzheimer's Disease,* 274–308.

96. Sabat, *Experience of Alzheimer's Disease,* 276, 308.

97. Sabat, "Mind, Meaning, and Personhood in Dementia," 287–302; cf. Kitwood, *Dementia Reconsidered,* 48.

98. Post, *Moral Challenge of Alzheimer Disease,* 80–82.

spiritual aspects of well-being that are open to them."[99] Like Sabat, he recognizes these "fragile clues" to selfhood which remain until the late stages of dementia.[100] Post also chooses to develop a case for the role of spirituality within Judeo-Christian faith in illuminating our understanding of persons with dementia, and the important co-operative role of faith communities in enabling the maintenance and expression of their personhood.[101] He builds an ethical framework for the respect and care of persons with dementia which arises from faith foundations.

Roman Catholic philosopher Spaemann brings another perspective to this discussion with the question, "Persons: someone or something?"[102] Being someone is not dependent on certain capacities but is inherent for all human beings.[103] Spaemann's proposal shares common ground with Kitwood, Sabat and Post: the nature of being human is social and therefore relational. But this social aspect is not the starting point for his definition of what it is to be human. He asserts that every human being is *a priori* "someone" and shares human rights and worth with all humankind, irrespective of capacities, because of their shared genealogical heritage. Although he writes as a Christian, this premise is accessible to all whether or not they own a particular faith. Nevertheless, he asserts that the term "person" takes us to the heart of Christian theology.[104] For the person anticipating their journey ahead with dementia, this issue can be profoundly disturbing. I will reflect further on this in the theological reflections.

The ideas of personhood are deeply associated with the concept of self-identity and its connection with memory. The experience of dementia provokes a particular interest and concern in considering the relationship between these.

Perspectives on Memory and Identity

In the early to moderate stages of dementia, the loss of memory may be a deeply troubling concern for those feeling the immensity of the

99. Post, "Fear of Forgetfulness," 72, discussed in Sabat, *Experience of Alzheimer's Disease,* 320.

100. Post, *Moral Challenge of Alzheimer Disease,* 25.

101. Post, *Moral Challenge of Alzheimer Disease,* 29, 137–42.

102. See Spaemann, *Persons.*

103. Spaemann, *Persons,* 236–48.

104. Spaemann, *Persons,* 17.

challenge of the decline which is in progress.[105] Both Wallace and Bryden write of how their diagnoses brought immediate, sharp awareness of how the label dementia changed their own and others' perceptions of them.[106] Bryden, as her dementia developed, contested this, asserting not only her continuing sense of identity, but also her strong sense of purpose.[107] Increasingly the literature of philosophy draws attention to the fragile clues of a person's identity which persist deep into their journey with this disease. It reveals unexpected perspectives about our memory. The literature uncovers its embeddedness in who we consider ourselves to be.

The idea of autobiographical memory with its recall of events in chronological order has been a benchmark in western literature's consideration of identity. Augustine wrote about memory containing our world and identity: "There . . . I meet myself."[108] Post writes that for Augustine it is "the temporal glue between past and present."[109] It is "the source of all the connections between past and present experience that allow us to have self-identity and autobiography." The Lockean definition of the human person has also influenced modern, western thinking about identity and this understanding has persisted in some ways into modern neuroscience. Psychologist Schacter sums up what he considers to have been the standard view: "Our sense of ourselves depends crucially on the subjective experience of remembering our pasts."[110] Brockmeier highlights the significance of this statement: if people lose their capability of autobiographical remembering, they also lose, their sense of their being in time and, therefore, their sense of autobiographical time.[111] Ultimately, he concludes, they lose their sense of self and identity. However, he also proposes that the Western "archival" idea of memory dependent on factual, time-ordered recall is undergoing change and is moving "beyond the archive."[112]

---

105. Post, "*Respectare*," 223.

106. Wallace, "Maintaining a Sense of Personhood," 26–27; Bryden, *Dancing with Dementia*, 156.

107. Bryden, *Dancing with Dementia*, 161–63; Bryden and MacKinlay, "Dementia: A Spiritual Journey," 71.

108. Augustine, *Confessions* 10.8 (186).

109. Post, "*Respectare*," 223.

110. Schacter, *Searching for Memory*, 34.

111. Brockmeier, "Questions of Meaning," 69.

112. Brockmeier, *Beyond the Archive*.

The assumption of identity of self being dependent on a chronological, grasp of autobiography is challenged by dementia. Post suggests that with a diagnosis of dementia "past, present, and future begin to disconnect.[113] We begin to lose the stories of our lives." Brockmeier's emphasis on meaning, provides a different perspective for thinking about the issue of the memory of faith for those who are living with dementia.[114]

As I discovered early on in this journey, the different strands begin to interweave. Identity and memory lead inevitably to questions of time. This later component is explored eloquently in Swinton's book *Becoming Friends of Time*, and his discussion raises important issues for theological reflection on this topic which will be considered later.[115]

In the following, I focus on the ways in which the literature uncovers how other kinds of remembering reveal identity. These are expressed in different ways but depend on a holistic understanding of the person and their identity. Shamy suggests that the whole person—the body-soul self—seems to have other ways of "knowing."[116] These understandings all illumine my perceptions of the identity of the person with dementia and deepen awareness of how that self is expressed.

The Embodied Self and Implicit Memory

Whilst dementia undoubtedly brings severely incapacitating cognitive loss and forgetfulness, there is increasing recognition that memory is also, with its accumulated and resulting sense of identity, embedded in every aspect of who we feel ourselves to be. Swinton, exploring this idea, comments: "Memory is, in fact, something that lives within our bodies."[117] For example, the literature of pastoral care reveals how the body's memory is revealed especially in Christian worship—through singing of familiar hymns, hands raised in praise, joining in with prayer, or expressing the wish to receive communion through acquiescent gesture.[118] In the spiritual caring of those with dementia, faith response is visible not only through

---

113. Post, "*Respectare*," 225.

114. Brockmeier, "Questions of Meaning," 83.

115. See, e.g., Swinton, *Becoming Friends of Time*, 133–46.

116. Shamy, *Guide to the Spiritual Dimension of Care*, 104–5.

117. Swinton, "What the Body Remembers."

118. Shamy, *Guide to the Spiritual Dimension of Care*, 93–119; Williams, "Knowing God in Dementia," 9.

brain-dependent capacity, but is expressed through bodily movement, emotional expression and gestures.[119] It is this embodied memory which can sustain and prompt moments of clarity in the experience and practice of faith. Swinton comments that it "potentially acts as a powerful conduit for knowing Jesus even if one has forgotten who Jesus is."[120] Such moments expressed in embodied memory can be significant for the experience of faith and connection with God in dementia.

Phenomenological writing (considered further in the following chapter) helps in understanding and recognizing this kind of remembering. Merleau-Ponty's notion of the embodied self offers insight for our understanding of the experience of faith in dementia. He distanced himself from Cartesian dualism where mind and body are "separate and distinct things."[121] Rather, he conceives the notion of person, as Matthews has expressed, as "a unified being who expresses their 'subjective' thoughts, feelings, and so on, in bodily form—speech, in gesture, in behaviour, in interactions with their environment."[122] Kontos draws on Merleau-Ponty's concept of embodiment to demonstrate how expressions of faith are sometimes seen in persons living with dementia.[123]

Others have reflected this interweaving of identity and memory. Sapp, in his account of *Living with Alzheimer's*, argues that memory, and the identity which arises from it, come from the "experiences that the person has had in and through his or her body . . . [thus] creating memories and a personal history."[124] Schacter speaks of implicit memory in which past experiences unconsciously influence our perceptions, thoughts, and actions.[125] He proposes that the subjective sense of remembering evokes the reality of past experience. Summa and Fuchs propose the concept of implicit or body memory which endures into dementia.[126] Whilst explicit memory is dependent on cognitive re-call, they argue that in dementia, body memory of the self is seen in familiar habits and practices, and also in corporeal interaction with others.[127] Kontos's focus on "the expressions

---

119. Swinton, *Dementia*, 237, 251.

120. Swinton, "What the Body Remembers."

121. Matthews, "Dementia and the Identity of the Person," 173.

122. Matthews, "Dementia and the Identity of the Person," 173.

123. Kontos, "Alzheimer Expressions," 3–4.

124. Sapp, "Living with Alzheimer's," 54–60.

125. Schacter, *Searching for Memory*, 161.

126. Summa and Fuchs, "Self-experience in Dementia," 396.

127. Summa and Fuchs, "Self-experience in Dementia," 399–400.

of the gestural body" similarly implies her assumption of human interaction. Swinton extends these ideas in ways which help make sense of what is happening in the faith-ed self in this context.[128]

For those living with dementia, as cognitive capacities diminish, identity found and expressed in the body and the relational becomes increasingly significant for the expression of self and for the understanding of others who care. These factors disclose new understanding of the experience of faith in dementia.

The Relational Self

The relational self draws us again to the phenomenological philosophy of Heidegger: Our being is *with* others. Leadbeater simplifies, "who we are depends not simply on our self-reflective ability to marshal our memories but, crucially, on our relationships with other people."[129] The question "Who am I?" finds its answer in relationships. Resonant with Fuch's discussion of implicit memory, Sabat proposes that, as dementia brings deterioration to cognitive capacities, the self requires interpersonal interaction and the social recognition given by others.[130] The vulnerability of self as dementia advances demands from others respect and care as fellow human beings. For those who live with little social interaction, the dangers are clear. For the Christian believer, relationship is fundamental, but, as Buber's concept of "I-Thou" assumes, this is encompassed in relationship with God.[131] Theological responses to this question bring different perspectives on the nature of self and will be considered later. Nevertheless, this beginning of understanding of the self in dementia brings particular challenge to communities of faith about how they will find ways of supporting the faith identity of those who are living with dementia.

As this literature review moves on in its work of attuning to the phenomenon, the questions and possible answers found in the literature discussed so far bring deeper and more specific questions about the nature of faith and how that is experienced in dementia. In the following section I bring insights and understandings from the small body of literature and

128. For example, Swinton, "What the Body Remembers."

129. Leadbeater, "Disremembered."

130. Sabat, *Experience of Alzheimer's Disease*, 275, 295.

131. Buber, *I and Thou*.

research which has described and explored the role and experience of religion and spirituality in dementia. I focus on that which in particular bring the voices of those who live with dementia.

The Experience of Spirituality, Religion, and Faith in Dementia

As the person of faith diagnosed with dementia begins to wrestle with the question of their identity, questions about the security of their faith and relationship with God also surface. In the following the voices of those with dementia begin to respond to this second question.

Perspectives from Research

Whilst there is an increasing body of work in the broader area of spirituality and dementia, there are still a relatively small number of studies which have sought to hear the voices of those who are living with dementia. Often, work which is insightful and compassionate about the experience of living with the illness, still leaves the reader feeling that, in the end, the focus is on the carer rather than bringing subjective understanding of the person living with dementia.[132] Whilst these important works provide significant insights into the experience of dementia, perhaps especially of the later stages from pastoral and theological perspectives, they do not give specific focus to the subjective, essential experience of those who are living with dementia in its early to moderate stages. There is a small number of studies which have set out to do this. These include, for example, those by Dalby et al., Katsuno, Snyder, Stuckey and Gwyther, Beuscher and Grando, and MacKinlay and Trevitt, each contributing different perspectives.[133] Even these, whilst addressing issues of faith and faith practice, often do so as part of a broader category of religion and spirituality, rather than the specific focus in this research of evangelical faith.

---

132. See, for example, Goldsmith, *Hearing the Voice of People with Dementia*; Keck, *Forgetting Whose We Are*; Mast, *Second Forgetting*.

133. See Dalby et al., "Lived Experience"; Katsuno, "Personal Spirituality"; Snyder, "Satisfactions and Challenges"; Stuckey and Gwyther, "Dementia, Religion, and Spirituality," 291–97; Beuscher and Grando, "Using Spirituality to Cope"; MacKinlay and Trevitt, *Finding Meaning*.

In this broader category, spirituality and religion are often described as coping resources, and also as ways of finding meaning in dementia. The autobiographical testimonies of Christians living with dementia, such as those of Bryden and Davis, bring important understanding about the subjective experience of living with this disease.[134] I will first consider some of the findings from research texts which I have found particularly significant.

Coping

Stuckey and Gwyther stress the importance of spirituality and religion as "significant resources—across a wide spectrum of faith perspectives—for coping with a diagnosis of dementia."[135] Whilst they acknowledge that these are not panaceas for the experience of dementia, nevertheless, the small body of work in this area agrees that they are "crucial coping strategies."[136] Studies often highlight this word "coping." For example, Beuscher and Grando, Katsuno and Snyder all emphasize the role of spirituality and religion in this way. Interestingly, it does not seem to be a word which is used by Christians who are themselves experiencing dementia. The word "coping" could suggest an "*ad hoc*" resource which may be used in times of great need, rather than faith, which is an all-life encompassing relationship.[137] This doesn't deny the struggles and grief of dementia, but the subjective accounts from Christians suggest rather that it is situated as part the ongoing relationship with God who sustains them in their faith (for example, Davis, Bryden, Bute). The conclusions of Beuscher and Grando nevertheless suggest some of the important elements of what spirituality, as a coping resource, means. These include finding reassurance and hope; staying connected with church. Snyder identifies similar qualities: giving hope, belief in the afterlife, enabling acceptance and bringing relief.[138] Katsuno also speaks of personal spirituality enabling the person living with dementia to manage their feelings of helplessness.[139]

134. Bryden, *Dancing with Dementia*; Davis, *My Journey into Alzheimer's Disease*.

135. Stuckey and Gwyther, "Dementia, Religion and Spirituality," 291.

136. Stuckey and Gwyther, "Dementia, Religion and Spirituality," 295.

137. Stuckey, "Blessed Assurance," 71, 72.

138. Snyder, "Satisfactions and Challenges," 303–7.

139. Katsuno, "Personal Spirituality," 315–16.

Meaning

The search for meaning is recognized, often implicitly, by these writers, as participants in the studies seek to understand the purpose of dementia in their lives. MacKinlay and Trevitt have focused on this particularly in their work of spiritual reminiscence.[140] They argue that this facilitates one of the central tasks of ageing, but have used it with those in the early to moderate stages of living with dementia. Their work shows how in and through the experience of dementia, the person living with dementia can find meaning, hope and growth. Snyder and Katsuno also draw attention to this function of spirituality.

Identity

Whilst the questions of identity and personhood emerge philosophically for those trying to understand what this disease is doing to the person living with dementia, those who are living with dementia, whilst they are still able to speak, assert their continuing sense of self. This sustained sense of personal identity is a strong focus of MacKinlay's and Bryden's work, both individually and in their co-operative writing: "I can seek an identity by simply being me, a person created in the image of God."[141] Beuscher and Grando also highlight this notion of identity and how "staying connected" with others, for example, with church, is important for maintaining the sense of identity.[142] Bryden has written several years into her journey with dementia, of her perception of the I-Thou relationships in which she is sustained both through her relationship with God and others.[143]

Experience

Dalby, Sperlinger and Boddington's study of the lived experience of spirituality and dementia in those living with mild to moderate dementia has been particularly helpful in my own hermeneutic phenomenological

---

140. MacKinlay and Trevitt, *Finding Meaning.*
141. Bryden, *Dancing with Dementia*, 152.
142. Beuscher and Grando, "Using Spirituality to Cope," 591.
143. Bryden, "Spiritual Journey into the I-Thou Relationship," 7–14.

research journey.[144] They have taken an interpretative phenomenological approach, seeking to understand more deeply the subjective experience of six people living with dementia. They identify five themes which emerged: the experience of faith is understood as relationship with God; the search for meaning which is seen as a spiritual challenge; "I'm not as I was," bringing changes to the experience of self and relationships with others; "staying intact," including strategies for coping, staying hopeful, recollecting self and family relationships; current-pathways to spiritual connection and expression, such as spiritual practices and belonging to spiritual community.

Beuscher and Grando and Katsuno's studies conclude that faith itself is sustained in and through dementia.[145] Katsuno reports that belief remained strong and there was a sense of being supported by God, feelings of security and comfort. The majority of participants in Beuscher and Grando's study said that "cognitive losses did not affect their spirituality or beliefs." Belief and relationship with God had begun in childhood and were continuing to sustain them now in their coping with Alzheimer's Disease. They give this example, spoken by an eighty-four-year-old woman: "The Lord helps me get through this. I don't dwell on sitting around worrying and all that kind of stuff because God has been good to me. He brought me from a long ways. Definitely, my faith is the power of my life."[146]

They found that for some, the experience of Alzheimer's Disease brought a "heightened spiritual sense": "Religion has always been a part of me, and it gets stronger and stronger."[147] MacKinlay and Trevitt conclude that spiritual growth is possible in dementia. Karen MacKinlay, a chaplaincy worker and deacon in the Anglican church, concludes similarly from her small study that dementia does not stop spiritual growth: God has not "finished" with them.[148] The challenge, she suggests, is to provide and allow opportunities for this.

144. Dalby et al., "Lived Experience," 80.

145. See Beuscher and Grando, "Using Spirituality to Cope"; Katsuno, "Personal Spirituality."

146. Beuscher and Grando, "Using Spirituality to Cope," 591–92.

147. Beuscher and Grando, "Using Spirituality to Cope," 591–92.

148. MacKinlay, "Listening to People with Dementia," 99.

Practice

However, whilst faith itself often provides a means of "coping" and sustains the sense of well-being, there is agreement across the pastoral literature (discussed earlier) and evidence in the studies of those living with dementia, that religious or faith practice can present difficulties. Beuscher and Grando mention cognitive impairment (short attention span, declining ability to comprehend, memory loss) which effect a range of faith activities such as Bible reading, listening to sermons and involvement in church activities.[149] Katsuno and Dalby, Sperlinger and Boddington mention similar difficulties. Whilst many found personal prayer helpful, for others, loss of concentration was making this difficult.[150] Katsuno highlights the implications that these findings bring for healthcare and religious practitioners.[151]

Doubt

Research in this area has looked at the broader area of religiosity, rather than the experience of those with a personal, committed faith. Studies suggest that whilst challenges to faith are experienced, as revealed by the participants in this research, these do not result in actual loss of faith.[152] Katsuno's research found that "doubt in faith was not definitive, but rather temporal in nature." She concludes, "Even lifelong religious people might have doubt in their faith when they face extreme physical and emotional stress."[153]

However, such stress does not undermine personal belief.[154] Dalby, Sperlinger and Boddington conclude that rather than polarities of disillusionment with faith or faith growth, people were seen to be in an ongoing process of living their faith in the context of having dementia.[155] In a personal email exchange, Stuckey, reflecting on this, wrote:

149. Beuscher and Grando, "Using Spirituality to Cope," 589–93.

150. See also MacKinlay, "Listening to People with Dementia," 98.

151. Katsuno, "Personal Spirituality," 332–33.

152. Snyder, "Satisfactions and Challenges"; Katsuno, "Personal Spirituality"; Dalby et al., "Lived Experience."

153. Katsuno, "Personal Spirituality," 330–331.

154. Katsuno, "Personal Spirituality," 323–28.

155. Dalby et al., "Lived Experience," 90.

Even amid that negativity, there was an overall sense that their
faith provided them with an anchor—a frame of reference—that
permitted them to find meaning (if not happiness) in their difficult situations.[156]

Perspectives from Personal Narratives

The research which focuses on the lived experience of those with dementia, begins to uncover the essence of spirituality and religious practice
in dementia. However, its interpretation, inevitably depends on the situated researcher who brings her own choices and understandings to the
conversation around the question. The person living the experience has
a unique and authoritative view on the nature and meaning of their experience. Bryden writes: "As survivors of the journey with dementia, we
can share with you the insider's knowledge that we have. . . . Let's work
together to share our insights as equal partners."[157]

Whilst each person's experience is unique, in similar cases there will
be a resonance of understandings of the meaning. Christine Bryden and
Robert Davis's autobiographical work have been especially significant
in this field. Both are committed Christians. Davis was a Baptist pastor.
Their narratives are significant for the purposes of this study, because
they come to terms with living with dementia within the horizons of
their faith.

Reactions: Fear and Stigma

Bryden spoke of the fear she experienced when first diagnosed as having dementia, the "fear of losing self, of a future without knowledge of
identity."[158] She describes the depression which followed as she reflected
on her medical prognosis. She was also angry with the stereotypes that
others imposed on her, no longer expecting her to be able to contribute
opinion or insight: "I had become a labelled person, defined by my disease overnight."[159] She argues strongly that stereotypical views of those
living with dementia and the resulting stigma is because these "are based

156. Stuckey, email with the author, August 24, 2016. Quoted with permission.

157. Bryden, *Dancing with Dementia*, 171.

158. Bryden, *Dancing with Dementia*, 10.

159. Bryden, *Dancing with Dementia*, 156; see also 39–40.

on the end stages of dementia," unaware that dementia is a journey, "with many steps along the way."[160]

For Davis, the immediate shock and fear had more to do with his personal spiritual life. He had been a successful pastor ministering to a large congregation. As the effects of dementia became apparent, his work became impossible and he found that he had lost his sense of close relationship with God.[161] His increasing difficulties with memory took away the comfort he might have found in Scripture reading. The peace and joy he had felt as a Christian disappeared. He speaks of "blackness and darkness" which turned "every night into a living hell."[162]

These accounts of the early years with dementia make clear the initial struggle and anguish of discovering that you are living with the developing symptoms of dementia.

Acceptance and Growth

MacQuarrie in her study into the experience of Alzheimer's Disease noticed a paradox of understanding that included both acknowledgement and resistance, which was neither denial or acceptance.[163] In some ways, this paradox has resonance in the lived experience of faith for both Davis and Bryden. Their accounts as Christians demonstrate that struggle was part of their journey in living with dementia. But they both found relief and peace as they chose to accept their illness and in doing so experienced spiritual growth.

Davis describes how, in his struggle, he had an encounter with Christ which lifted from him the sense of darkness and helplessness: "My new and simple service to him was to rest in him and moment by moment take his peace and use his strength to simply live."[164] He felt at this point that he had a choice to make between a life that could be frustrating and frightening, or peaceful and submissive.[165] He chose to say to God,

---

160. Bryden, *Dancing with Dementia*, 40. Wallace writes of similar responses to people living with dementia in Wallace, "Maintaining a Sense of Personhood," 27.

161. Davis, *My Journey into Alzheimer's Disease*, 47.

162. Davis, *My Journey into Alzheimer's Disease*, 48–49.

163. MacQuarrie, "Experiences in Early Stage Alzheimer's Disease," 430–441.

164. Davis, *My Journey into Alzheimer's Disease*, 55.

165. Davis, *My Journey into Alzheimer's Disease*, 57.

"Thy will be done."[166] Davis notes that his acceptance was not "blind resignation" but an intentional "recommitment to a loving Father" who had called him and empowered him for God's service.[167]

For Bryden, working with MacKinlay, she has found meaning and purpose in her writing and speaking about the experience of dementia.[168] Her journey with dementia has been different to that of Davis, but again the darkness and depression following realization that she had this disease found resolution in making a choice to accept her condition: "I'm choosing to live my life positively."[169]

Identity and I-Thou Relationship

Bryden has been an advocate of growth in her identity and also of finding this in her relationship with God and others in the body of Christ. From the beginning of her journey with dementia, she asserted: "This unique essence of 'me' is at my core, and this is what will remain with me to the end. I will be perhaps more truly 'me' than I have ever been."[170] Kevern gives the insightful example of Kath Morgan, an academic living with dementia, who has a similar sense of her enduring identity: "Even when you appear to have lost everything, faith will still be there, in the essence of you, like a perfume always remembered."[171] I am interested that this sense of identity for Christians is centered on their faith-ed self. Lisa Snyder gives another example from an African-American Baptist:

> God is a foundation that I have. My faith is solid. It's within me and it is me. . . . As a child when you're brought up with the scripture and the teaching of the holy word, that puts a foundation under you. . . . I'm steeped in it now. You couldn't pull me away from it now.[172]

Bryden refutes "the toxic lie of dementia,"[173] by which she means the loss of self. Instead, she argues, as the layers of cognition and emotion are

166. Davis, *My Journey into Alzheimer's Disease*, 58; cf. Matt 6:10.

167. Davis, *My Journey into Alzheimer's Disease*, 72.

168. Bryden and MacKinlay, "Dementia: A Journey Inwards," 134–44.

169. Bryden, *Dancing with Dementia*, 164.

170. Bryden, *Who Will I Be When I Die?* 64.

171. Kevern, "I Pray that I Will Not Fall," 285–86.

172. Snyder, *Speaking Our Minds*, 101.

173. Bryden, *Dancing with Dementia*, 156.

stripped away, she experiences her journey as being drawn into a deeper and more trusting relationship with God. In her experience, it is one of "becoming," with her true self "held in the grip of the divine."[174] In her recent writing, many years after her diagnosis of dementia in 1995, she explores her sense of the I-Thou relationship, in which her relationship with God is growing: a "walking with God in the garden at the time of the evening breeze."[175]

Throughout her work, she acknowledges and depends on her relationship with others in helping her to know God's presence with her: "I need you to relate directly to my spirit, and as I travel this journey of dementia, I will rely on others increasingly to support my spirituality."[176]

Sense of Purpose

At the beginning of this research journey, my thinking was about how the community of the church can care spiritually for those who are living with dementia. Increasingly, as I have met and read the stories of people with dementia, I have learnt of the driving sense of purpose which sustains and motivates their lives. For example, I've been drawn to the writing of Bryden who has worked for many years to help others understand dementia and to grow in their own faith as they learn. She writes: "Many of us find self-validation in giving of ourselves to others. . . . I am called to help others, to love others as Jesus loves them."[177]

Bute has recently written of her own long journey with dementia which, like Bryden, she describes as "a gift."[178] Her focus is also on helping others to understand both the nature of the experience of dementia and how to help those living with dementia pastorally. Like Bryden, Bute recognizes that life as a Christian is not a solitary one. She also emphasizes that she is part of "the body of Christ."[179] Her emphasis, as a person living with dementia, is on her sense of calling to serve others from within her

---

174. Bryden, *Dancing with Dementia*, 161–62.

175. Bryden, "Spiritual Journey into the I-Thou Relationship," 10.

176. Bryden, *Dancing with Dementia*, 153.

177. Bryden, *Dancing with Dementia*, 167.

178. Bute, "My Glorious Opportunity."

179. Bute, "My Glorious Opportunity," 22–23; Bryden, *Dancing with Dementia*, 153.

experience of dementia: "I have come to see that dementia is a glorious opportunity to demonstrate God's love for the whole body of Christ."[180]

Other insights from Bryden and Bute will also inform the later considerations of theological response and the pastoral implications of their experience. In this chapter, I have considered the broad context in which the phenomenon of faith experience in dementia is located, and have listened to those reflecting on the issues which dementia brings to our awareness. Consideration of how the issues of spirituality affect the lives of those living with dementia leads to the specific phenomenon of faith in the lives of those who took part in this study.

Conclusion

In this account of the literature, I have sought to uncover the conversation about the nature of faith within the experience of dementia. The literature reveals that there is increasing agreement that attention to the whole person, which includes their spirituality, is essential for the well-being of those living with dementia. The different perspectives considered have sought to show that dementia itself asks questions about what it means to be a person and, therefore, about the nature of faith. If the spiritual is important for all people, how can we understand the spirituality of those with dementia? If spiritual growth is important for all human beings, then how can this be seen in the experience of dementia? These questions are of great significance for how we regard the person with dementia, and, in particular, those whose core identity is found in their Christian faith. Deeper understanding of the phenomenon under investigation contributes to our relationships, our knowledge of being-with and our care for those facing the particular challenges of this disease.

The Gap

There has been, as testified by the existing literature, a limited number of investigations into the role of spirituality, religion and faith in dementia. There are even fewer studies which address the particular issue of committed faith, or look specifically at the theology of dementia. There is little in the research which sets out to listen to the voices of Christians from an evangelical tradition to learn about their specific faith experience. There

180. Bute, "My Glorious Opportunity," 23.

are few investigations into the role of such faith whilst the person with dementia is still able to reflect and express their thoughts. In my study I set out to listen to people with early to mid-stage symptoms of dementia because this provided an important opportunity to listen and learn, both for the bettering of spiritual care offered in the present, and also in the funding of faith as resource for later stage dementia. Bryden writes of this potential opportunity:

> After diagnosis, there is usually a journey of several years, in which we are battling the decline. And in this journey many of us can still speak.
>
> All of us travelling this journey have a right to be heard, to be listened to, and to be regarded with respect. There is no time to lose to hear our voice as we struggle to communicate.[181]

The account of the experience of Christians who live with dementia, using a hermeneutical phenomenological approach, will seek to make use of this opportunity. In doing so, the study aims to uncover deeper understanding and new insights in response to questions concerning the faith experience of those from an evangelical tradition who are living with early-mid stage symptoms of dementia. Later in the book, the theological reflections arising from this study and the central question of the research will seek to contribute fresh theological and pastoral thinking in order to deepen understanding and response to the questions posed by those who are living with dementia.

In the following chapters I first discuss and describe the methodology and methods which have been used to enable the gathering of my research participants' experience.

181. Bryden, *Dancing with Dementia*, 48.

4

Methodology and Research Approach

Introduction

IN THIS CHAPTER I describe the methodology and research approach used for the qualitative study which begins to uncover response to the question and goals outlined in chapter 1. I will first discuss the rationale for using a qualitative approach, then consider the methodology of hermeneutic phenomenology which I have selected as the most appropriate means for investigating the lived experience of evangelical Christians living with early to moderate symptoms of dementia.

In the midst of the complex web of lived experience and situated understanding, the hermeneutic phenomenologist seeks to understand not only the nature of an experience, but also its meaning and ultimately to consider what does this phenomenon reveal in response to the fundamental human question: "Who am I?" Such a question, in contemplating the progressive loss of cognitive capacity, is fundamental for those living with the early to moderate symptoms of dementia. For the Christian believer, with understanding of their identity being in relationship to God, there are additional questions which arise from the human condition in relation to faith, perhaps aptly expressed as David Keck suggests: "*Whose are we?*"[1]

---

1. Keck, *Forgetting Whose We Are.*

In this chapter I will describe this methodology and its underlying philosophical foundations. I will then consider key aspects of how the approach of hermeneutic phenomenology is used in empirical research, considering "lived experience," situated understanding and the importance of reflexivity. First, I begin with discussion of the context for this phenomenological approach.

The Qualitative Research

The Rationale for the Qualitative Approach

In the context of the book, the qualitative research is a component of the reflective circle and critical conversation of practical theology, discussed in chapter 2. This approach was deemed most appropriate to the research question,[2] and as Swinton and Mowat suggest, is a natural dialogue partner for practical theology, having "potential to be fruitful and illuminating."[3] As in Practical Theology, and also phenomenology, the starting point for the research is human life. Here, this is to do with the "lived experience" of individuals regarding their personal experience of faith. Whilst scientific modes of inquiry have an important complementary role, these cannot access the experiential knowledge that is available through a qualitative approach to human sciences, particularly in the area of spiritual experience. Qualitative research recognizes the complexity of the human world with its multiplicity of meanings. McLeod summarizes:

> Qualitative methods have traditionally been considered as most appropriate for research which seeks to uncover the meanings embedded within a slice of social life. . . . Qualitative research is seen as contributing to the growth of understanding, rather than to the collection of factual knowledge and construction of causal explanation.[4]

In this particular study, where the focus is the spiritual understanding and faith experience of individual evangelical Christians living with dementia, a qualitative approach was therefore considered as having most potential for enabling in-depth understanding of the lived experience of

2. Swinton and Mowat, *Practical Theology*, 56; Denscombe, *Good Research Guide*, 83.

3. Swinton and Mowat, *Practical Theology*, 28.

4. McLeod, *Qualitative Research*, 178.

participants. Swinton has written compellingly of the necessity of finding ways which enable us to investigate "the spiritual dimension that can dig into the hidden depths of human emotion."[5] As he writes, the use of such methodology has the potential to "reveal aspects and perspectives that are unavailable to other ways of doing research."[6] The fresh insights and new perspectives afforded through this particular study seek to affirm the methodology for the purpose described here, as well as contributing understanding that is potentially transformative for the lives of people with dementia.

Whilst the rigour of quantitative research rests on criteria of falsifiability, replicability and generalisability,[7] these are not the appropriate criteria for this qualitative inquiry which looks at the individual lived experience of faith. Yet, there is demonstrable rigour. McLeod speaks of qualitative research as "a process of careful, rigorous inquiry" which leads to "new ways of understanding the world," and which comprise "knowledge that is practically useful."[8] Here, the criteria for qualitative research are the senses of identification and resonance in others experiencing similar situations. Such criteria may then result in a degree of transferability. Swinton and Mowat make the point well:

> Qualitative research can therefore claim a degree of transferability insofar as it often raises issues and offers insights beyond the reach of the particularities of the situation. It frequently (arguably, always), creates a resonance with people outside of the immediate situation who are experiencing phenomena which are not identical, but hold enough similarity to create a potentially *transformative resonance.*[9]

Before proceeding to a discussion of the particular methodology, I will first discuss three important facets of the qualitative approach which are of special relevance to this study: the epistemological basis, the interpretative paradigm and the issue of reflexivity.

---

5. Swinton, *Spirituality and Mental Health Care*, 93.

6. Swinton, *Spirituality and Mental Health Care*, 93.

7. Swinton and Mowat, *Practical Theology*, 40–41.

8. McLeod, *Qualitative Research*, 3.

9. Swinton and Mowat, *Practical Theology*, 47.

Epistemological Foundations

Knowledge of the other and understanding of their experience is elusive. This is particularly the case in a study of spiritual experience in the context of persons with diminishing cognitive capacity. Whilst the nomothetic truth of quantitative research can be objectively, measured, quantified and compared, the ideographic truth of qualitative research begins with different presumptions. As Swinton and Mowat have proposed: "meaningful knowledge can be discovered in unique, non-replicable experiences."[10] This kind of knowledge is of particular importance to the work of Practical Theology, being integral to "the experiences and situations that Practical Theology seeks to reflect upon." It is also integral to the nature of Scripture and tradition, where truth about God is disclosed in ways which are clearly ideographic (for example, in the incarnation of Christ, his death and resurrection).[11] As Schultz and Meleis have proposed: "There are different ways of knowing, different propensities of knowers . . . and different aspects to be known about the same phenomenon."[12] McLeod concurs, suggesting three categories "within which qualitative research can produce new forms of knowing: . . . *knowledge of the other . . . knowledge of phenomena . . .* [and] the production of *reflexive knowing.*"[13] These forms of knowing are integral in this research and in the hermeneutic phenomenological approach used in this study.

As Swinton and Mowat discuss, "knowledge of the other" brings focus on particular individuals, exploring their experiences in-depth.[14] McLeod notes that it gives those who may not usually be given a voice the opportunity to tell their stories and to have that experience documented.[15] As previously highlighted, there have been few studies which allow the voices of persons with dementia to be heard. One participant in this study, a former medical practitioner, underlined the importance and potential value of hearing the perceptions of those with dementia in the following:

---

10. Swinton and Mowat, *Practical Theology*, 43.

11. Swinton and Mowat, *Practical Theology*, 43.

12. Schultz and Meleis, "Nursing Epistemology," 217–21.

13. McLeod, *Qualitative Research*, 3.

14. Swinton and Mowat, *Practical Theology*, 35.

15. McLeod, *Qualitative Research*, 3–4.

> I think it's a privilege to understand dementia from the inside.
> You know, I knew about it from the outside. And I've also
> learnt so much that illness from the inside is very different
> than from the outside . . . and it's . . . I mean, as a doctor, I
> tried so hard to help people and to identify with them, but one
> doesn't really understand.[16]

In setting out to hear such testimony, the knowledge gained through
qualitative research enables deeper understanding and has the potential
to contribute, in the particular case of this study, to better spiritual and
pastoral care. Knowledge of phenomena, McLeod suggests, is concerned
with particular categories of phenomena, for example, in this study,
the faith experience of evangelical Christians who live with dementia.[17]
Conversation with participants reveal the meaning which they find in
this and, in so doing, add to pre-existing understanding and knowledge.
McLeod's third category, the production of reflexive knowing, involves
constant deliberate reflection on and awareness of the researcher's own
world and how that is constructed, in order to bring about deeper and
clearer understanding of the research participants' worlds. Reflexive
knowing is embedded in practical theology's pastoral cycle.[18] It is a key
dynamic in the work of qualitative research, and is essential in the particular chosen methodology of hermeneutical phenomenology. Reflexivity
is an important component in this study and will be considered in greater
depth at a later point in this discussion.

The Interpretative Paradigm

Denzin and Lincoln emphasize the inherent interpretative role which is
interwoven in qualitative research.[19] Swinton and Mowat develop this in
the light of Practical Theology:

> Human beings are by definition "interpretive creatures." . . .
> The ways in which we make sense of the world and our experi-
> ences within it involve a constant process of interpretation and
> meaning-seeking.[20]

16. Extract from transcript of research interview with Alice.
17. McLeod, *Qualitative Research*, 4.
18. Swinton and Mowat, *Practical Theology*, 59.
19. Denzin and Lincoln, *Sage Handbook*, 3.
20. Swinton and Mowat, *Practical Theology*, 29.

The value of this methodology therefore depends significantly on the researcher's interpretative skill as she reflects on the data gathered. However, it is not the case that such meaning-seeking is remote from the life-world. The researcher herself, as highlighted in earlier discussion of contextual factors,[21] was "inevitably enmeshed"[22] in this lived reality, including the lived experience of faith: "Qualitative research recognizes 'the world' as the locus of complex interpretive processes within which human beings struggle to make use of their experience including their experiences of God."[23] This highlights a fundamental aspect of the interpretative paradigm. Whereas the scientific mode of quantitative research depends on a positivist understanding of the world, qualitative research draws on the premise of constructivism. Within this perspective the qualitative researcher must acknowledge both their own as well as the research subject's embeddedness in their context. Denzin and Lincoln describe it being concerned with "the socially constructed nature of reality, the intimate relationship between the researcher and what is studied, and the situational constraints that shape inquiry. . . . They seek answers to questions that stress how social experience is created and given meaning."[24] Constructivism is one aspect of the interpretative paradigm within which qualitative research functions, and is part of the framework for this particular study where hermeneutic phenomenology is the approach. From this perspective, the researcher's own embedded role in the research means that her contribution inevitably becomes part of the data.

Swinton and Mowat bring nuance to their discussion of constructivism, being careful to emphasize the activity of interpretation. Constructivism assumes, as Swinton and Mowat note, "the existence of multiple realities," and that there are "various interpretations" which can be given to the same phenomena.[25] This study, depending on description of lived experience, assumes an appreciation of the essential role which such situated understanding plays in how the world is interpreted.[26] It also recognizes that the researcher becomes "an active . . . co-creator of the

21. See chapter 1.

22. Swinton and Mowat, *Practical Theology*, 37.

23. Swinton and Mowat, *Practical Theology*, 29–30.

24. Denzin and Lincoln, *Sage Handbook*, 10.

25. Swinton and Mowat, *Practical Theology*, 35–36.

26. McLeod, *Qualitative Research*, 2.

interpretative experience."[27] Swinton and Mowat conclude that it is from "this constructivist perspective" that meaning arises "from the shared interaction of individuals within human society."[28]

There is a further significant element in the interpretative paradigm used in this study of faith experience. In his discussion of "Christopraxis"[29] Root emphasizes the place of "critical realism." Here, there is an assumption that reality is not only socially constructed; it recognizes that divine intervention is also a possibility. This paradigm acknowledges that "there is a real world that human minds cannot possess." As such, it allows the honoring of the "evangelical experience" of encounter with Jesus, but also recognizes the need for "judgement and discernment" which is found in the ongoing conversation between experience, theology and ministry.

These factors—qualitative research's epistemological basis with its emphasis on meaning arising from lived experience, the interpretative paradigm with its situated understanding, contextually embedded interpretation and "critical realism"—bring potential for fresh insights and transformation, and lead compellingly to the particular phenomenological methodology and method selected for this study.

Phenomenology and Its Philosophical Foundations

Phenomenology is both philosophy and methodology and has given rise to a number of distinctive approaches in human science research. All are concerned with uncovering the meaning of "lived experience,"[30] but there are different emphases which encompass a spectrum of the purely descriptive through a range of different interpretative assumptions. Phenomenologist Finlay summarizes phenomenology as "a continuum with pure rigorous, scientific description on one end and lucidly poetic interpretation at the other."[31]

This methodology has been widely used as an approach for research in the human sciences, particularly by practitioners in the fields of education and health care, but less so in research into the human experience

---

27. Swinton and Mowat, *Practical Theology*, 35 (my italics).

28. Swinton and Mowat, *Practical Theology*, 35–36.

29. Root, *Christopraxis*, xiv–xv. See also my discussion in chapter 2.

30. Finlay, *Phenomenology for Therapists*, 10.

31. Finlay, *Phenomenology for Therapists*, 19.

of spirituality.[32] However, Manen, drawing on the work of Chrétien,[33] has mooted "a phenomenology of religious experience" as being necessary for "a highly relevant human concern."[34] Also seeking a methodology which is able to investigate spiritual experience, Swinton has described his use of hermeneutic phenomenology in research into spiritual experience in the area of mental health. He has proposed that this approach enables focus on the experience of spirituality from the perspective of the person with the particular illness, and it is this "lived experience" which is the starting place.[35] Building on this model, I use it here as a means to explore the particular faith experience of evangelical Christians living with early to moderate stage dementia.

Some researchers, for example Paley, working in the area of nursing inquiry, have criticized phenomenological studies for being mere rhetoric which pay lip service to phenomenological philosophy.[36] Aware of such criticism, Marilyn Ray has highlighted that it is important to demonstrate the philosophical foundations for this methodology.[37] Finlay also emphasizes this, suggesting that "research focusing on lived experience could only be considered 'phenomenological' if it embraced underpinning theory and philosophy in some way."[38]

In response to such discussion, before looking further in detail at the practice of hermeneutical phenomenology as used in this study, I will first consider its philosophical foundations. I will look, in particular, at the work of Husserl, Heidegger and Gadamer and also refer to the philosophy of Merleau-Ponty, which has contributed to my understanding of the phenomenological approach used in this research.

Edmund Husserl

In the early development of phenomenology, Husserl proposed his transcendental phenomenology as a rigorous scientific way of investigating

---

32. See, for example, Manen, *Researching Lived Experience*; McLeod, *Qualitative Research*, 62; Swinton, *Spirituality and Mental Health Care*, 99.

33. See Chrétien, *Ark of Speech*, 17.

34. Manen, *Phenomenology of Practice*, 173.

35. Swinton, *Spirituality and Mental Health Care*, 93–101.

36. Paley, "Phenomenology as Rhetoric," 113–14.

37. Ray, "Richness of Phenomenology," 123.

38. Finlay, *Phenomenology for Therapists*, 43.

human experience which begins in the "lifeworld":[39] "not as a science of matters of fact, but a science of essences (as an 'eidetic' science)"[40] He insisted on first going to "the things themselves"[41] in order to discover "the essence of a thing."[42] Husserl's approach was to be pre-reflective and pre-theoretical.[43] It was essential, therefore, that all fore-understandings arising from our situated-ness must be suspended, in order "to see the world anew."[44] However, whilst seeking to be purely objective in his description of essences, Husserl's approach eventually hesitates uneasily when it is confronted with "the assumptions upon which all human understandings are grounded."[45] Moran comments, "Even Husserl eventually had to concede that his attempts to found an absolutely presuppositionless first philosophy—phenomenology—had ended in failure."[46]

Human understanding is inherently contextually-shaped and—mediated and true objectivity is, therefore, not possible. Husserl's student, Heidegger, subsequently understood this situated-ness as a strength rather than a weakness in the search for truth. This understanding is embedded and necessary in hermeneutic phenomenology, which assumes an interpretative role for the researcher.

Martin Heidegger

In his seminal work *Being and Time* a key notion in Heidegger's thinking is that of *Dasein*, or "being-there," and *Mitsein* or "being-with."[47] His philosophical methodology begins with the understanding that human beings are in and part of the everyday world. Further, this concept, as Finlay explores, is inherently and inescapably relational:

---

39. Moran, *Introduction to Phenomenology*, 12; Finlay, *Phenomenology for Therapists*, 45.

40. Husserl, *Ideas Pertaining to Pure Phenomenology*, xx. For further discussion, see Manen, *Phenomenology of Practice*, 90–91.

41. Husserl, *Logical Investigations*, 1:168; Finlay, *Phenomenology for Therapists*, 3; Moran, *Introduction to Phenomenology*, 108.

42. Ray, "Richness of Phenomenology," 119.

43. Manen, *Researching Lived Experience*, 7, 184.

44. Finlay, *Phenomenology for Therapists*, 23.

45. Manen, *Phenomenology of Practice*, 91.

46. Moran, *Introduction to Phenomenology*, 189.

47. Heidegger, *Being and Time*, 149–68.

The world of *Dasein* is a "with world" (*Mitsein* or Being-with). Even when we are physically alone or we ignore others, we remain in-relation through our everyday engagement in our common world. . . . In sharing the world with others, just as my own existence is an issue for me, we also develop a care or concern (what he called *Sorge*) for others' welfare.[48]

In contrast to Husserl's insistence on "bracketing,"[49] Heidegger recognized that such a project was impossible: we are inescapably situated in and with the world. More than this, he understood that it is in the investigator's awareness of their own presuppositions that there is the possibility of finding meaning and understanding in the phenomena being investigated.[50] Emerging out of her thinking on Heidegger's work, Ray has concluded: "Presuppositions are not to be eliminated or suspended, but are what constitute the possibility of intelligibility or meaning."[51] Rather than the objectivity of traditional scientific approach, which Husserl sought in his eidetic transcendental phenomenology, Heideggerian phenomenology, in contrast, is founded on the investigator's awareness of being *in* the world.[52] It is this *Dasein* which enables the researcher to interpret and make sense of the phenomena they investigate.

Integral to the methodology of phenomenology is the activity of description and, therefore, of writing which seeks understanding, or "unconcealment."[53] Heidegger's concept of *poiesis*[54] imagines a work of disclosure. Whereas Husserl's[55] hunt for truth depended on "exhaustive description" of the essence of a particular phenomenon with presuppositions recognized and suspended, Heidegger took an opposite approach, which assumes fore-understandings: "Understanding is always from a perspective, always a matter of interpretation. . . . We can never get beyond our language. . . . Our understandings are embedded in culture."[56] In Heidegger's work the methodological approaches of both phenomenology and hermeneutics are brought together: "Both . . . seen

48. Finlay, *Phenomenology for Therapists*, 50.
49. Finlay, *Phenomenology for Therapists*, 46–49.
50. Heidegger, *Being and Time*, 182–95.
51. Ray, "Richness of Phenomenology," 120.
52. Ray, "Richness of Phenomenology," 121.
53. Ray, "Richness of Phenomenology," 131.
54. Heidegger, *Introduction to Metaphysics*; Pippo, "Concept of Poiesis," 3.
55. McLeod, *Qualitative Research*, 38.
56. McLeod, *Qualitative Research*, 56.

as integral, complementary aspects of any satisfactory way of knowing about human existence."[57]

Critics of phenomenology have contended that such a context-mediated understanding limits the implications of this approach. For example, Paley writes that such methods, used in nursing research, "entitle them to very little other than tentative assertions about how things seem to a handful of people."[58] However, this argument fails to grasp the epistemological and ontological understandings of phenomenology, as described previously here. The questions of interpretation and understanding and how these are achieved is central to hermeneutic phenomenology, and is key to the work of philosopher Hans Georg Gadamer to which I now turn.

Hans Georg Gadamer

Building on the work of his mentor Heidegger, Gadamer[59] premises his work on his founding belief that all "human beings are by definition interpretative creatures."[60] The underlying contention is that interpretative-ness is an ontological, inescapable characteristic of being human and is how we "make sense of the world."[61] Husserl's phenomenological approach had emphasized an orientation towards the world of lived experience allowing the researcher to gain understanding "of the world as it is."[62] Hermeneutic phenomenology, on the other hand, recognizes that the researcher is "in the world" and that it is this prior understanding itself which enables the disclosure of new insights and transformative understanding.[63] Four key elements arising from Gadamer's philosophy and methodology are significant for the conduct of this study. These are: *prejudice, the fusion of horizons, the hermeneutical circle* and Gadamer's *emphasis on language and the interpretation of texts.*

---

57. McLeod, *Qualitative Research*, 59.
58. Paley, "Phenomenology as Rhetoric," 113.
59. Gadamer, *Truth and Method*, xx.
60. Swinton and Mowat, *Practical Theology*, 107.
61. Swinton and Mowat, *Practical Theology*, 107; Hekman, *Hermeneutics*, 117.
62. Ray, "Richness of Phenomenology," 120.
63. Ray, "Richness of Phenomenology," 121.

Prejudice

Gadamer does not ignore the pre-understandings that human beings bring to any situation under investigation. Of course, for researcher and research subject alike there are areas of commonality and, inevitably, unseen biases. Gadamer brings these to our awareness, describing them as "prejudices." In this project where both researcher and participants shared a common understanding of faith, it was inevitable that this commonality influenced the encounters and mutual understandings. As Swinton and Mowat write: "It is naïve to believe that one can ever be truly detached from the object of interpretation."[64] Bound by our own perspectives, "understanding is always from a particular position or perspective. . . . [It is] always a matter of *interpretation*."[65]

A challenge, then, is how to distinguish between the contextualized understandings of the investigator and those of the research subject, in order to gain new insights into the truth of a particular experience. Gadamer writes: "To try to escape from one's own concepts in interpretation is not only impossible, but manifestly absurd. To interpret means precisely to use one's own preconceptions so that the meaning of the text can really be made to speak for us."[66] Unlike Husserl's bracketing of foreunderstandings, Gadamer finds solution to the presence of prejudices in "the fusion of horizons" which informs the practice of hermeneutic phenomenologists and resonates with the work of practical theology.

Fusion of Horizons

The "horizon" of each person denotes the perspective on life given by their historical and particular cultural situated-ness.[67] That horizon includes what has gone before in their experience and, based on that *habitus*,[68] the imaginative understanding of life experience in the future. The solution for the intrusive presuppositions which accompany the researcher in their investigation is, Gadamer suggests, not as Husserl

---

64. Swinton and Mowat, *Practical Theology*, 114; Gadamer, *Truth and Method*, 354.

65. Swinton and Mowat, *Practical Theology*, 107; Gadamer, *Truth and Method*, 356.

66. Gadamer, *Truth and Method*, 398.

67. Gadamer, *Truth and Method*, 301–6.

68. See Bourdieu's discussion of his concept of *habitus* which arises from sociocultural factors, in Bourdieu, *Outline of a Theory of Practice*.

proposed, to suspend presuppositions, but rather through "the dialectic of experience"[69] to bring about a "fusion of horizons":

> The historical movement of human life consists in the fact that it is never absolutely bound to any one standpoint, and hence can never have a truly closed horizon. The horizon is, rather, something into which we move and that moves with us. Horizons change for a person who is moving.[70]

As "horizons" fuse, development and transformation happen for all participants, researcher and participants in their purposeful conversation. Inherent in this idea is another key element in the methodology of hermeneutic phenomenology: the hermeneutical circle.

The Hermeneutical Circle

Gadamer proposes that this fusion of horizons must be worked out as a "hermeneutical situation": "This is what takes place in conversation in which something is expressed that is not only mine or the other participants, but common."[71] Here, there is resonance with the dialogical process of the hermeneutical circle which is also key to the work of Practical Theology. Swinton and Mowat comment: "The fusion of horizons is a version of the hermeneutical circle . . . in that it is a crucial dialogical process that takes place between interpreter and text."[72] Gadamer describes the hermeneutical circle as a process of moving backwards and forwards from the "whole to the part and back to the whole."[73] It is this back-and-forth process of conversation and reflective engagement with the text, which brings about new and transformative understanding presented by the changed horizon. In the ongoing process of this book, this process has been characteristic. Gadamer describes the transformative conversation of the hermeneutical circle in this way:

> To reach an understanding in a dialogue is not merely a matter of putting oneself forward and successfully asserting one's

---

69. Gadamer, *Truth and Method*, 350.

70. Gadamer, *Truth and Method*, 303.

71. Gadamer, *Truth and Method*, 390; see also 305.

72. Swinton and Mowat, *Practical Theology*, 114.

73. Gadamer, *Truth and Method*, 291.

own point of view, but being transformed into a communion in which we do not remain what we were.[74]

The language used in research encounters and the resulting phenomenological texts are key in this dialogical process.

Language and Interpretation of Texts

In Gadamerian thought, language and its interpretation is inescapably a fundamental factor in our understanding of the world: "Our experience of the world is bound to language."[75] Ray comments with reference to this: "All human consciousness is historical and sociocultural and is expressed through language (text)."[76]

For Gadamer therefore, the work of interpretation of text, caught up in the hermeneutical conversation, is key to finding understanding and truth: "language is the universal medium in which understanding occurs. Understanding occurs in interpreting."[77] He goes as far as imagining the text itself as a participant in the hermeneutical conversation. The partner to the text is the translator, or, as Gadamer asserts, the interpreter. The translator-interpreter carries the responsibility of finding ways of expressing the meaning of the text truthfully: "Nevertheless, in being changed back by understanding, the subject matter of which the text speaks itself finds expression."[78] It is through this fusion of horizons brought about in the hermeneutical circle that the text is enabled to speak in ways which can be heard in our world:

> What we can do is to extend the horizon of our culture-based understanding, or achieve a *fusion* of horizons through allowing ourselves to learn from our immersion in the "text" being studied and thereby permitting the world expressed by the text to speak to our world.[79]

Whilst Gadamer was suspicious of "method," believing it imposed limits on understanding the true nature of the phenomenon under

74. Gadamer, *Truth and Method*, 371.
75. Gadamer, *Truth and Method*, 445.
76. Ray, "Richness of Phenomenology," 118.
77. Gadamer, *Truth and Method*, 390.
78. Gadamer, *Truth and Method*, 389.
79. McLeod, *Qualitative Research*, 56.

investigation, his work resonates with that of Sartre, who concluded that "writing is the method."[80] It is, as Manen explores, the writing and re-writing of the texts which "allow a rigorous interrogation of the phenomenon" and is, therefore, a central facet of this research methodology.[81]

The above aspects of Gadamerian thought are fundamental to the understanding of the methodology which facilitates this study. These philosophical foundations, particularly the thought of Heidegger and Gadamer, underpin the methodology of hermeneutic phenomenology as used in the qualitative study, to which I now turn, drawing particularly on the works of Manen and Finlay.

Hermeneutic Phenomenology: Key Elements

In this study it is hermeneutic phenomenology which allows the uncovering of the experience of faith "within the context" of dementia.[82] Of prime importance are the voices of those who live with dementia and the narratives of their "lived experience."

In the following, I describe three key elements which are integral in this hermeneutic phenomenological approach: lived experience, situated understanding and reflexivity.

Lived Experience

Resonating with previous discussion, Manen asserts that phenomenology begins with "lived experience," and it is this which is at the heart of the phenomenological search into what it means to be human.[83] This term has emerged from the phenomenological tradition. In Gadamer's exploration of the German term *Das Erlebte*,[84] he proposes that it is "something real" which is lived through and immediately experienced:

> The word suggests the immediacy with which something real is grasped—unlike something which one presumes to know but which is unattested by one's own experience, whether because it is taken over from others or comes from hearsay, or whether it is

80. Manen, *Researching Lived Experience*, 126.

81. Manen, *Researching Lived Experience*, 131.

82. Swinton, *Spirituality and Mental Health Care*, 93–94.

83. Manen, *Researching Lived Experience*, 35, 36.

84. Gadamer, *Truth and Method*, 53.

inferred, surmised, or imagined. What is experienced is always what one has experienced oneself.[85]

Yet, the meaning of such experience is not transient:

> The form "*das Erlebte*" is used to mean the permanent content of what is experienced. This content is like a yield or result that achieves permanence, weight, and significance from out of the transience of experiencing.[86]

Manen suggests that lived experience gathers hermeneutic significance as it is transformed into text and as it is reflected upon.[87] As he explores, this is "not a matter of formal intellect alone," but about "depth of the soul, spirit, embodied knowing and being."[88] The lived experience is set in a complex social world which means that while we may bring understanding of aspects of the lived experience, our knowing is always fluid and as Manen writes "ultimately mysterious."[89] Nevertheless, the rigour of hermeneutic phenomenology is distinguished "by its courage to stand up for the uniqueness and significance of the notion to which it has dedicated itself."[90]

In this study, the phenomenological accounts of evangelical Christians living with dementia, raise unique questions and bring unique *understandings* which inform, with authority and integrity, the wider understanding of this particular human experience. "Lived experience," once one is aware of it, inevitably prompts inquiry: "What is it like?"[91]

Arising from the thinking of philosophers such as Heidegger and Merleau-Ponty, Manen has proposed four existentials which suggest a framework for understanding and investigating the structure of the "life-world"—*spatiality, corporeality, temporality* and *relationality*.[92] Appropriate as descriptors of all human life experience, each of these categories was evident in the research conversations, and each raised pertinent questions for those facing the future with dementia.

85. Gadamer, *Truth and Method*, 53.

86. Gadamer, *Truth and Method*, 53.

87. Manen, *Researching Lived Experience*, 36–39.

88. Manen, *Researching Lived Experience*, 14; Bollnow, "Objectivity of the Humanities," 3–18.

89. Manen, *Researching Lived Experience*, 16.

90. Manen, *Researching Lived Experience*, 18.

91. Manen, *Researching Lived Experience*, 39, 40.

92. Manen, *Researching Lived Experience*, 18, 101–6.

Spatiality

Manen explains spatiality as "felt space."[93] The research conversations took place in the participants' own homes where they felt secure and things were familiar. As researcher, I was an invited guest into that place of "secure inner sanctity."[94] The participants therefore felt relaxed, even though some aspects of their experience were painful to narrate to the researcher.

In order to understand a person and their experience of the present, the research conversations explored the participants' wider world and history, for example, the places where their faith had been expressed with others. This *habitus* is especially significant for those with dementia for whom sedimented memories bring meaning to the present.[95]

This felt space is also about the wider context in which, as Manen, proposes "human beings move and find themselves at home."[96]

Corporeality

This "existential" draws particularly on the philosophy of Merleau-Ponty whose work has made a significant contribution to the practice of phenomenology through his emphasis on the body-subject. He has built on Heidegger's work, agreeing that understanding emerges from our "being-in-the-world." Merleau-Ponty's famous dictum "I am my body"[97] starkly asserts his holistic view of what it means to be human, and it has particular resonance where cognitive aspects of corporeality may be diminishing. Finlay extends this holistic perception of self in her writing about the body in lived experience: "Our body is the vehicle for experiencing, doing, being and becoming. . . . Through our bodies, we perceive the world and relate to others, and—in the process—we learn about ourselves."[98] She also talks about the "subtle and profound ways person—body and others—world are intimately intertwined." This intertwining was particularly significant in the research encounters of this

---

93. Manen, *Researching Lived Experience*, 102.

94. Manen, *Researching Lived Experience*, 102.

95. See the note regarding Bourdieu's *habitus* above.

96. Manen, *Researching Lived Experience*, 102.

97. Merleau-Ponty, *Phenomenology of Perception*, 231.

98. Finlay, *Phenomenology for Therapists*, 29.

study, where the relationship needed to be quickly established so that the participants felt relaxed and confident with the researcher and fruitful interchange was made possible.

Corporeality is closely intertwined with a third category of Manen's existentials, relationality.

Relationality

The "being-with" of Heidegger and the embodied self of Merleau-Ponty both insist on the essential relationality of lived experience. Finlay, discussing Manen's lifeworld existentials, writes: "They argue that we all have an embodied sense of self which is always in relation to others, while our consciousness is shared with others through language, discourse, culture and history."[99] This aspect of human experience raises challenging questions for people living with dementia as their symptoms develop. In this study where participants were those with early to moderate symptoms, their narratives revealed complex webs of relationality which have shaped lives from infancy through to the present and provide a sense of security and confidence as they look towards the future.

For example, for those who were living with their spouses, the importance of their joint identity as a couple was evident in the way that they spoke to and of one another. Hellström has highlighted this factor of couplehood in her discussion of caring in dementia.[100] Other significant relational networks for the participants in this study included their church communities, friends and a wider range of significant others who knew or had known them in particular roles and contexts.

This existential of relationality also becomes apparent in the relationship between researcher and the research participants.[101] Finlay and Evans have highlighted that this embodied encounter is a crucial aspect of phenomenological research: data emerges out of that relationship which is "co-created . . . in the embodied dialogical encounter."[102] This factor was of particular significance in this study where the participants and researcher shared a common faith and sense of purpose. Interestingly,

99. Finlay, *Phenomenology for Therapists*, 20.

100. Hellström, "I'm His Wife Not His Carer!," 53–66.

101. See discussion of this in Finlay and Evans, *Relational-Centered Research*.

102. Finlay and Evans, *Relational-Centered Research*, 29.

Manen also extends his understanding of relationality to include "religious experience of the absolute Other, God."[103]

These aspects of relationality will become evident in the account of the research process and the lived experience. The fourth existential category of lived experience to which Manen refers is temporality.[104] This, as the other categories, raises issues of particular interest for those with dementia who are also persons of Christian faith.

Temporality

Finlay summarizes our lifeworlds as: "We are thrown into the world in order to live: we act, make choices, strive, become. And ultimately we die."[105] Yet, within the bounds of this human temporality, past and present experience and future anticipations are significant for who we are as persons: "We experience time in our recollection of past joys and trauma. We also anticipate what is to come in the future."

For Heidegger, being and time are fundamentally interlinked.[106] Through time-bound life, we are always "becoming."[107] Drawing on Heideggerian thought, Finlay highlights the paradox of who we are in the present which emerges from past experience and also our anticipation of the future: "In our existence we are constantly projecting ourselves into the future, yet at the same time the 'who' we are becoming emerges from our past."[108] Like other phenomenologists, Manen speaks of this merging of past, present and future: "The temporal dimensions of past, present, and future constitute the horizons of a person's temporal landscape. Whatever I have encountered in my past . . . forgotten experiences . . . somehow leave their traces on my being."[109] In this study, I was interested to hear from participants about their past faith-life experience, in order to discover how this might be affecting them in the present, and in their expectations of their future faith life.

---

103. Manen, *Researching Lived Experience*, 105.

104. Manen, *Researching Lived Experience*, 104.

105. Finlay, *Phenomenology for Therapists*, 19.

106. Finlay, *Phenomenology for Therapists*, 50.

107. Finlay, *Phenomenology for Therapists*, 50.

108. Finlay, *Phenomenology for Therapists*, 50.

109. Manen, *Researching Lived Experience*, 104.

For the person living with developing dementia, the future reality is likely to be one in which only the present moment will be of importance. However, at the time of the research, the participants in this study were still able to place themselves in a temporal time frame. Thus questions about the past were important for eliciting stories which have contributed to their still-developing identity in the present and also give confidence for the future. Heidegger speaks of our existence as "being towards death,"[110] bringing uncomfortable anxiety. Yet, he also recognizes that to face death "gives life its intensity, urgency, meaning and potential for authenticity." However, the Christian hope of resurrection and eternal life with God proposes that human felt life experience transcends temporality.

Situated Understanding

A second key element in this approach to the research is situated understanding. The earlier discussion of the philosophical foundations for phenomenology makes clear the unavoidable nature of human situatedness, our history, our culture, our relationships, our values, our religious beliefs, our embodied experience through life. All of these form who we are and contribute to our understanding of the present and our imaginings of the future. The researcher and the participants inevitably had presuppositions deeply embedded in who they had become and who they were. As discussed earlier, phenomenologists have taken different approaches to this situatedness. Husserl initially insisted on the possibility of pure eidectic description, going to the "'thing'" itself, made possible through the practice of "bracketing." However, Heidegger and Gadamer, understood the impossibility of pure objectivity. Gadamer in particular recognized the inherent interpretativeness of human being. The human researcher can neither escape their situatedness, nor their interpretativeness.

In this study, the recognized situatedness, both of researcher and participant contributes to the possibility of the research. Similar to the standpoint theories of feminism, understanding is made possible by common situated-ness with the subject under investigation.[111] In this study, the participants and researcher have a common background within the evangelical tradition. The sharing of familiar experience enables the

110. Heidegger, *Being and Time*, 299–311; Finlay, *Phenomenology for Therapists*, 51.

111. Park, "Towards a Pastoral Theological Phenomenology," 7–8, 11.

researcher to understand and identify more deeply with her participants. Their common Christian beliefs and motivations for the research enable trust and openness to be established. Gadamer, in particular, highlighted the interpretative quality of human being, and argued that again this is an unavoidable component of our situatedness. It is these very qualities which enable us to learn from one another, as explored earlier, through the fusion of horizons.

The hermeneutic phenomenological approach, therefore, involves both careful description and interpretation. However, one of the conundrums of this approach is how these two elements are held in balance.[112] For Finlay, as discussed earlier, this is partly resolved by the continuum between researcher embeddeness and reflexivity.[113]

Reflexivity

Gadamer argued that, rather than the suspension of the researcher's own presuppositions, it is these which enable the understanding of the situation under investigation. However, there is, of course, a corollary to this that, unless those presuppositions are acknowledged, then the understanding and learning arising out of the fusion of horizons cannot take place. Hermeneutic phenomenologists then stand open to Paley's charge of "naïve realism"[114] who argues that unbiased understanding is, in reality, impossible and purported learning and discovery cannot be substantiated. However, this methodology does not expect final answers but is on a continuum of discovery.[115] This concern is answered in part, as discussed above, in Gadamer's fusion of horizons. However, it is apparent that the questioning of one's own beliefs, values and responses to the participants' contributions is an essential discipline which is integral to this work. Swinton and Mowat define this aspect of the research in this way:

> Reflexivity is the process of critical self-reflection carried out by the researcher throughout the research process that enables her to monitor and respond to her contribution to the proceedings.[116]

112. Dreyer, "Knowledge, Subjectivity," 90–109.

113. Finlay, *Phenomenology for Therapists*, 19.

114. Paley, "Phenomenology as Rhetoric," 10.

115. Dreyer, "Knowledge, Subjectivity," 92.

116. Swinton and Mowat, *Practical Theology*, 59.

More than this awareness, Swinton and Mowat suggest that all "research is, to an extent, autobiography."[117] The methods of hermeneutic phenomenology research aim for closeness to (not distance from) the research subjects. A mutual influencing is inevitable.

Reflexivity was therefore a significant part of this project. Gadamer writes: "The important thing is to be aware of one's own bias, so that the text can present itself in all its otherness and thus assert its own truth against one's own fore-meanings."[118] Throughout the period of the research, a research journal, annotation of reflective commenting on the interview transcripts, and my supervisor's rigorous questioning of my suppositions maintained this reflexive stance. In the final section of this chapter I begin to consider how this methodology has informed my approach to the research.

Research Tools

Gadamer was distrustful of the possibility of "method" which follows the traditional methodological conventions of research.[119] He felt that the perspective of any method "necessarily imposes limitations."[120] This, at first glance, is perplexing for researchers using the methodology of hermeneutic phenomenology. Finlay writes:

> In fact, there is no actual *method* of how to do hermeneutic phenomenology. "Method" seems almost proscribed by this approach. As Gadamer (1975/1996) argued in his *magnus opus* *Truth and Method*, method—particularly scientific method—is seen as incapable of guaranteeing "true" understanding.[121]

Yet, of course, in order to research into the particular topic of this study, where the object is to discover deeper understanding of lived experience, method is integral to the methodology and its philosophy. Hence, building on the work of the philosophers discussed above, particularly following Gadamerian phenomenology, and drawing on the work of phenomenologists Finlay and Manen, there follows discussion of the

117. Swinton and Mowat, *Practical Theology*, 60.

118. Gadamer, *Truth and Method*, 271–72.

119. Gadamer, *Truth and Method*, xx–xxi.

120. Swinton and Mowat, *Practical Theology*, 110. See the discussion in Gadamer, *Truth and Method*, xx–xxxiv.

121. Finlay, *Phenomenology for Therapists*, 115.

research tools I have used in this study. These are summarized as: *the phenomenological attitude*; *the embodied encounter*; *the hermeneutical circle*; *writing: re-writing and uncovering of themes.*

The Phenomenological Attitude

From the outset I adopted, as Finlay describes it, "the phenomenological attitude."[122] This makes use of the tension between the purely descriptive approach of Husserl and the situated, interpretative, philosophical approaches of Heidegger and Gadamer. The challenge of these approaches is to what extent bracketing of the researcher's presuppositions should be applied.[123] In hermeneutic phenomenology, Finlay envisages: "a kind of dance between the reduction and reflexivity."[124] Whilst I was aware of my own "pre-understandings," I was careful to manage the intrusion of these. Finlay proposes that this "dance" is "a source of insight."[125]

Ashworth, writing of this, proposes that from the beginning, the researcher's and participants' presuppositions are presumed.[126] He speaks of the "shared inter-subjective world and the existence of a social reciprocity of perspective." Finlay, drawing on Ashworth, talks about "a shared focus" and "cultural meanings" which are not set aside.[127] In this study, participants and researcher had an awareness of mutual faith understandings and shared goals for the research.

This focus, held within the dance between reflexivity and reduction, involves empathic, compassionate understanding, and also an open approach which is ready to be surprised.[128] Initial pre-conceptions may be overturned and transformed, new insights emerging from the fusion of horizons.

The phenomenological attitude is one which takes the lived experience of the participant as reality. The particular experience described is their "truth."[129] As researcher, I respected the participant's account as be-

---

122. Finlay, *Phenomenology for Therapists*, 74.

123. Finlay, *Phenomenology for Therapists*, 73.

124. Finlay, *Phenomenology for Therapists*, 74.

125. Finlay, "Dance between the Reduction and Reflexivity," 1–32.

126. Ashworth, "Presuppose Nothing!," 21–22.

127. Finlay, *Phenomenology for Therapists*, 76.

128. Finlay, *Phenomenology for Therapists*, 77.

129. Finlay, *Phenomenology for Therapists*, 77.

ing true, as she understood and wished to present her experience. In the case of this study, experience described was being formative of the participant's identity in her own current situation of living with dementia.

Embodied Encounter

In this research, data was gathered in the context of embodied encounter with each of the eight participants in their own homes. The initial meeting and greeting were significant in establishing a context which felt respectful and safe for the person with dementia and for their loved-one who, in six of the cases, was present in a nearby room. As my hosts, the participants or family members present provided welcoming drinks and moments of general conversation. This time provided opportunity for relationship and trust to be established. It also became clear during this time for the researcher the extent to which the dementia was affecting aspects of physical mobility and communication. In all cases, patience and sensitivity were required by the researcher, and attention to the effects of tiredness on participants' concentration.

The atmosphere of the home and interactions of the participant with the spouse or other family members present gave me important clues and understandings of how the advent of dementia was being understood and the challenges that were being faced. For example, at the end of the formal part of the interviews, two family members, having overheard the exchanges between their loved-one and the researcher were moved and tearful, evoking empathic response from myself.

As Finlay draws out, the embodied encounter allows an "intertwining" of researcher and participant which enables a co-creation in what is being expressed and understood. In this study, during the conversations, facial expressions and gestures added significantly to the felt meaning that participants contributed at various stages in their accounts. My own bodily movements instinctively reciprocated, for example, when one of the participants was moved to tears as he spoke, I instinctively reached out and held his hand. He responded by grasping my hand tightly. In some conversations there were frequent silences where the person with dementia hunted for elusive words or the ideas they wanted to express. My own bodily responses in movement and facial expressions allowed silence, encouraged further response and aimed to communicate my felt empathy and compassion with the experience being described.

Nevertheless, as Gadamer has highlighted, "language is the universal medium in which understanding occurs."[130] At this stage of early to moderate dementia, conversation was still possible and this provided an important opportunity for investigating the lived experience of dementia.[131] The focal point of the encounter was the research conversation, which took the form of an in-depth, semi-structured interview, allowing the participant freedom to tell their stories, guided by the interviewer.

The presence of early to moderate symptoms of dementia meant that lapses in concentration or short term memory sometimes resulted in difficulty in finding a word or thought. This caused both hesitation, or, conversely, lengthy digression and repetition. Nevertheless, the choice of words was revealing. As Heidegger's emphasis on language in *Being and Time* suggests, the style of speaking and choice of language reveal and show the mystery of being.[132] In the case of two of the participants where symptoms of dementia were becoming more advanced, careful listening and attention to gestures was especially important. Gadamer has made the point that sometimes gesture may have a synonymous-ity with language. He writes of "an articulated use of gesture that represents articulated vocalized language."[133] However, in this study, language was the bedrock for the ongoing and interpretative activity of textual analysis.

The Hermeneutical Circle

The function of the hermeneutical circle has been discussed earlier in the context of practical theology and qualitative research. Here, in spite of Gadamer's misgivings about the use of the word "method," it is integral to the use of a hermeneutic phenomenological approach. Swinton and Mowatt[134] draw on Gadamer's description: "The hermeneutical circle refers to the interpretive process wherein the scholar moves backwards and forwards from 'whole to the part and back to the whole.'"[135]

---

130. Gadamer, *Truth and Method*, 390.

131. Robinson, "Should People with Alzheimer's," 104.

132. Heidegger, *Being and Time*, 34, 203.

133. Gadamer, *Truth and Method*, 442

134. Swinton and Mowat, *Practical Theology*, 116.

135. Gadamer, *Truth and Method*, 291.

Finlay, drawing on Heidegger, expounds the circle process as one of interrogating experience and as a challenging of initial understandings, leading to "an interpretative revision of the fore-understanding."[136]

> The hermeneutic circle thus moves between question and answer; between implicit pre-understandings and explicit understandings; between the reciprocal relationship between the interpreted and interpreter; between understanding parts and the whole. Understanding deepens by going round the circle again and again.[137]

Swinton locates this reflective cycle with focus on the back-and-forth movement "between the meaning of the words and the meaning of the wider text."[138] This process cannot be hurried. Finlay talks about "dwelling" with the research.[139] This first enables attentive listening to the participants, then the discovery of ever deeper levels of meaning being discovered in the texts. These are then opened up for the reader of the phenomenological text. In this study, this "dwelling" took place over several months and was enabled first through unhurried conversation with participants, then careful, transcription of the texts myself which involved repeated listening to the recordings of the research conversations, bringing awareness of the ways in which words were expressed and their accompanying emotions. Finlay suggests that, whilst a laborious process, transcription by the researcher "provides an opportunity to hear the interview again and to remind oneself of tone and other nonverbal noises or silences which are so useful when grappling with implicit meanings."[140]

The resulting texts were then read and re-read, beginning the process of analysis and discovery of structures of meaning.

Writing: Description Seeking Understanding

Hermeneutic phenomenological research is not complete when the data has been collected. Echoing Heidegger and Sartre, Manen asserts, "Writing is the method."[141] "Creating a phenomenological text is the object of

136. Finlay, *Phenomenology for Therapists*, 53.
137. Finlay, *Phenomenology for Therapists*, 53.
138. Swinton, *Spirituality and Mental Health Care*, 104.
139. Finlay, *Phenomenology for Therapists*, 228.
140. Finlay, *Phenomenology for Therapists*, 229.
141. Manen, *Researching Lived Experience*, 126.

the research process."[142] Reflective immersion in the text involves writing and re-writing, editing and re-editing, aiming to provide rich description which evokes the phenomenon under study, and in its interpretative style, sets out to uncover new insights and fresh understandings. Carefully crafted language is the medium, the use of which is "inevitably an interpretive process."[143] In the process of this research, writing and re-writing involving "re-thinking, re-flecting" were essential tools in the interrogation of the data.[144] Resonant with the dynamic and dialectic of the hermeneutical circle, this process of crafting the phenomenological accounts has the potential to bring to light ever deeper meaning and understanding.[145]

The immersive reflection on the texts, prompting memories of context and voices, slowly revealed emergent themes which provided "structures of experience."[146] These facilitated the writing of the phenomenological account which, in this study, set out to uncover something of the nature of being a Christian living with dementia. Paley has spoken disparagingly of a "liturgy of common themes" which, he complains, this research approach sometimes results in.[147] When this happens, he argues, it provides a general framework of categories in which all uniqueness, all "lived experience," completely disappears. However, the themes of true hermeneutic phenomenology are not mere generalizations. Rather, the thematic analysis "offers the opportunity to highlight important conceptual features or nuances of lived experience."[148] Manen describes the themes as being "more like knots in the webs of our experiences, around which certain lived experiences are spun," and which enable exploration and fresh understanding of nuanced, rich, distinctive aspects of the experience under investigation. He writes:

> Themes are the stars that make up the universes of meaning we live through. By the light of these themes we can navigate and explore such universes. Themes have phenomenological power when they allow us to proceed with the phenomenological descriptions.[149]

142. Manen, *Researching Lived Experience*, 111.

143. Manen, *Researching Lived Experience*, 181.

144. Manen, *Researching Lived Experience*, 131.

145. Manen, *Researching Lived Experience*, 131, 132.

146. Manen, *Researching Lived Experience*, 79.

147. Paley, "Phenomenology as Rhetoric," 108–9.

148. Finlay, *Phenomenology for Therapists*, 236–37.

149. Manen, *Researching Lived Experience*, 90.

Throughout the research process and writing, it was necessary to hold onto commitment to the subject under inquiry. Manen speaks of this as "maintaining a strong and oriented relation" which results not only in thinking but in action.[150] In line with practical theology's goal of faithful service to God, Heidegger's insistence on *sorge*, and Finlay and Manen's emphasis on thoughtful, relational caring and attention, the phenomenological accounts have a transformative goal. As with all writing, its goal is to let us and others see: "It is in and through the words that the shining through (the invisible) becomes visible."[151] To be transformative, as with other forms of writing, the phenomenological accounts resulting from this research aim to provoke attentive and responsive reading.[152]

Conclusion

This chapter has set out to describe the methodology and approach used in this study. I have described the nature of qualitative research, and the methodological tools found in phenomenology which have been used in pursuit of the goals of the research. I have discussed the philosophical foundations of phenomenology, seeking to show why I have used the approach of hermeneutic phenomenology in this study. The chapter has also begun to suggest how the methodology has shaped the methods and process of the research project.

In the following chapter, I give an account of the research design and process which enabled the gathering of the phenomenological accounts of the lived experience of Christians living with early to moderate symptoms of dementia.

150. Manen, *Researching Lived Experience*, 90, 154.
151. Manen, *Researching Lived Experience*, 130.
152. Manen, *Researching Lived Experience*, 130–31.

$$5$$

The Research
Design and Process

Introduction

IN THIS RESEARCH PROJECT I was seeking ways of finding understanding
and insight into the lived experience of Christians from the evangelical
tradition who were living with dementia. In this chapter I give an account
of the research process, describing the design, introducing the participants and discussing issues of ethics and auditability.

I had initially planned to interview individuals who were living with
dementia and then conduct small group semi-structured interviews with
family members or close friends of the individual participants. I had also
envisaged second interviews with each of the individual participants.
However, in the early stages of the research design it became evident that
some changes were necessary partly for methodological reasons, and
partly because of the sensitive nature of dementia, and its impact on both
caring supporters and the persons with dementia. Reflections on these
decisions were noted in my research journal.

Early Changes in the Development
of the Research Design

Group Interviews

The rationale for gathering data from small group interviews had been that these would provide a multi-perspectival understanding of the experience of living with dementia, with regard to their loved-ones' faith experience and practice. However, I decided eventually not to use this data in the analysis and presentation of the lived experience. It became clear during the research period that the group interviews were not the best tool for generating material which focused on the precise topic under investigation. On reflection, the following reasons for this emerged:

- The chosen methodology of hermeneutic phenomenology sets out to examine the lived experience of those who are experiencing the phenomenon. Whilst family and friends were compassionate witnesses to the experiences of their loved ones, it was nevertheless, not their own experience. Consequently, any description was from their own point of view which sometimes differed from the participant's own account. This was interesting, but not in keeping with the methodology which trusts the participant's own account as being true to their own experience. Finlay has commented:

> Phenomenological researchers believe that what participants say about their own experience is their "truth" and that is the starting point of any explorations. We accept (i.e., do not morally judge) our participants and assume that what is given in research is their reality—at least as they understand or wish to present it.[1]

- The different levels of relationship between individual group members made open discussion about this emotive and painful subject difficult, especially in two of the groups. Some participants expressed reluctance to share frankly in the presence of "strangers." One participant, for example, felt uncomfortable expressing her own personal views openly in the presence of another member of her church. The different relationships with the person living with dementia also resulted in inconsistent kinds of contribution to the

---

1. Finlay, *Phenomenology for Therapists*, 77.

discussion. For example, husbands and wives were much more intimately aware of the developing difficulties of their loved ones, than those who were a caring child, sister or friend.

- However, in one group in particular, where people had not previously known each other well, discussion of the issue of faith and dementia was animated, committed and mutually supportive. In this group, there was the danger for me as researcher, that the group became focused on mutual pastoral caring. The conversation was a positive, albeit at times, emotional experience for the loved-ones gathered. However, it gave particular insight into the feelings and perspectives of the supporters rather than the experience of the person with dementia. Whilst for these reasons, the data from this group discussion has not been presented, it had the positive outcome of allowing the group members to voice their understandings and experiences, and of establishing helpful and supportive contacts for their future support.

Whilst not presenting data from the group interviews for the above reasons, these nevertheless did provide the researcher with useful background and further understanding of the focus of the investigation: the lived experience of individuals living with dementia.

Second Interviews with Persons Living with Dementia

Initially, I had considered conducting second interviews with each of the participants, aiming to explore more deeply some of the issues raised in the first interviews. However, after three of the second interviews, I decided not to pursue this pattern, for the following reasons:

- For the person with dementia to participate in the research in this way was emotionally and physically demanding at a very stressful and difficult time of their lives. I did not feel that it was useful to repeat the process of the interview with its very sensitive questioning for an additional occasion, adding to the pressures of the participants' daily living.

- In the four second interviews which were undertaken, participants tended to repeat what they had already said using similar words, although they were invited to expand or explore further. Although, I have no medical expertise, my experience in working in ministry with those with dementia, led me to feel that this was probably due to incipient difficulties with memory, and the repetition of familiar anecdotes, characteristic of those living with dementia.[2]

- A third issue was that all participants had *developing* dementia and their experience of dementia and faith was likely to change during the period which would separate our encounters. Their capacity level for communication and short-term memory was also inevitably diminishing and therefore the research process and methodology would no longer necessarily be the most appropriate. Hermeneutic phenomenology recognizes the transience of lived experience and its nature, that it is always developing and changing.[3] This is especially true in the lived experience of dementia.

I now turn to a description of the research methods, design and process which resulted in the phenomenological accounts and their analysis presented in the next chapter.

Outline of the Research Process

The nine stages of my research process are outlined and summarized below.

1. A series of eight in-depth interviews were carried out in line with the general principles of phenomenological interviewing.[4]

2. These were recorded during the research meeting and then transcribed by the researcher to create texts for further reflection and the interpretative task.

3. The transcripts were then returned to the participants for their confirmation of accuracy and further comments or clarification. Where a loved-one had been present in the home during the interview, they also read the transcript on behalf of the person with dementia. All of their comments and thoughts were fed back to the researcher and were incorporated in the transcript texts and notes.

---

2. Caring.com, "What You Should Know about Alzheimer's Disease."

3. Finlay, *Phenomenology for Therapists*, 223.

4. For example, Finlay, *Phenomenology for Therapists*, 199; Manen, *Researching Lived Experience*, 66–68; Swinton and Mowat, *Practical Theology*, 120.

4. The researcher then immersed herself in these texts, repeatedly listening to the recordings, reading and re-reading the transcripts, looking for nuances and unspoken meanings in the words, silences and remembered gestures and expressions.

5. Following the reflective process of the hermeneutical circle, I moved backwards and forward between the contributions of the different participants and different sections of the texts, looking for repeated words, patterns and emerging themes which seemed to evoke the essence of the lived experience being investigated.

6. I chose not to use software available for data analysis, preferring to "dwell" with the text over a period of several weeks.[5] Reflections were recorded in my research notes and also in my comments added through "Tracking" as I read the texts over and over again. I also used the "Find" function in Word to track the usage of particular words and phrases which seemed to be key and occurred in several of the interviews.

7. During this process I began to construct a thematic analysis, first of each transcript and then of the collected complete transcript, looking for patterns which unified the texts.

8. This process enabled the construction of the phenomenological text, facilitating a descriptive and interpretative account of the phenomenon under investigation.[6]

9. As discussed earlier, writing is fundamental to the hermeneutic phenomenological approach. It was through writing and re-writing that the final account was produced.[7]

---

5. Finlay, *Phenomenology for Therapists*, 228.

6. Manen, *Researching Lived Experience*, 111.

7. Manen, *Researching Lived Experience*, 126.

The Cohort

Selection of Participants

Participants in the research project were selected purposefully[8] the sample being chosen "because it offers the best chance of answering the question."[9] Patton writes:

> The logic and power of purposeful sampling lie in selecting *information-rich cases* for study in depth. Information-rich cases are those from which one can learn a great deal about issues of central importance to the purpose of the inquiry, thus the term *purposeful* sampling. Studying information-rich cases yields insights and in-depth understanding rather than generalizations.

The cohort included four men and four women, all chosen intentionally because they met the criteria for the study. All were Christians whose faith was of an evangelical tradition, although at the time of the interviews they were attending a variety of local churches, including Anglican, Baptist or other free churches. All were living with mild or moderate symptoms of dementia, and were aware of their diagnoses.[10] In these stages of living with dementia, all had capacity for use of language and the sense of linear time, although in some cases these were beginning to be obviously diminished by their illness.[11] This, therefore, presented a window of opportunity for hearing the voices of persons with dementia and for gaining understanding of their lived experience, both in the present and in their anticipation of the future. The small numbers of the cohort were appropriate to the thick description of qualitative research[12] and that of hermeneutic phenomenological methodology,[13] and also to the time limitations of this small-scale study.

As Cotrell and Schulz have emphasized, the small sample size was also an appropriate strategy for research with people living in the earlier stages of dementia.[14] It was important in communication with those

8. See Patton, *Qualitative Research*, 230.

9. Swinton and Mowat, *Practical Theology*, 69.

10. Goldsmith, *In a Strange Land*, 60–65; Shamy, *Guide to the Spiritual Dimension of Care*, 50–53.

11. Alzheimer's Society, "Progression of Alzheimer's Disease."

12. Denscombe, *Good Research Guide*, 220.

13. Swinton and Mowat, *Practical Theology*, 108–9.

14. Cotrell and Schulz, "Perspective of the Patient with Alzheimer's Disease," 205–11.

with dementia to demonstrate focused attention on the person, and to be patient in allowing time for response. It was therefore particularly important that the research conversation should not, in any sense, be hurried.

The research participants were living in their own homes in different regions of Southern England. Three of the participants were living on their own in supported-living retirement residences; the others were living with their spouses. Participants were located through the researcher's contacts with churches and Christian networks. All the participants volunteered to take part in this study, in some cases following discussion with a family member who was the "gatekeeper." All were aware of the reasons for the research and wished to contribute to its aims and outcomes.

One of the participants who consented to being interviewed for the research, with the support of her husband, understood that she had a diagnosis of dementia, but preferred that in our interview I spoke of this in terms of "memory loss." Bartlett and Martin have highlighted such examples, citing the difficulty of working within "the limitations of a society that still stigmatizes dementia," making those facing the challenges of the disease unwilling to name it, or to accept their diagnosis.[15]

Introducing the Participants

The names of the participants and their family members used here are not their real names, in order to protect their anonymity.

Alice, a retired GP, was living independently in her own home which was part of a supported-living community. Her husband had passed away a few years before our conversation. Her upbringing had been in the evangelical tradition. At the time of the interview, she was part of an evangelical, "ecumenical" (Alice's description) church. She had been diagnosed with dementia ("mainly Alzheimer's") about five years before the first interview.

Bill, a former policeman, was living with Carol, his wife. As a child, he went to a local Anglican church. At the time of the interview, he was part of an evangelical Baptist, charismatic church of which Carol is the pastor. He had received a diagnosis of early onset dementia (Alzheimer's) about 18 months before the research interview.

David, a retired teacher, was brought up in the Methodist denomination. For many years he and his wife, Gail, had been part of an evangelical

---

15. Bartlett and Martin, "Ethical Issues in Dementia Care Research," 59.

Anglican church. He had received a diagnosis of dementia (combined vascular and Alzheimer's) about one year before the research interview.

Jess was living with Andrew, her husband. They were part of an evangelical Anglican church. Neither of them had had a Christian up-bringing. Jess was diagnosed with Alzheimer's about two years before the research interview.

Jill was living independently in her own home in a supported-living community. Her husband had passed away several years before the research interview. She was brought up in a "nominal" Christian home, and became a committed Christian in her early twenties. In recent years she had been part of a local Anglican church. She had been diagnosed with dementia about two years before our conversation. Her dementia was mainly Alzheimer's with some Vascular.

Matthew had been brought up in the Anglican church. Broadly, of an evangelical tradition, he and his wife, Wendy, were part of their local Anglican church. He had Alzheimer's Disease which was diagnosed about six years before the research interview.

Ron was living with Clare, his wife, at the time of the interview (he has sadly passed away since then). He attended a Baptist church as a young person, although his parents were not regular church-goers. He had been converted whilst living in Rhodesia [Zimbabwe]. He and Clare belonged to a Baptist church at the time of the interview. He had been diagnosed with Vascular dementia about three years before this.

Rosemary, a former teacher, was living independently in her own home, part of the same community as Alice. Her upbringing had been in the Plymouth Brethren, which she had left as a young adult. She didn't go to church regularly as an adult. However, following a serious illness about ten years before the research interview, her sense of relationship with God had grown. She had been diagnosed with vascular dementia during the ten years preceding our conversation.

The Interviews

These began informally as I was welcomed to the home of the person with dementia. In some cases their spouse or other close relative was present. Each meeting began with informal introduction and conversation about the research topic and its goals and an explanation of the research process and interview. This informal time gave opportunity for a relaxed atmosphere and mutual trust to be established.[16] Supporting family members left the room when the research interview was about to begin.

The interviews with individuals were lightly structured in order to provide guidance for a purposeful exchange on the topic under investigation, within an informal setting. Keeping focused on the research question about the lived experience of Christian faith in the context of dementia was important. Even though participants were all in the early to moderate stages of the disease, participants to greater and lesser degrees, sometimes digressed from the research topic. On occasions, it was evidently difficult for the person to find the precise word or expression for which they were hunting, or memory lapses interfered with fluency.[17] Participants' delivery was, in some cases slow, hesitant and repetitive. In one case, delivery was rapid, but with gaps in sentences or a running together of ideas. Another participant occasionally used a positive or negative when context, and later conversation with the family, confirmed that the opposite was intended. Sometimes it was necessary to repeat or re-phrase a question.[18] In all of these situations, the researcher gently recalled the participant to the point in question, or prompted through word, gesture or expression of empathic understanding. It was important for the researcher to stay aware of the effects of tiredness on participants' concentration.

The lightly structured interview included questions about past faith experience, present faith experience with dementia, and feelings about faith experience in the future in the light of their developing dementia. Questions aimed to enable exploration of the impact of dementia on faith experience and aspects of faith practice, including how these contribute to the lived experience of faith. As discussed in the Introduction, practices of evangelical Christians such as Bible reading and being part of small groups are integral to the sense of relationship with God and, therefore, the personal lived experience of faith. It was important therefore to explore the significance of these for participants.

The interviews, with one exception, were face-to-face encounters in the participants' own homes. There was an exception with one participant who was unwell on the planned interview date. We subsequently talked via Skype with visual and audio links, the research participant being

16. Clarke and Keady, "Getting Down to Brass Tacks," 37–38.

17. MacKinlay, "Listening to People with Dementia," 101, 104.

18. See discussion regarding challenges of data collection from people living with dementia in Clarke and Keady, "Getting Down to Brass Tacks," 34–41.

in her own home. Some research has suggested that the lack of three-dimensional presence makes rapport between researcher and participant more difficult.[19] However, other research suggests that this is dependent on the personalities of individuals involved and, in some cases, may allow the participant to speak more freely. In this case, I had met the participant on a previous occasion and she was a confident person who wanted to find a way of contributing to the research.

All interviews were recorded and field notes made. In the case of the Skype interview, the initial recording failed after 20 minutes. Extensive field notes were made of the interview immediately following our conversation. A subsequent interview via Skype re-visited some of the questions which had been discussed and the recording of this interview was entirely successful.

Each interview lasted from approximately forty-five minutes to one hour. Interviews were transcribed by the researcher, facilitating initial reflection and creation of texts for further reflection and analysis as appropriate to the methodology of hermeneutic phenomenology, and to the dialogical focus of practical theology.[20]

Ethical Issues

Ethics Guidelines and Approval

Ethical considerations of the research have been addressed and requirements fulfilled in line with the University of Aberdeen's guidelines.[21] In the early stages of the research two previously unforeseen situations arose which were referred back to the Ethics Committee who approved the solutions I suggested with the support of my supervisor, Professor John Swinton. The research was explained to the participants in advance of the research. Information sheets giving the reasons for the research and its goals were supplied. Participants have been assured of their anonymity being safe-guarded in the data, the PhD thesis itself, and in any publication of the research, such as found in this book.

---

19. For further discussion of this, see Iacono et al., "Skype as a Tool for Qualitative Research," 6–7.

20. Finlay, *Phenomenology for Therapists*, 229.

21. ESRC, "Framework for Research Ethics"; PEC, "Guidelines."

Consent

Consent forms indicating understanding of the project and willingness to take part were signed before the research began. As Bartlett and Martin have argued, "lack of competence" to give written consent "cannot be assumed just because a person has a diagnosis of dementia."[22] In the light of participants being in the earlier stages of dementia, they were able to read and understand the documents supplied and give consent on their own behalf. They all knew that they had received diagnoses of dementia and were happy to confirm details of these. Nevertheless, in cases where the participant was living with their spouse, or the gatekeeper was a family member, their additional consent was given before the interview began, following the "practice of 'double consents'" identified by a study in the USA.[23]

Participants were informed that they could withdraw from the research at any time and for any reason. Ethical concerns and procedures were discussed and agreed throughout, both with the Ethics Committee of Aberdeen University and following the guidance of my supervisor, Professor John Swinton.

Issues of Power

Whilst my research methodology assumes a relational approach, it was important at all times to remain reflexively aware of inevitable "power imbalances" in the researcher/participant relationship.[24] Finlay speaks of the need for the researcher to "work hard to relinquish their 'power' and yield to whatever might emerge in the relational moment."[25] As the researcher, leading our interview conversation, I needed always to be conscious of my "duty of care" which involved empowering participants to speak of their experience, but also being protective of them in restraining them from "too much exposure."[26] Within this delicate balance, as researcher, it was necessary to remain humble, recognizing the expertise of my participants

---

22. Bartlett and Martin, "Ethical Issues in Dementia Care Research," 51.
23. Bartlett and Martin, "Ethical Issues in Dementia Care Research," 58.
24. Finlay, *Phenomenology for Therapists*, 217.
25. Finlay, *Phenomenology for Therapists*, 219.
26. Finlay, *Phenomenology for Therapists*, 220.

who are the ones living with dementia. As Finlay comments, "We need to appreciate the gift they are giving us by sharing."[27]

A further dimension to this study were the ethical issues of power involved when researching the experience of those living with dementia. As Wilkinson has explored, there are particular power inequalities that need to be addressed in "the relationships between people with dementia and others."[28] As discussed earlier in chapter 1, the voices of those living with dementia are rarely heard, although this is changing.[29] Wilkinson challenges the medicalized view of people with dementia which objectifies them, seeing them as "diseased brains rather than individual people."[30] Giving a voice to people living with dementia is an empowering activity which is one consequence of this study.

The ethics approval procedure for this research highlighted a pertinent issue concerning the involvement of people with dementia in research. The initial procedure proposal was that participants with dementia would have a family member or other nominated supporter nearby during the research interview and that they should also sign a consent form to confirm the person with dementia's informed consent. However, three of the participants with dementia were living independently. Wanting to safeguard ethical concerns, I asked if the first of these would like to invite a friend to be present in her home with her during the research interview, and if such a person would also sign a consent form confirming her consent to participate. This person was at first surprised and then affronted by this suggestion, protesting that, as with other aspects of her life, she remained entirely capable of making her own decisions. Her reaction raised the ethical principle of autonomy and competence to consent which is challenged by early dementia.[31] However, as Bartlett and Martin note: "lack of competence cannot be assumed just because a person has a diagnosis of dementia."[32] They highlight that consent in this area of dementia needs to be not a single event but a continual, ongoing process between the researcher and participant. This situation was

27. Finlay, *Phenomenology for Therapists*, 221.

28. Wilkinson, "Including People with Dementia in Research," 10.

29. Robinson, "Should People with Alzheimer's," 104; Bryden, *Dancing with Dementia*, 48.

30. Wilkinson, "Including People with Dementia in Research," 11.

31. MacKinlay and Trevitt, *Finding Meaning*, 71.

32. Bartlett and Martin, "Ethical Issues in Dementia Care Research," 51.

discussed with the Ethics committee and my supervisor consulted, and an amicable compromise was found.

This participant's reaction to my suggestion made me aware of how presuppositions about those living with dementia may be based on incorrect stereotypes that disempower them and risk excluding them from contributing their unique perspectives.[33] Whilst the ethical considerations prompted appropriate reflection and concern to safeguard the well-being of the research participants, the prescriptive characteristic of some of the measures suggested endangered some participants' freedom to choose to be involved. As Bartlett and Martin discuss, there is a "tension between the opposing notions of 'empowerment' and 'risk.'"[34] It is important to recognize that dementia is a progressive disease. In the early to moderate stages of dementia, memory lapses and other incipient symptoms of dementia may be beginning to be apparent, requiring researcher sensitivity and patience. However, if language facility and linear temporal awareness remain as in the early stages of dementia, hermeneutical phenomenological research remains possible and profoundly transformative of our understanding of the experience of dementia as, it is hoped, this study will demonstrate.

The power of gatekeepers is also especially relevant to this study. Some participants, as discussed above, were living independently and made autonomous decisions about their involvement in the research. For others, who were living with a spouse or were beginning to be more obviously affected by their dementia symptoms, the spouse or other family member was the gatekeeper. Here, where the gatekeepers were the loved-ones of the person with dementia, they were appropriately protective. Pratt makes the point that they "have a valid protective role" and are a valuable resource "in supporting people with dementia into research."[35] Conversely, in the search for potential participants, the power of the gatekeeper was in some cases, a barrier to the research, perhaps because their own distress in face of the dementia diagnosis meant they were overprotective of their loved-one, and they were unwilling for me to contact a potential participant directly. Or, during some research meetings, it was clear that when present in the same room, the gatekeeper with good intentions, sometimes found it difficult to allow the person with dementia

---

33. Wilkinson, "Including People with Dementia in Research," 10.

34. Bartlett and Martin, "Ethical Issues in Dementia Care Research," 58.

35. Pratt, "Nobody's Ever Asked How I Felt," 167.

to speak for themselves.[36] However, the influence of the gatekeeper was powerful when perceived as "valuable collaborators in the research process," as was the case with participants in this study.[37]

Issues of Validity

As discussed earlier in the consideration of the interpretative paradigm of qualitative research, its validity depends on different criteria from those of quantitative research. It is not concerned with the nomothetic truth of the natural sciences, but ideographic truth which leads to understanding. This is particularly the case in a hermeneutic phenomenological study where "the object . . . is to gain *understanding* of the experience of research participants, rather than to *explain* the experience."[38] As discussed earlier, the senses of identification and resonance in others experiencing similar situations, together with maintaining a reflexive mode, are part of the rigour and ultimate transferability of the research and its outcomes.[39] In this study I have followed the established validation criteria which "fit with the philosophical assumptions, purposes, and goals" and demonstrate the trustworthiness of the hermeneutical phenomenological methodology.[40] In the following, I draw on Swinton who proposes that "trustworthiness" includes "credibility, auditability and fittingness":

> For a study to be trustworthy it must be credible, it must be possible for an external person to audit the progress of the work and it must have a sense of fit or resonance with the experiences of the participants or others experiencing similar phenomena.[41]

Credibility

In order to substantiate its credibility, the research account must, as qualitative methodological writing affirms, "be able to present a thick,

---

36. Pratt, "Nobody's Ever Asked How I Felt," 167.
37. Pratt, "Nobody's Ever Asked How I Felt," 169.
38. Swinton and Mowat, *Practical Theology*, 121.
39. Swinton and Mowat, *Practical Theology*, 47.
40. Leininger, "Evaluation Criteria and Critique," 97.
41. Swinton and Mowat, *Practical Theology*, 122.

rich and recognisable description of the subject matter."[42] In line with the hermeneutical phenomenological approach, this thick description "seeks to capture the essence of a phenomenon in a way that communicates it in all its fullness."[43] As discussed earlier, the research is not only about data gathering, but is also ongoing in the writing, reflection and analysis. Swinton affirms this: "The process of writing, reflecting and accurately interpreting the data is not simply epiphenomenal to data presentation and analysis. It is a crucial part of the process."[44]

Participant and Independent Validation

The research participants were inspired and motivated to participate in the research because they wished their experience to contribute to increasing the well-being of others in similar situations, and to helping the Church be better equipped in providing spiritual support for those facing the challenges of living with dementia. As researcher who had received their hospitality, I was aware of my responsibility to tell their stories well. It was important, therefore, to demonstrate that their contributions were being received respectfully and handled carefully.

As Swinton notes, "a vital part of the validation process was the use of the participants' own words and narratives as a prominent aspect of the final text."[45] It is those words which are used as a basis for the reflection and interpretation. All interviews were recorded, as described earlier, and then transcribed. These transcriptions were returned to all the participants, which some chose to share with others who knew them. I requested confirmation that these were accurate and this was given. Some chose to make additional comments or made amendments at this stage, all of which were incorporated into my notes on the transcripts and formed part of my ongoing and final reflection.

Whilst I had some ongoing, informal contact with the research participants and their primary supporters regarding the progress of the research, I did not conduct further interviews with the participants for the reasons given previously above regarding second interviews with participants. Qualitative research data in any case is context specific. As

42. Sandelowski, "Problem of Rigour in Qualitative Research," 27–37.
43. Swinton and Mowat, *Practical Theology*, 123.
44. Swinton, *Spirituality and Mental Health Care*, 109.
45. Swinton, *Spirituality and Mental Health Care*, 109.

Finlay notes, "What may have been 'true' for them at the time of the interview may no longer be the case."[46] The experience described was that given and agreed at the time of the interviews.

Independent validation by those who are expert both in the spiritual care of those with dementia and as hermeneutic phenomenologists was important for prompting awareness of distortions in the interpretation and personal reflexivity. The development of the Ethics proposal was monitored by the Aberdeen Ethics Committee. Throughout the study my supervisor, who was the lead researcher for this project, read and reflected on my research and the themes emerging. I noted and reflected on all of these comments which were discussed.

Issues of Auditability

As the literature suggests, auditability is an important component of the research process.[47] In line with this, I have sought at each stage of the research to create an "audit trail" which can be followed by others.[48] Throughout the research process, the transcripts, my initial reflections, comments and themes were shown to my supervisor for confirmation of their validity. In my research journal I have recorded my reflections both on the emerging data and the developing research process, making it clear where the latter was changing and giving the reasons for the decisions I made regarding this. As stated above, initial approval was sought and given from the Ethics Committee of Aberdeen University. The committee was also consulted about subsequent changes which became necessary as the research process progressed and developed.

In addition, I was required to give short, annual reports to my sponsoring organization who part-funded my research, and I also contributed a paper at a conference for their doctoral researchers.[49]

46. Finlay, *Phenomenology for Therapists*, 223.
47. Swinton and Mowat, *Practical Theology*, 124; Koch, "Story Telling," 1182–90.
48. Koch, "Story Telling," 1187–88.
49. Bible Society, Stonehill Green, Westlea, Swindon, SN5 7DG.

"Fittingness"

"Fittingness," or resonance, is a further way which Swinton suggests as a criterion for establishing the trustworthiness of the research.[50] This looks beyond the data gathering, the reflection and the thematic analysis to the final phenomenological account and, in some ways, brings the research back to its starting point. The goal is to reflect "something of the essence of the experience described."[51] This is the objective in chapter 6 which sets out to describe the lived experience of Christians with early to moderate symptoms of dementia. Dependent on the perspectives of methodology and method, some aspects of the research discussed below might be seen either as limitations or as strengths.[52]

Limitations of the Approach to This Study

The size of the cohort was small, but this enabled the necessary depth of conversation and its subsequent analysis within the timescale available. The hermeneutic phenomenological approach is not seeking results which can be measured quantatively. Rather it is about seeking deeper understanding of the essence of experience, bringing insights to the ongoing, wider conversation. The number of the participants was also in keeping with the qualitative goals of the research, and the guidance from the limited research writing available about people living with dementia.[53]

Selection of participants was purposive, conducive to the narrow field of inquiry. Patton comments: "Qualitative inquiry typically focuses on relatively small samples . . . selected *purposefully* to permit inquiry into and understanding of a phenomenon *in depth*."[54] The criteria for inclusion in the study inevitably limited the number of potential participants. However, the small number of participants allowed a strong focus on the issue under investigation. They were selected intentionally because: they were Christians from the evangelical faith tradition,

50. Swinton and Mowat, *Practical Theology*, 122; Guba and Lincoln, "Paradigmatic Controversies," 205–9.

51. Swinton and Mowat, *Practical Theology*, 124.

52. Swinton and Mowat, *Practical Theology*, 110; Crowther, "Sacred Joy at Birth," 247.

53. For example, Cotrell and Schulz, "Perspective of the Patient with Alzheimer's Disease," 205–11; Clarke and Keady, "Getting Down to Brass Tacks," 34.

54. Patton, *Qualitative Research*, 46.

living with early to moderate stage dementia, and willing and able to participate in the research.

It proved difficult to find those for whom dementia was bringing negative feelings about their faith. Nevertheless, other research in this area reports that whilst challenges to faith are experienced, as revealed by the participants in this research, these do not result in actual loss of faith.[55] For example, rather than polarities of disillusionment with faith, Dalby, Boddington, and Sperlinger speak of people being in an ongoing process of living their faith in the context of having dementia.[56] The participants, who had volunteered themselves to take part in the study, in some cases encouraged by their spouses, were strongly committed to their faith, and were motivated to participate in a project which they felt would be helpful to others.

Gadamer points out that all methods are limited by particular perspectives.[57] My own situated-ness in the context of the evangelical tradition was potentially a limitation and my empathic understanding made it important to retain my reflexive researcher stance. However, as discussed previously, it was also a strength as it enabled mutual understanding and a sense of co-operation which may not have been possible had I not shared the participants' faith.

Conclusion

This chapter has set out to describe the research design and process used in this study. I have sought to build on the methodology discussed in chapter 4 and to demonstrate that this is both useful and appropriate to the task of this research. I recognize that research with people with dementia is a developing field and, as Wilkinson's work proposes, there is more to be done in finding ways of enabling their voices to be heard.[58]

In chapter 6 I present the analysis of the phenomenological accounts gathered through the methodology and research tools I have described. In doing so my aim is to deepen understanding and uncover fresh insights into the lived experience of Christians from an evangelical tradition, who are living with early to moderate stages of dementia.

55. Snyder, "Satisfactions and Challenges"; Katsuno, "Personal Spirituality."

56. Dalby et al., "Lived Experience," 16–17; Snyder, "Satisfactions and Challenges"; Katsuno, "Personal Spirituality"; Snyder and Stuckey, email exchanges with the author.

57. Gadamer, *Truth and Method*, 325.

58. Wilkinson, "Including People with Dementia in Research," 9–24.

6

The Lived Experience
of Faith in Dementia

"Whenever we enter into another person's experiences
of suffering, we need to tread very carefully
for we tread upon sacred ground."[1]

Introduction

IN THIS CHAPTER I present the contributions of the participants, revealing their experience of faith whilst living with dementia. Their commitment to faith was the starting point for their response to their illness, and
it is this which had motivated them in wanting to be part of the research
project. Rosemary said her goal in speaking to me was that she wanted to
"just bring glory to him." For these human beings, what is the nature of
their experience of faith whilst living with dementia, and how is that faith
to be understood in relation to their dementia?

As researcher, in accord with the methodology of hermeneutic methodology, I have the privileged task of seeking understanding of the essential
meaning of that experience.[2] The encounters and the participants' words
begin to disclose the hidden nature of this phenomenon.[3] I was also aware,

1. Goldsmith, "Tracing Rainbows," 122.
2. Manen, *Researching Lived Experience*, 77.
3. See Heidegger, *Being and Time*, 49–62.

as we spoke, of the expression of subjective thought and feelings through the whole unified, embodied being, not just through their words.[4] These gifts of the participants' personal narratives are an invaluable resource and form part of the dialectical hermeneutical circle. The perspectives of both the research participants and the researcher come together in a fusing of horizons to deepen our understanding and bring new insights.[5]

In the wider scope of practical theology, this lived experience contributes to Osmer's descriptive and interpretive tasks.[6] In the following analysis, I follow Manen's approach in using a thematic approach as a tool which aims to enable "a process of insightful invention, discovery or disclosure."[7] The themes provide structure and are "a means to get at the notion we are addressing."

The research participants' words and the commentary are structured using five themes which emerged from our conversations, as follows:

Theme 1: Transforming faith: responding to dementia
Theme 2: Memory funding faith
Theme 3: Knowing God in dementia
Theme 4. Faith in practice
Theme 5: Finding meaning in dementia

Each theme is followed by a brief summary of emerging insights.

Theme 1: Transforming Faith: Responding to Dementia

In this first theme, the participants' words show something of how living with early to moderate dementia was affecting their own (and others') perception of self and their faith identity. Their words revealed how their faith was responding to the experience of dementia, and the transcendence of faith which was enabling resilience and bringing hope. Their contributions and my commentary are organized in three inter-linking subordinate themes, as follows:

- Identity: knowing who I am
- Enduring faith: laughter, loss and struggle
- Transcending faith: acceptance, thankfulness and hope

4. Matthews, "Dementia and the Identity of the Person," 172–73.
5. Gadamer, *Truth and Method*, 305.
6. Osmer, *Practical Theology*, 4.
7. Manen, *Researching Lived Experience*, 78–79.

Identity: Knowing Who I Am

Whilst the participants knew that the focus of the research was about their experience of faith, some chose to speak at length about the difference the diagnosis of dementia was making to their sense of identity as people, and how they felt others regarded them. This data is included here because it provides context and background for the exploration of how dementia was affecting the participants' sense of faith identity. It is important to acknowledge that their faith experience was not a separate aspect of their selves, but was framed in the context of this wider issue of how they understood their identity within dementia. In all the conversations, aspects of the participants' faith stories are interwoven in the discussion of the different themes identified for this analysis.

"I'm the Same Person"

Near the beginning of our conversations, both David and Bill told me about their initial sense of shock on hearing of their probable diagnoses:

> DAVID: I was quite staggered by this. . . . I was very cross with him [GP] actually . . . but I was really quite shocked.

However, at the time of their interviews, over a year since their diagnoses, they asserted strongly that dementia was not affecting their sense of who they were. David said that his dementia was "not a problem," and Bill said it was making no difference, "apart from these memory lapses." However, in spite of their emphases on not being changed by dementia, I wonder if these assertions reflected a fear of the changes which dementia was bringing. Their comments resonated with Bryden who writes of diagnosis as bringing the "horror of prognosis" which is "a turning point in our lives."[8] They both chose to minimise their awareness of difficulties.

> DAVID: The way I look at it is, it's one part of the brain, it's just one part. . . . Now if that one part (or those two bits), they don't work—but the rest of the brain does.

> BILL: I think what has surprised me is that I still feel I'm the same person before it was diagnosed. Now I've got the medication I think it's bringing it down to a stable.

---

8. Bryden, *Dancing with Dementia*, 155.

In these early stages of the disease, David and Bill were seeing dementia as a medical condition which was contributing to changes in their lives, but feeling that these were not significant for their identity. It is as though seeing dementia in this way was enabling them to keep their biological diagnoses separate from the person they felt themselves to be, and to retain control over their lives. At the beginning of their journeys with this illness, I wondered, as Kitwood has highlighted, if their medical diagnoses were beginning to define who they felt themselves to be.[9] Nevertheless, Bill's surprise that he felt like "the same person" suggested his awareness of stereotypical images of people who live with dementia. Their protests that there was "no problem," suggested their desire to assert their sense of continuing identity as they were encountering the changes that dementia was undoubtedly bringing.

"When I Was Labelled 'Dementia'"

The words of Jess and Jill expressed their perspective on this experience. I became aware that they had a consciousness, even concern, about how others might see them because of their dementia.

At the beginning of our conversation, Jess told me that she would prefer that I used the term "memory loss" rather than the word "dementia" because of negative associations with childhood memories of her grandmother's dementia.

> JESS: She was put in a sort of prison . . . hospital . . . and there she died. And the only thing I remember about her is her crying and saying . . . that it's not right that she has to leave her children . . . and she can't see her children.

With such memories—the exclusion, the disempowerment of her grandmother—it was not surprising that Jess's diagnosis made her want to reject this designation:

> JESS: I do agree that I have "memory loss" . . . but it doesn't affect me . . . when I knew . . . that I had memory loss . . . when I was labelled "memory loss."

Her emphasis on the word "labelled," spoken with an ironic emphasis, suggested that she strongly objected to having her identity summarized

---

9. Kitwood, *Dementia Reconsidered*, 9. See also Kevern, "Alzheimer's and the Dementia of God," 241.

with a medical label. In contrast, she asserted her identity as a person embedded in social relationships:

> JESS: Just because you can't remember things it doesn't make you not human. You're still a human, you're still a parent, wife . . . husband. . . . I'm just me.

The strength with which Jess spoke suggested her concern that others might regard dementia as a threat to the person she felt herself to be. Her words conveyed a confident understanding of who she was, which was not affected by impaired physical capacity, but was found in relationships: "you're still a parent, wife."

Jill was surprised that I wanted to talk to her about her dementia. Her response might have been an expression of humility, arising from the feeling that the advent of dementia in her life was not important to other people. Or, maybe she was feeling uncomfortable about speaking of this with others. Like Jess, Jill's words showed a concern about how her diagnosis might affect the ways others see her. She spoke about the embarrassment that others might feel when they knew of her diagnosis:

> JILL: Yes. I think they're embarrassed about naming it . . . [laughs]. . . . You see, nobody has asked me questions like you ask me. . . . I haven't been asked those sort of things. . . . Very rarely do people acknowledge that I have dementia.
>
> RESEARCHER: Is it helpful to have it acknowledged?
>
> JILL: As long as I'm not made to look a fool [laughs] . . . or as if it's my fault.

Whilst Jill recognized that it might be helpful if others acknowledged her dementia, I sensed a reticence in speaking about this. She feared that it might be embarrassing and that she might "be made to look a fool." She was concerned that having this illness might make others think less of her or, even, that it is her fault. Her concerns raised questions about her own response to discovering that she had dementia. This felt stigmatizing seemed to have brought anxiety for Jill's own self-perception. Yet, her words also conveyed that she did not believe herself "a fool," and did not regard having this illness as her own fault. Like other participants in the study, Jill's response to the sense of unspoken judgement of others arose out of her faith. Later she said, "He [God] doesn't blame me."

I noticed that both Jess and Jill were beginning to feel the impact of the isolating tendency of the reactions of others to their illness.

Whilst both were confident in their own sense of personal identity, there seemed to be underlying concern about how others might see them. It was interesting that Jill's fear was not so much of the disease itself, but of the possible responses of others to this which might lead to stigmatizing reactions.

For the person of faith, in addition to Sabat's malignant social positioning, there is an additional source of stigma which Swinton has named as "malignant spiritual positioning" in which others make negative assumptions about one's spiritual life.[10]

"Loved by God"

Unlike Jill, Alice had lived with dementia for several years, and was accustomed to speaking about it to other people. Her prime sense of identity was found in her sense of relationship with God. She was: "a child of God, that is fact." She was "loved by God, no matter what."

In spite of this illness, and reactions of others to it, her identity remained secure in the love of God. I noticed that Alice instinctively, expressed her belief in God's love for her as being prior to her own capacities:

> ALICE: Our worth and value never changes, that when God so loved the world he gave his Son, that . . . our worth and value doesn't depend on how good we are, or what we do, or what our health is like, or the state of our bodies. . . . He just loves us for who we are . . . so we are complete in him.

For her, this was the central and most important aspect of who she was. A former GP, Alice understood the nature of her illness and its consequences from a medical perspective. Yet, in spite of this, she believed and felt that she was "complete in him" [God].

She recognized that the physical imperfection brought by dementia is part of life, but this didn't diminish her sense of identity. Her emphasis on wholeness resonates with the insistence in the literature on seeing the whole person rather than the illness.[11] Her words reflected a sense of wholeness brought about through her faith in Christ.

10. Sabat, "Mind, Meaning, and Personhood in Dementia," 287–302; Swinton in Barclay, "Psalm 88," 90.

11. See, for example, Kitwood, *Dementia Reconsidered*, 7; Shamy, *Guide to the Spiritual Dimension of Care*; Swinton, *Dementia*, 41–48.

Enduring Faith: Laughter, Loss, and Struggle

The positive nature of participants' response to their dementia was surprising and humbling. Shared laughter and smiles were often part of our conversations, but this was within the context of acknowledging the anguish that dementia was bringing to the participants and their loved-ones. In spite of their strong faith in God, as some participants (and their loved-ones) disclosed, there was also sadness and struggle.

"Faith Has Laughter"

David clearly enjoyed being with people and the experience of laughing together with others. His responses in the research interview were punctuated with self-deprecating laughter. This characteristic was helping him to cope in his early experience of his illness.

> DAVID: I'm quite often able to see people and talk to them about something . . . but I might forget who they were [laughs]. . . . There's lots of laughter. And, you know, faith has laughter. I mean, I'm sure that Jesus must have laughed . . . and the disciples must. . . . It's a bit like that. . . . And so all of that encompasses the dementia bit as well because there's so much laughter. And you know it is . . . laughter that makes the dementia, in a sense . . . more bearable. . . . So, it's not "you've got dementia . . . right, so put you to one side," but actually, embrace it and say, we can enjoy it.

As other research has suggested, humor was playing an important role in coping with painful reality.[12] Underneath the smiles of our exchange, there was the unspoken recognition of the pain that he was dealing with. The playful humour pointed to David's trust in Christ for what is not understood. He acknowledged his memory difficulties, but coped by laughing at his own mistakes and being intentionally positive. It seemed to be a choice he had made. His reflections on Jesus, suggested that he saw laughter and fun as part of his God-created humanness, although these were also particular aspects his own personality. The fun and laughter were also a coping strategy; they make "the dementia in a sense . . . more bearable." He knew dementia is a burden, but laughter was helping.

---

12. MacKinlay and Trevitt, *Finding Meaning*, 109–13; McFadden et al, "Actions, Feelings, and Values," 76–78.

David was aware that some people might discount the significance of those with dementia: "It's not, 'You've got dementia . . . so put you to one side.'" Like the implications of Jess's and Jill's words, he had a negative view of how others might regard his dementia, but he also refused to accept this implied judgement.

His words "embrace it" suggested positive and intentional acceptance of this aspect of his life. It was not a burden to be borne, but a new challenge which David seemed determined to welcome, not just for himself but, as the "we" indicates, for those close to him. Laughter and fun are intensely social and are made possible through mutually rewarding relationships with others:

> DAVID: I still think that in this house we have an awful lot of laughter. . . . [We] do laugh a lot at each other [chuckles]. . . . We do such silly things.

"I Had a Memory . . . I Haven't One Now"

In spite of the positive and friendly manner of the participants, the concerned and sometimes tearful responses of their nearby loved-ones disclosed the anxiety and sorrow they felt as they supported their family members. I was particularly conscious of this in the home of Ron and Clare.

Ron's words revealed a sense of the sadness of loss which dementia was bringing. Wrestling with his understanding of memory, he said:

> RON: And I know you're at least not what you should be, but what you are then, you are not now, and hence the reason why . . . it's because I had a memory then, I haven't one now . . . and it's not funny . . . thing is, life is not funny.

Despite, his warm and positive attitude, living with dementia "is not funny." He struggled with the meaning of memory and, throughout our conversation, his hesitant (and sometimes misplaced) words suggested the frustration he was feeling.[13] At this point on the journey with dementia, there was for Ron, a realization of the implications of memory loss.

> RON: Yes, it is something that is debilitating, but I know dementia is debilitating because if you can't discuss . . . the actual

---

13. MacKinlay, "Listening to People with Dementia," 101, 104.

> dementia does . . . and that is take away your memory . . . it's
> tough luck.

Ron recognized the loss that dementia was bringing. He was aware in himself that discussion, logical exchange with others, was now less possible. In spite of his faith, life now was "tough."

In spite of his determined cheerfulness, David also recognized the difficulties of his memory loss.

> DAVID: For years and years I relied on memory. . . . But now it's much harder. Well, it's not much harder, but I know that I've got to . . . I have a routine for example. . . . And if I put it in the wrong place I spend ages trying to find it.

He was finding strategies to cope, but living with his poor memory is getting "much harder."

Bill also acknowledged his loss of memory and had resolved to face it:

> BILL: There is something going on here that perhaps I'm not too . . . want to know about, but I've got to deal with it.

He understood that this struggle would be a feature of life from now on:

> BILL: It's a matter of having to come to realization that it would always be with me now until the day I die—unless somebody comes up with some miraculous treatment.

For each of the above, the losses which dementia was bringing were difficult. But each of them was making a choice to accept the challenges which living with dementia was bringing.

"I Just . . . Crumpled Underneath It"

Rosemary, living independently, was particularly conscious of her memory difficulties and the struggles this was bringing to her life:

> ROSEMARY: I've had dementia now until I consider that my memory is so awful. . . . I know God is helping me . . . because I asked him to . . . to be as fluent as I could without overdoing it, honest, brief if I could and to just bring glory to him [Rosemary loses track of what she wants to say]. . . . I'm just trying to think I'm want to really say. . . . You asked me something. . . . What did

you say? You can ask me something and I'm with it and then it will fade away.

Her struggle was reflected in her communication with me during this interview. It was clear that she was aware of her difficulties and this was frustrating and distressing, yet she "know[s]" that God was with her in this.

> ROSEMARY: And my memory was so shocking and I couldn't remember where I'd left anything. . . . I lost my keys, I haven't got my bag . . . I just . . . crumpled underneath it.

The frustrations of losing her belongings made her feel overwhelmed and defeated. Her dementia was making daily living a struggle:

> ROSEMARY: The analogy which I often say to people is the best one I can think of is every day is a form of challenge. . . . It's a form of struggle to go up an escalator which I feel is coming down and that's perhaps the most difficult thing if you imagine it. (I used to race up escalators in London when I was in my student days.) You know . . . but now I just see it as a weary . . . I must get up . . . how can I move on? How can I do . . . how can I complete all these tasks today? It's a difficult thing.

She felt as if life was working in opposition to her ("to go up an escalator which is coming down"). Whilst, it was evident that she relied on her faith in God ("I know God is helping me"), life was a struggle and she felt "weary."

Beyond the practical problems, her failing memory was bringing a sense of lost-ness of self and, sometimes, of separation from God:

> ROSEMARY: It's a very minor thing, but . . . I . . . still . . . do experience sometimes . . . when it's a . . . deep down . . . feeling . . . of the worst of it all . . . when I can't . . . find myself . . . in that state where God . . . seems to have shut . . . and you read about it in Psalms.[14] . . . "Oh God, where are you? Why have you . . . ? I'm calling out to you and I can't at this moment connect." . . . Yes, of course, there's the dark night of the soul . . . it's always been used to describe people who have moments like that . . . but they're not dominating my life. My life is dominated by the Lord. But he knows. . . . And sometimes when I'm feeling those dark nights of the soul I can cry out to God and say "Where are you God?" Where is this feeling of joy which I so often get, which I'm just not feeling now. Is it like the sun that's gone behind the clouds?

---

14. For example, "My God, my God, why have you forsaken me?" (Ps 22:1).

Rosemary's sense of struggle with dementia and her frustration was apparent. A key characteristic of this was the sense of separation from God and her own sense of lost-ness. Evidently, this was not, as she sought to minimise "a very minor thing." In these "dark" times she felt alone and sad. Her words echoed those of the pastor Davis, discussed earlier, whose dementia initially brought a similar sense of loss.[15] For Rosemary, whilst these feelings sometimes overwhelmed her, she was remaining resilient because of her faith in God: "My life is dominated by the Lord.

Transcending Faith: Acceptance, Thankfulness, Hope

Despite the stigma, the struggles and sense of loss resulting from dementia, each participant talked courageously about how their faith was enabling them to transcend the challenges of their illness. Their responses were characterized by their expressions of trustful acceptance, thankfulness and hope.

"God Gives You the Strength"

I asked Rosemary about the effort needed to maintain her faith as she lived with dementia.

> RESEARCHER: What about your faith? Is it hard work maintaining your faith?
>
> ROSEMARY: [Pauses.] No. I don't think it's hard work. It's something God gives you the strength. . . . It's constant. . . . It's everything. . . . I've got [Bible] texts around me everywhere. I can't refer to them now, but they will come into my head and I'll say them: "You are my strength and my joy. . . . You are my rock and my salvation."[16] Goodness me, if you say those words and don't get anything from it . . . even in the midst of difficult . . . yes!

Rosemary seemed to differentiate here between the struggle of daily living with dementia and her faith life which was not "hard work." In spite of the difficulties, she had the sense that "God gives you the strength." She had developed strategies for encouraging herself in her faith, such as

---

15. Davis, *My Journey into Alzheimer's Disease*, 47–48.

16. Rosemary is referring to verses from the Psalms (e.g., Ps 27:1; 95:1).

displaying Bible texts around her home and finding inspiration from the verses she was choosing to display.

"I'm Very Grateful"

Surprisingly, thankfulness for dementia was reflected several times in the participants' words. Goldsmith has highlighted this apparent paradox: "There is a strange relationship between suffering and gratitude."[17] Rosemary spoke about this:

> ROSEMARY: I'm so grateful for what God's offered me and given me that I can relax and just say, "What will be, will be . . . when it comes, in your time Lord and your will." . . . Very many positives. . . . I'm not saying it's a good thing. Far from it, because that would be absurd. Of course, had God not willed me to have this part of my body affected . . . The organ in my mind . . . a skull here, my brain.

Rosemary knew that dementia was not "a good thing." Nevertheless, she felt that it had been allowed by God. She emphasized that it was only a part of her physical body that was affected, implying that her essential identity remained intact. Underlying her words was the sense that God was in control. She had a feeling of God having a personal commitment to her: "What God's given me." This enabled her to feel safe. Within this sense of security, she was able to express gratitude for God allowing dementia to come into her life.

For Alice, too, her faith was enabling her to respond with thankfulness towards God in the light of her dementia:

> ALICE: Well dementia is something that's happened. It might be anything else. . . . [For] some people it's cancer. And I think, well Lord, this is something that you've allowed me to have (I don't believe that God beats us up, or gives us bad things). He allows things in this broken world, and so he's allowed it. So I say, "Thank you Lord, this is your gift for here . . . therefore I will accept it as this gift and with your help I will do what I can in order to reflect your glory in it."

Alice's words were founded in her faith presupposition that God is sovereign and in control. The "Lord" had "allowed" dementia into her life. Her words reflected a theological understanding of a fallen or "broken"

17. Goldsmith, "Tracing Rainbows," 132.

world with hints of God as Creator, and her acceptance of suffering as a normal part of human experience. Despite her illness, she believed in a loving God who does not "beat us up." Her faith was enabling her to accept dementia with thankfulness, as a "gift" from God, because, she felt, it was given with a purpose.

"The Presence of God . . . within This"

Jill's words revealed a humility as well as courage. These qualities, with her thankful attitude, seemed to be helping her cope with dementia.

> JILL: You know, I don't want to be privileged or have life any easier than anybody else because I'm a Christian. Why should I? That's not the point at all. And in some ways I think I'm lucky knowing the presence of God . . . near me . . . within this.

Jill seemed to feel that she should accept her dementia as a normal part of the human experience of living in a difficult world. The knowledge that she had dementia wasn't making her doubt God's care. She didn't consider that her faith in God should privilege her over others who didn't share her faith. Her words seemed to suggest an acceptance that human life is a struggle. Like Rosemary and Alice, there was an assumption of God being a real presence who was near her "within this." I noticed again the sense of seeking purpose in this experience of dementia. Jill's awareness of the "presence of God" suggested that she was able to transcend the knowledge of her illness because of her faith. Unlike those who might not have this sense of God in their experience of dementia, she considered herself "lucky." Facing the developing and ongoing symptoms of her illness, such an assertion was striking.

I asked Jill how her faith was important as she came to terms with her diagnosis. Her response was preceded with a long, thoughtful pause.

> JILL: Well, I couldn't live without it. . . . It's the foundation of my life . . . my Christian faith is. And . . . I think having . . . dementia with . . . it gives me hope . . . and a knowledge that God is with me in it . . . I can't imagine how awful it would be without.

> RESEARCHER: Can you say why your sense of knowing God is helping you?

> JILL: Dementia is outside of my control, it's something that has happened . . . and the fact that God is with me and knows about

it and . . . is there is very important. . . . God knows about it. . . . He is my strength in order to carry on with life. . . . He doesn't blame me or any of these things. . . . That's what I think.

Faith was foundational and sustaining Jill in her life as she faced dementia: "I couldn't live without it." Her belief that God was with her in this countered, what would have been for her, the unimaginable awfulness of having no sense of God's presence, both at this stage and as she imagined her future. She recognized that the coming of dementia into her life was outside of her control, yet there was a sense of security because "God . . . knows about it." For Jill, her belief that he knew about her illness and is with her gives her strength "to carry on with life."

I was interested that Jill introduced the word "blame." This word suggests a self-questioning about whether others might think she was responsible in some way for the advent of her illness. Or perhaps, like the word "fault" Jill used earlier, it reflected her fears of how others might perceive it. Yet she knew that this was not a matter for blame and found reassurance in her confidence that God knew what was happening to her. In these early years of dementia, it seemed that Jill's faith understanding was already growing in ways which were equipping her for its future development.

Summary

Theme 1: Transforming Faith: Responding to Dementia

- In these early to moderate stages of the journey with their disease, the positive responses of participants suggested that faith was giving them a strong sense of their continuing identity in their understanding of self in relation to God and to others.

- Responses to dementia which were helping them to remain resilient included: laughter and fun, acknowledgement of loss, and acceptance of struggle facilitated by their trust and hope in God.

- Faith in God was bringing a sense of strength, and the surprising response of thankfulness. Resilience and transcendence were enabled by their sense of God's presence with them in their illness.

- Faith in early to moderate dementia was enabling these individuals in their hopeful imagination of the future.

- However, their positive words also revealed struggles of living with dementia, and the losses it was bringing which were sometimes concealed beneath their smiles.

Theme 2: Memory Funding Faith

In my encounters with the literature as I looked for meaning in the experience of dementia, the interweaving of memory, identity and faith had caught my attention.[18] I was interested to discover how memories of pre-dementia faith experience shapes individuals' present experience of faith in dementia and their feelings about the future. Most of the participants were eager to tell me their personal faith stories, revealing how these memories were funding experience of faith in the present. Their words and my commentary are structured around the following subordinate themes:

- Engrained faith: this is my story
- Commitment to Jesus
- "Tough times" remembered
- Other ways of remembering
- Memory funding future faith

Engrained Faith: This Is My Story

For most of the participants, church-going had always been a part of their lives from childhood, and adult faith commitment has arisen out of that background. These biographical memories provided and created the context for understanding the advent of dementia in their lives. For example, David recognized that his early involvement in Christian activity was significant for his later and present faith commitment and understanding.

"So Engrained"

David spoke in detail about his life and developing faith story. He had a Methodist background and had been brought up in a church-going family.

18. For example, Summa and Fuchs, "Self-Experience in Dementia," 396.

DAVID: But I had that background. . . . . It's much easier if you have a background of church-going as a child . . . that core at the beginning of having that understanding of Jesus as a child, I think, is always there after that, and funny enough, probably if the dementia became much . . . got worse and worse, I suspect it would come back to being the child of Jesus.

David's words suggested that his present faith awareness had developed from his childhood experience and memories. His phrase "child of Jesus" suggested his feeling that faith was about relationship with Jesus, who cared for him as for a child. This, he believed, was the most significant aspect of his faith as the dementia symptoms affected him more.

He instinctively used the word "Jesus" to indicate his sense of relationship with God. For him, this seemed to be the central focus of what it meant to have faith. His memories from his Christian upbringing suggested the importance of faith memory for his experience of faith now. He felt that this simple relationship with Jesus was what would endure as his dementia progressed.

DAVID: That is so, so now engrained in what I believe . . . because it's so all-encompassing.

His choice of word "engrained" suggested the significance of his faith identity formed in childhood. Out of this engraining had developed the all-encompassing nature of his faith experience as he was living with dementia. It was not a cerebral belief alone, but something which was "engrained" throughout his whole person.

"Always, Always"

Alice's family had been deeply committed in their faith. Her parents had always been involved in various kinds of Christian ministry. She had always had a sense of relationship with God and this seemed to have grown from childhood onwards.

ALICE: Always, always. Even when I was little. . . . I can still remember that God was the center of our home. And talking with God about everything. He wasn't a member of the family in the sense he was equal with us. We were all . . . he was . . . always in charge . . . in love . . . and . . . yes, always.

The nurture of Alice's faith in her family was clearly significant. This wasn't based on church-going, but in its sense of relationship with God who was in control, "in love." Her sense of the reality of God's presence in her family's life was embedded in her daily existence. Her deeply held belief in a loving, but authoritative, God was evident in how she was responding to her dementia in the present.

For others, faith in early childhood was "nominal" but, nevertheless, clearly important for their faith development. For example Bill, Jill and Ron were taken to church regularly, although they didn't recall their families having a strong sense of personal faith.

> BILL: I was Church of England to start off with. . . . I just went because I was taken. I went to Sunday school, sang in the choir.

Bill's words "I just went because I was taken" suggested that faith practice at this point was not a matter of his personal choice, but dictated by parental choice and family culture.

Jill also had had a nominal Church of England upbringing:

> RESEARCHER: Were you brought up in a Christian family?
>
> JILL: Nominally . . . [chuckles].
>
> RESEARCHER: Was it a Church of England family?
>
> JILL: Yes . . . we went to church as a family. My dad was a definite. . . . He had had a great experience of God when Billy Graham who came to this country. . . . He made the commitment at the Billy Graham crusade. . . . My mum was not quite so sure of things . . . but she took us to church.

Church had been a normal part of life through Jill's childhood. She had also witnessed the significance of her father's conversion experience and faith commitment[19] during her childhood.

Ron had grown up in the chapel culture of South Wales in the middle years of the twentieth century. He spoke with a marked Welsh accent. His parents' faith had been nominal:

> RON: My mother and father wasn't. . . . They were churchgoers . . . but never professed much on it. . . . It was I . . . of the family . . . [who] actually participated in the church.

---

19. The large, evangelistic Billy Graham Crusade at Harringay Arena, London, in 1954.

I was interested that even in childhood, though his parents were not committed to faith, Ron chose to take part in church activity. The interview didn't reveal the reason for this. However, his independence is reflected in his later life choices, for example, going to work in Rhodesia [Zimbabwe] and, eventually, making a personal faith commitment there to Christ.

Commitment to Jesus

For all the participants, there was a difference between knowing about God and commitment to relationship with Jesus. For some, characteristic of Christians from an evangelical background, this development was marked by a conversion experience of being "born again" or other memorable encounter with God.[20] As other sections of this analysis reveal, this sense of a recognized relationship with Jesus was deeply significant for how the participants were responding in the present to their dementia.

"I Knew about Jesus, but I Hadn't Really Taken It on Board"

David's faith had become more significant when he met Gail (his wife):

> DAVID: When I met Gail . . . it really was. . . . She challenged me, she brought me to faith. But I had a background already, so it wasn't in the same way. I'd come from a Methodist background, but it didn't matter. To me, whatever, denomination is, it doesn't matter really. . . . I think my faith came really strongly when I met Gail I knew about Jesus, but I hadn't really taken it on board.

I noticed that David differentiated between his Christian upbringing and coming to personal faith as an adult in his late twenties. However, his Christian background was clearly important for him, preparing him for an adult personal faith response. His description "knew about" suggested a movement from cognitive, factual knowing to a deeper understanding of faith and implicit sense of relationship with Jesus. For him, this seemed to be the central focus of what it meant to have faith; it is not dependent on a particular church tradition. It was this sense of relationship, as revealed in other sections of the analysis, that was now sustaining him in his experience of living with dementia.

20. Harris, "Beyond Bebbington," 204; McGrath, *Evangelicalism*, 55–56.

Bill also remembered a time of conversion which came about through a leader of a Christian youth group:

> BILL: They were living words as opposed to what I perceived to be dead words. . . . It was through him, I think, that I made that "conversion" (from want of a better word), from being a pew-sitter to somebody who actually had a faith. . . . That was the point I . . . believed in Jesus as being my Savior without a doubt.

The "dead words" of his past experience were replaced in this context with "living words" which led to personal faith and a sense of relationship with Jesus and dependence on him ("my Saviour"). Like David's experience, this faith development was triggered by his social interaction and relationship with others.

Jill's coming-to-faith experience as a young adult was also not the direct result of her Church-going upbringing:

> JILL: Not through the family. I went to a [Christian conference center] and I became a committed Christian there. . . . I was in my twenties, my early twenties.

Whilst Jill can't now remember details, nevertheless she does recall her commitment to faith as a specific event in her life.

"Something That Doesn't Leave You"

For Ron the experience of conversion came as a young independent adult when he was working in Rhodesia [Zimbabwe]. He is further on in his experience of living with dementia than some of the participants and, as a result, his words and recall were not always fluent. He describes his experience of being "born again":

> RON: Well, that was where I got converted . . . "born again." And the thing is that . . . it's a lovely feeling. . . . But I did feel that I was nearer to God than what I wanted. . . . Not because I wanted it but because God accepted it. . . . It was because there was always . . . can I say, a way that you could rest upon with a faith that you know fully well . . . worthwhile . . . not because it was with Jesus Christ himself . . . nobody else . . . it was a personal thing . . . that I said to the Lord, "Thanks a lot" . . . because I always had someone that I could turn to.

RESEARCHER: You've been talking about the experience of being "born again" and . . . that was different to your Christian upbringing.

RON: There's . . . there is no satisfaction in the way that you would get if you wasn't "born again" . . . and it is something that doesn't leave you.

RESEARCHER: So what is the "satisfaction"?

RON: The satisfaction is that you've got someone to lean upon . . . it's a permanent way . . . you've got it, you can't lose it.

As for other participants, there was a clear memory and sense of coming to faith during a particular time in a definite way. A key aspect of this commitment was the sense of personal relationship with Jesus which this had brought. Whilst struggling to recall, Ron reiterated several times that he believed the transformation of conversion was permanent. It is something "that doesn't leave you." Ron used the word "satisfaction" to describe the contentment he felt came as a result of being "born again." Now, several years into his experience of dementia, he asserted that this was still characteristic of his faith. The personal aspect of his faith was indicated in his expression of dependence on God: "you've got someone to lean on."

Rosemary's story of coming to personal and active faith had not been straightforward. In contrast to other participants, she remembered a strict Christian upbringing, and her childhood fears of hell. In adulthood, she had faced various challenges and, for a time, moved away from active commitment to faith. Ten years before our conversation a serious illness had brought a fresh encounter with God:

ROSEMARY: I was sixty-eight when I had my near-death experience—exactly ten years ago. . . . [I'm] coming up to seventy-eight. It's ten years ago and all that time it's been a time of learning from God and being shown, every day, every day something happens.

Conversation with Rosemary's family supports her account of a sense of changed relationship with God through this experience. Now, in her dementia, she expressed a sense of faith which was vibrant and energetic, sustaining an evident sense of joy and peace. Her present faith experience in dementia was building on understandings of faith that had arisen from her experience of childhood and youth, and a continuing "learning from God."

"Tough Times" Remembered

Some of the participants talked in detail about difficult times in their lives. Their memories of adversity seem to have prepared them in different ways for faith in God in coping with the challenges that dementia is bringing.

For Jess, unlike other participants, church-going was not part of her early experience. She described instead a difficult early life:

> JESS: I had . . . a difficult childhood. . . . [Says quietly] I don't want to remember it actually [chuckles].

Unlike the experience of other participants, habitual faith practice had not been instrumental in shaping her adult faith. However, in the light of the adversity of her childhood situation, Jess recounted her experience of a transformative encounter with God when she was a teenager:

> JESS: No, I'm not a Christian because I go to church. I'm a Christian because when I was about fifteen I had a vision. And it changed me completely. And the thing . . . the trigger that makes me know this is that I stopped swearing. I never swore after that.

Jess's early awareness of God had come from outside of herself and her situation. She felt that God had intervened to help her at a difficult time. The encounter was remembered as a significant turning point in her life which changed her behaviour. Her family later revealed that they didn't think Jess had spoken of this to them before, yet the memory recounted in our conversation clearly reminded her of God's faithfulness to her when she was growing up.

In contrast to Jess's experience, Alice's family had had a profound commitment to faith, yet the experience of adversity was also formative throughout her childhood. Her mother died when she was a young child.

> ALICE: My experience of church and Sunday school was very positive . . . but I don't remember a great deal about it because, when my mother died, my father . . . it was very sudden . . . struggled a bit to start with and he gave up being a Baptist minister. . . . Initially, we [Alice and her sisters] were distributed round the family—grandparents and aunts and uncles.

In spite of the disruption brought to her family life by the death of her mother, memories of Sunday School and church remained unquestioned, positive aspects of normal life.

"I'm Very Grateful for All These Dreadful Experiences"

Gratitude and faith marked Alice's responses to the difficult memories of childhood and youth. With reference to a particular incident, she says:

> ALICE: Because if I hadn't had that I wouldn't have understood people who have these dreadful experiences. . . . And, in a sense, I've always said my shattered remains were nailed to the cross . . . and . . . I'm very grateful for all these dreadful experiences.

Alice felt that experiences of adversity had given her understanding of others' difficult experiences. She chose to resolve difficult experiences and their destructive results by perceiving these as caught up in the suffering of Christ on the cross.

Coping with adversity and her choice to be thankful seemed to have equipped Alice for subsequent events in her life and now, at this stage of her life, the experience of living with dementia.

Other Ways of Remembering

As discussed in chapter 3, there is a growing amount of research and reflection which speaks of how memory is embodied. This recognizes that identity and expression are seen in and through the *whole* person, not just cognitive activity dependent on reason and recall.[21] In my conversations with the participants in this study, I was interested to notice the role of embodied memory, even in these earlier stages of their dementia.

"A Memory Is There and It's Not There"

The exchanges with participants highlighted the significance of other ways of remembering in their dementia. Rosemary talked about how she likes to sing.

---

21. For example, Sapp, "Living with Alzheimer's"; Kontos, "Alzheimer Expressions," 3–4.

> ROSEMARY: Music, songs, anything that . . . it just brings you into that peaceful sense of joy and happiness. . . . I just love singing those choruses and hymns. . . . I don't care even if somebody is walking past me, I'll still sing, "Praise my soul the King of heaven" . . . and know all the words. . . . You've learnt them and they come back to you.
>
> RESEARCHER: Do you think that's about memory, or is it about your experience of God as well?
>
> ROSEMARY: I think it's what your memory has deeply taken in from the early days . . . as you're going through the dementia you come more and more, come back into . . . and it means more to you all those early influences are so.

Rosemary recognized that it was memory which had laid down the familiarity of the music and words of the hymn, but once they were brought to her present awareness, she felt that they "mean more" to her now, bringing peace and joy in the present moment.

Ron's words reflected his puzzling about the nature of memory. He was aware of his memory loss and reflected on that in relation to his faith:

> RON: Dementia firstly is something that you know. . . . Clare would tell me in the kitchen go and do this or go and do that for me . . . and I've gone into the kitchen and . . . [speaking to self:] "What did she just say she wanted?" And it's . . . dementia deprives you of all your memory. You haven't got a memory.
>
> RESEARCHER: You can remember a long time ago . . . ?
>
> RON: Well . . . that is dementia . . . a memory is there and it's not there.

Ron knew that he was losing his short term memory, but had an awareness of the presence of memory at the same time. His words began to disclose the complexity of memory. The conversation focused on how this was affecting faith in the present:

> RON: The only difference I would say . . . is because the fact that I've got no memory, that is because of dementia, but I've got it and I know fully well I shan't lose it. So it doesn't do me any matter for me, really.

Ron seemed to be aware here of a difference between kinds of memory. "I've got no memory" seemed to refer to the short-term memory lapses because of his dementia. However, "but I've got it and I know fully well

I shan't lose it" referred to his present experience of faith. His words, "It doesn't do me any matter for me, really," suggested perhaps that his "memory" of faith is of more importance to him than the short-term cognitive loss. He then spoke of prompts which were helping him to access this faith memory:

> RON: Why I say that is because it's given me a memory which I haven't got, but by going to church, it has . . . it's there.

The memory prompt of going to "church" translates into his present experience: "It's there . . . "

Memory Funding Future Faith

Faith seen in relationship with memory raises interesting questions for the mingling of past and present experience. I had begun to encounter this in some of the literature discussed earlier.[22] In these conversations, all of the participants, at this stage of their dementias, still retaining self-awareness, were able to different degrees, to speak of the future.

"Not Concerned about the Future"

In our conversations, speaking as Christians living with dementia in the present, the participants spoke about their beliefs and faith for the future.

> DAVID: As I go on, maybe the dementia gets worse, but that part of me will belong to Jesus. I feel very strongly. When you've got that sort of faith, it's there.

David felt secure in his faith for the future. Even though he knew that dementia would affect him more, his relationship with Jesus would remain. His past and present faith were funding his faith for the future.

> DAVID: If we have faith now . . . and dementia sets in, I believe, that the dementia . . . Jesus will know the dementia . . . and just becomes . . . he loves me . . . that's it . . . yeah.
>
> RESEARCHER: So right now you believe that's safe [your faith] . . . ?

22. For example, Brockmeier, "Questions of Meaning," 83; Swinton, *Becoming Friends of Time*, 147–61.

> DAVID: Yes, but . . . as . . . it gets worse that faith will still be there, because of the background, yes . . . and maybe that's just the one thing that hangs on.

Envisaging his future, David believed that his faith was safe with Jesus. His cognitive incapacity does not affect Jesus' love for him. His faith background was part of who he was and he believed that his faith would remain in spite of the worsening effects of dementia.

Ron was also clear about his sense of future hope:

> RON: I am not concerned about the future . . . because I know that I am born again. I know where I'm going without any shadow of doubt . . . and that in actual fact is what keeps me going. [Researcher prompts Ron to help him continue.] . . . The thing is I don't know where I'm going in the way that you know where you are going. But I know myself that being a Christian I shall be going . . . to heaven.

He was sure of his faith and of the specific event in the past which brought him to faith ("being born again") and this was sustaining him in present. His past knowledge and experience of faith gave him the sense of certain hope for the future and was enabling resilience. He recognized difference between himself (with dementia) and others (the researcher, without dementia), but asserted his certainty of faith in spite of his memory loss. His trust in God and hope of heaven, were funded by his faith memory, bringing resilience, confident assurance and contentment for the present.

"He's Never Deserted Me"

Jill also drew on past experience of God as she thought about the future.

> JILL: He's never deserted me. He keeps his word . . . his promises. [Quietly to self:] He keeps his promise. . . . And if I acknowledge him then I will be given peace even in great trauma . . . I will be given peace.

I noticed that Jill addressed herself to encourage herself. She asserted her trust in the promises of God which, she reminded herself, had proved reliable in the past. She didn't expect solutions, but believed that in future "trauma . . . I will be given peace." Past and present faith memory seemed to be funding her faith for her future with dementia.

Thinking about the future, Alice recognized that she would need the help of others to remember.

> ALICE: I want . . . my family know all this . . . they have to remind me that God is never going to desert one, he's always there and that he has prepared a place for us.[23]

Alice expressed her belief that God's presence in her life was not affected by dementia. She appealed to others to remind her in the future of the hope of her faith. I noticed her use of remembered Scripture. Her words suggested that her memory of faith was bringing peace for the present, and in anticipation of the future.

Summary

Theme 2: Memory Funding Faith

- Faith memories were "embedded" in the stories of the participants and seemed to be core to their sense of identity.

- Certainty of relationship with God may have come about through an experience of "conversion" or through gradual spiritual growth. In whatever way this had happened, memory of this was bringing confidence in the unchanging nature of God's relationship with them, whatever happened to them in the future. This was clearly important for participants in these first stages of their experience of living with dementia.

- Tough times remembered suggested that a sense of God's presence was strengthening faith in their experience of adversity. Such memories were preparing individuals with dementia to trust in God's presence and his love in the present as they faced the challenges of their illness.

- The participants' faith memory seemed to be dependent on their experience of relationship with God, rather than ability to use words correctly or accurately, or their cognitive understanding. In these early to moderate stages of dementia, it seemed that it was important to find ways of accessing and strengthening this memory for sustenance of faith in the present.

23. See John 14:1–4.

- Memory of past faith experience was funding faith both for the present, and bringing hope for the future.

Theme 3: Knowing God in Dementia

I was interested to discover how the advent of dementia in a person's life affected their faith and sense of closeness to God. At the beginning of the research project, I had wondered whether Christians with dementia might feel more distant from their faith. However, for the participants in the study, as already recounted, this was not the case. Their words resonated with Stuckey's conclusion who found that faith itself does not seem to be under threat because of dementia.[24]

This is not to minimise the struggles of living with dementia which may *include* doubt and questioning. However, conversations with the participants in this study revealed, as Stuckey reflects, that faith increasingly seemed to provide an anchor in their lives. In fact, participants spoke about how the cognitive loss brought by their dementia was bringing a greater intensity to their sense of secure relationship with God. Individuals' stories reveal this strengthening sense of closeness to God and well-being through reflection on the following:

- Strengthening faith
- Relationship with God
- Knowing Jesus
- Experiencing God through feelings

Strengthening Faith

"It Makes Me Feel Stronger"

Matthew was further on in his journey with dementia than some of the other participants, having lived with dementia for at least six years at the time of the interview. He was physically frail, and throughout the interview, concentration to think and speak took time and effort. Nevertheless, his body language was welcoming and he wanted to participate

24. Stuckey, email exchange with the author, writing about his research in the area of faith and dementia. Quoted with permission. See further comments in chapter 3.

in this research. I asked him whether he felt dementia was making a difference to his faith. He replied:

> MATTHEW: Yes, it makes me feel stronger.
>
> RESEARCHER: It hasn't made you doubt?
>
> MATTHEW: [emphatically and strongly, sounding moved] No!

In contrast to what I might have expected, Matthew asserted that faith was growing as a consequence of the dementia. I wondered in what sense he was understanding the word "stronger"? He clearly did not feel that his evident physical frailty was weakening his faith. His "No" was expressed firmly, in a voice which was beginning to break with emotion. Doubting God was not part of his response to the experience of dementia. The breaking in his voice suggested a sense of his confidence in God in spite of his illness.

"Faith Is Growing"

David seemed puzzled by fact that whilst memory was becoming more difficult, his faith was growing at this point in his dementia.

> DAVID: For years and years I relied on memory . . . but now it's much harder. . . . But it's the faith bit that is really interesting I think, because faith is growing more for the moment.

He seemed surprised by this ("it's the faith bit that is really interesting"). We talked further about his sense of relationship with God.

> RESEARCHER: How has that [dementia] made you feel about your relationship with God?
>
> DAVID: I think there's much more of a closeness.
>
> RESEARCHER: More of a closeness . . .
>
> DAVID: Yes, because it becomes more important. I think it becomes more important.

David stressed his growing sense of relationship with God and its increasing significance for him. Could it be that his sense of experience of God and relationship with him was greater in adversity? This resonates in some ways with Heidegger's awareness of human temporality which brings a sense of urgency to the search for meaning.[25]

"Closer to God"

Alice was also aware of and surprised by this paradox.

> ALICE: The less I have, the more amazed I am at what he [God] does with it. Whereas . . . when I was working, I thought some of it was me [Alice laughs]. I thought God had given me many gifts and I was quite clever! [Alice laughs] But now I realise everything that happens is of God. So in a sense, I'm closer to God because there's less of me [chuckles].

I am struck by her implication that being aware of her own abilities in her pre-dementia experience of life had created distance between her and God. The lessening of her capacities had brought a greater awareness of her dependence on him. She highlighted the paradox that, "I'm closer to God because there's less of me." She seemed to suggest that, as the physical symptoms of her illness were increasing, her spiritual life was becoming more intense.

As I observed those beginning this journey, their apparent growth in faith may seem counterintuitive. Not only was faith a resource for coping in the present moment, the participants talked of their relationship with God continuing to grow. Rosemary chose to emphasize the mystery she felt there was in this. She responded to my question about the effect of dementia on her sense of relationship with God as follows:

> ROSEMARY: Closer to God. "Nearer my God to thee . . ."[26]

I prompted her to say more about her understanding of "God."

> ROSEMARY: God, Jesus his Son, and the Holy Spirit who indwells[27] . . . all . . . to me are a mystery . . . I don't think we're meant . . . yet . . . to have any understanding of that really, only by reading Jesus' account when he was speaking to his Father on

25. See Heidegger, *Being and Time*, 296–304. MacKinlay and Trevitt discuss the growing importance of finding life-meaning in "increasing age and frailty" (*Finding Meaning*, 23).

26. Rosemary is referring here to the hymn "Nearer My God to Thee" (1841), lyrics by Sarah Flower Adams.

27. For example, "Do you not know that your bodies are temples of the Holy Spirit, who is in you?" (1 Cor 6:19 NIVUK).

the cross,[28] and before it and with his ministry and everything.
. . . Then when, of course, he gave the Holy Spirit . . . So the
answer to that is, "Yes!"

Her acknowledgment of the "mystery" of the triune God resonated with
her positive acceptance of dementia. Her words hinted that she felt that
she didn't understand why dementia (or other life events) had come into
her life. But she accepted this as mystery, and was willing to trust God
without understanding. Her use of "we" seemed to suggest that she felt all
human life exists in this context of divine mystery.

Relationship with God

One of the distinctive characteristics of faith in the evangelical tradition,
discussed earlier in chapter 1, is the sense of relationship with God.[29]
Each of the participants spoke of their experience of faith, despite now
living with dementia, in terms of being in a continuing, loving relationship with God. This relationship seemed to be a central part of their experience of dementia.

"A Relationship to Someone . . . Who Loves Me"

I invited Alice to tell me what she felt was at the center of her Christian
experience.

> ALICE: Well, walking with God every day and having him at the
> center of my life . . . it's not a work, it's not a doing, it's a relation-
> ship to someone that I love and who loves me.
>
> RESEARCHER: So are you aware of God's presence with you?
>
> ALICE: Well in some ways, yes. . . . I mean I know that God is
> always with me, because he always has been and I know that
> there's nothing that can ever separate me from him.

It was loving relationship with God that was at the heart of Alice's experience of faith: "It's not a doing." Her sense that "nothing . . . can ever separate
me from him" (see Rom 8:38–39) was grounded in her past experiences
and her memory-funded faith. Again, I noticed that she instinctively used

28. See, for example, Luke 23:46.
29. Zahl, "Reformation Pessimism," 82.

words of Scripture to describe her experience. At that present moment, it was both her cognitive knowledge and her intuitive faith which were making her confident of continuing relationship with God.

> ALICE: But now, even when my brain falls apart . . . it doesn't matter.

In spite of her medical knowledge, Alice asserted that her faith superseded cognitive capacity. She felt that the experience of her relationship with God was transcending brain-limited knowledge. This conviction was resourcing Alice's faith and confidence in God as she faced the future with dementia.

For Rosemary, although she had had a Christian up-bringing, it was only in the last ten years since a serious illness, and now, as she was living with dementia, that her personal faith had grown. Yet, her words often showed her lifelong knowledge of faith, which, in part, was enabling her experience and expression of faith in the present.

> ROSEMARY: I love the Lord God with all my heart and all my soul . . . the Spirit of God is always in me. Now I am always conscious of that, even if it's really bad.

Rosemary was passionate about her feeling of love for and commitment to God. Her knowledge of scripture ("all my heart and soul") helped her to express the totality of this.[30] She loved God with the whole of her being, irrespective of failing cognitive capacity. I noticed that Rosemary did not use the word "mind" here which is included in Gospel reference to this verse, and might be assumed to suggest cognitive function.

Her deliberate reference to the Holy Spirit might have arisen from the understanding, from her evangelical tradition, that a defining characteristic of what it means to be a Christian is the in-dwelling presence of the Holy Spirit within the believer.[31] In spite of her dementia, she believed that the Spirit of God would always remain in her. Her experience was of a mutual relationship which was sustained by God the Holy Spirit, even when her symptoms of dementia were "really bad."

---

30. "You shall love the Lord your God with all your heart, and with all your soul, and with all your mind, and with all your strength" (Mark 12:30); "You shall love the Lord your God with all your heart, and with all your soul, and with all your might" (Deut 6:5). See also Matt 22:37; Luke 10:27.

31. "God has sent the Spirit of his Son into our hearts, crying, 'Abba! Father!'" (Gal 4:6); "Put his Spirit in our hearts as a deposit, guaranteeing what is to come" (2 Cor 1:22 NIVUK).

"It's Over to You Now Mate!"

Jess's words expressed her sense of relationship with God more informally. We talked about how dementia was affecting her experience of this.

> JESS: I think when I knew . . . that I had memory loss . . . I said, "God, it's over to you now mate! I'm all right!" [chuckles]. . . . You know, "You keep me going." . . . I feel that God has kept me going.

Whilst circumstances had changed for Jess, her conversational relationship with God remained constant. I noticed that she hesitated before saying "that I had memory loss," perhaps subconsciously choosing to register her dislike of the word "dementia." Her sense of close, informal friendship with God was giving her strength to cope with her illness. Her words revealed her dependence on God: "You keep me going."

> RESEARCHER: Do you feel that God is with you?

> JESS: Yes, I'm sure of that. And that's why the fact that I can't remember, my memory loss, doesn't matter.

For Jess, the sense of God being with her was more important than her memory loss. Her confidence in God's presence with her made her feel secure: "my memory loss doesn't matter."

"The Best Boss"

Each of the participants talked about God in terms of relationship, but their choice of words to describe this indicated differing aspects of their understanding of God. Bill used the word "Boss" to indicate God, arising from comparison with his experience of working under direction in the police force.

> BILL: "Boss" is a sort of colloquial . . . 'cause we, at the police station, we call whoever is in charge, we refer to him as the "Boss" . . . God . . . best boss.

Bill's words seemed to remove anxiety about his present experience of dementia. His questions arising from dementia were not about *why* God had allowed this in his life, but about *how* God wanted him to live with the illness.

Bill was also aware of God as the Trinity:

> BILL: Well when you're talking in terms of Trinity there are
> three bosses I suppose: Boss 1: Father; Boss 2: Jesus; Boss 3:
> Spirit . . . and they're all working together on our behalf.

Here, Bill thought of the different persons of the Trinity in relationship
with one another and with himself, "working together on our behalf."
God as Trinity was both in control, and also working for his well-being. I
noticed Bill's use of the first person plural ("on our behalf"), as he instinctively identified himself as part of community.

"Creator God . . . "

Some participants spoke about how creation played a part in their sense
of relationship with God. Matthew, who has limited mobility, spent much
of his time looking out of the window at his garden. I asked him if he
could tell me if his dementia was making him feel differently about God.
A long pause preceded his answer.

> MATTHEW: Yes, I think it has . . . because I can look out and I
> see the birds of the air.
>
> RESEARCHER: And what does that make you think?
>
> MATTHEW: Well, in the book of Genesis, God created the sea,
> things that . . birds that sweep over the sea . . . seagulls.

Matthew's words "the birds of the air" echo Jesus' words in Matthew 6:26
which speak of not being worried and instead trusting in God's care.[32]
Matthew was also thinking about God's role in creation and seemed to
relish this. His words seemed to suggest the evidence he felt he was seeing
of God's power and care.

Rosemary also spoke of creation as being significant in her relationship with God.

> ROSEMARY: I relate when I'm out in the country and I'm so
> aware of the beauty around me that I'm literally worshipping
> God the Father who's created this beautiful earth and it brings
> out the feeling of the Creator God in worship. I think that's
> very important.

---

32. "Look at the birds of the air; they do neither sow nor reap nor gather into
barns, and yet your heavenly Father feeds them. Are you not of more value than they?"
(Matt 6:26).

Seeing the beauty of the countryside, prompted gratitude for the gift of creation and inspired her worship of "the Creator God."

Knowing Jesus

More than the sense of knowing God, participants spoke of their sense of personal relationship with Jesus.

"I Know Jesus"

Whilst Matthew was beginning to struggle with recall and concentration, he retained a strong sense of relationship with Jesus.

> RESEARCHER: Do you feel you have a relationship with Jesus?
>
> MATTHEW: [very definitely] Yes, I do.
>
> RESEARCHER: And do you feel, as you go through this, he is close to you?
>
> MATTHEW: Yes.

For Matthew, as for other participants, the sense of Jesus accompanying him through the dementia was significant, and I was struck by his deliberate "yes" to my questions. Later, I discovered that Wendy had overheard his assertions of faith from a nearby room and was deeply moved, explaining that she had not heard Matthew speak in this way before.

David also spoke of his secure sense of relationship with Jesus as he anticipated the future:

> DAVID: I know Jesus, and that's the most important thing. I know Jesus very clearly and I know . . . as I go on, maybe the dementia gets worse, but that part of me will belong to Jesus. I feel very strongly. When you've got that sort of faith, it's there.

David's words, "I know Jesus," demonstrated that, for him, his faith was about relationship with God's Son Jesus. The statement suggested a transcendence, and his belief in a reality beyond human physical existence. He was confident in his relationship with Jesus as he imagined the future with dementia. His choice of words, "part of me" raised questions for me about which "part" of himself David thought might not "belong to Jesus." Nevertheless, his words and firm manner of speaking them conveyed a confidence. His trust in Jesus in the face of the unknown was sure in its expression. Thinking of other Christians who were further on in their journey with dementia, David talked about faith *holding* them: "But maybe it's sometimes that very thing that holds onto them." Rather than his holding onto faith, his words implied that he believed it was Jesus who would hold onto him.

"Jesus Is There"

When we meet for our first conversation, David had recently been unwell with a virus. The impact of this added to his reflection about his dementia.

> DAVID: And in this difficult time . . . you know, that Jesus is there. In the last few weeks it's been pretty dire and I know that he's there, that faith is there. It's not going to go away, just doesn't go away [dementia]. Once you've got it, you never lose it, and that's it.

David recognized the presence of dementia in his life and was accepting it, although this was not easy. But this did not threaten his sustaining sense of the presence of Jesus.

> DAVID: Dementia may be going one way, but there's Jesus there. . . . Even if the dementia gets worse, there'll still be Jesus. That's the important thing. We can still bring Jesus and dementia together [chuckles]. . . . Yes . . . [Long pause.] I think it's the core of everything now. The more I understand, the deeper it gets. . . . But the core is understanding Jesus, and knowing Jesus. . . . It's knowing Jesus personally.

In the adversity of dementia, David expressed his sense that in some way Jesus was present with him. It was as though David felt that the "knowing Jesus" was enabling him to make sense of his dementia and to live with it.

Jill responded thoughtfully to my question about relationship with Jesus. Her answer was preceded by a long pause.

> JILL: I know Jesus, but I would like to know him better. . . . I think that my difficulty in expressing it now is due to the fact that .. . . I've known Jesus for a long time [chuckles] . . . and I long to know him more in my illness.
>
> RESEARCHER: You're at the beginning of the journey [with dementia].

JILL: But . . . I look forward to knowing more through Jesus.

Jill's words suggested a humility in recognizing her imperfect knowledge and desire to "know him more in my illness." She expressed a confidence in a continuing development of her faith and relationship with God through Jesus. There was positive anticipation of knowing and understanding more about her relationship with him as a result of her developing dementia.

"God and Man"

For Bill, the incarnation of God in Christ was significant.

BILL: The person that I find it more easy to relate to is Jesus because he came to earth as a human being, so in a sense there is an identity between me as a human being and Jesus as a human being.

Here Bill expressed that Christ's humanity was strengthening his sense of relationship with Jesus because he felt that Jesus understands human experience. Jess also chose to emphasize the humanity of Christ.

JESS: I think God sent his Son into the world . . . and he chose Mary and Joseph to look after his Son . . . so he wanted his Son to be man. . . . He's God and man. . . . The only person that's been God and man.

She stressed her awareness that Jesus, as a human being, shared in common human experience.

JESS: He is the Son who came into the world to teach us about God and he paid the sacrifice of being a human being so that we could find God.

Jess's word "sacrifice" may first bring to mind the death of Christ on the cross. However, I noticed that Jess here applied it to the incarnated life of Christ. The sacrifice was in becoming human, so that in sharing human experience (including human suffering) he was able "to teach us about God."

Experiencing God through Feelings

Whilst evangelicalism has sometimes appeared to emphasize a cognitive understanding of faith, the conversations with research participants revealed that feelings and emotions seemed to be playing an increasing role in their experience of relationship with God.

"Feelings Remain When Facts Are Forgotten"

Alice spoke about the significance of feelings for the life of faith in dementia.

> ALICE: it's a matter of knowing you're loved. And because feelings remain when facts are forgotten, it's possible for anybody with dementia, no matter what the stage of their dementia, to know that they're loved and because God is God and it's not what I say but the Holy Spirit is alive and real God.

Here, Alice used the word "knowing" in a relational sense. Feelings were enabling a different kind of knowing. Alice asserted that this relationship depends on knowing one is loved by him, and that this relationship is dependent on the activity of God the Holy Spirit. Speaking from her own situation as a Christian with dementia, Alice believed that "feelings remain" and, in spite of facts being forgotten, these were a true indicator of relationship with God. Her insights suggested the importance for well-being of faith experienced through feelings.

Alice also talked of the ways in which the expression of her emotions had changed in dementia.

> ALICE: Some things I have very little emotion about that I would have in the past. But other things, I have more emotion about. . . . One's emotions do change. . . . Things that didn't upset me before, upset me now. . . . So, yes, my emotions have changed. . . . With dementia . . . the layers come off, so we become more vulnerable. . . . As a Christian, God accepts me as I am with all my mixed-up emotions, with all emotional unzipping.

I was interested that Alice felt her emotions were much closer to the surface in her life because of dementia. Dementia had brought a greater sense of vulnerability. There was an acceptance of this as part of the experience of dementia. Her belief that God accepted her with "all my mixed-up emotions" was enabling her to be resilient.

"Exquisite Joy" *

Sometimes participants' accounts revealed that their feelings were not to do with expression of emotions related to events, but were transcendent experiences of received love, peace and joy.

Rosemary told me about the feeling of great joy in her faith which she was experiencing as a Christian who was living with dementia. Her rapidly spoken words were preceded by a long pause and intake of breath.

> ROSEMARY: It's partly celebratory because I have something that is so wonderful that fills me very often with exquisite joy, and still allows me though to know the dark night of the soul. . . . How it makes me feel? Oh, I believe strongly, infinitely better than if I had been an intellectual type of person worried and concerned in every way about what was going to happen to me after death, what will I do and how will it be going through that dark tunnel of not knowing anything. . . . I think I have . . . sometimes a joyful time because I've got the dementia and I can accept it through God being with me. He will be with me . . . right to the end! Even if my . . . because my feelings are still as strong, if not stronger, as my mind becomes less intellectualized and able to . . . I shall be more filled with the feeling of the love of God.

Rosemary communicated passionately that her Christian faith was giving her great joy. Even though she sometimes experienced "the dark night of the soul" this did not overcome the sustaining sense of joy she felt that relationship with God was bringing her. Like Alice, she also felt that she was more aware of God because of the intensifying of her feelings in dementia: "infinitely better than if I had been an intellectual type of person." She also attributed the lessening of anxiety about the future being partly due to her increasing strength of feelings. The emotional experience of her faith was bringing increasing confidence in "the love of God" which would be with her "right to the end!" There was even a sense of gratitude that she had dementia because it was seeming to bring her a greater sense of relationship with God.

Ron also highlighted his feeling of joy in knowing God in his dementia:

> RON: The joy of being born again is always there. You can't separate one or the other . . . and therefore, I'll never lose that joy, but I have lost my memory.

When he came to faith he felt that he had received a special kind of joy which was still with him, in spite of his dementia. This sense of coming into relationship with God was synonymous with his experience of joy. His confidence in its permanence was striking. There is paradox here: "I have lost my memory," but he felt certain that he would "never" lose the joyful sense of God's presence in his life. Ron's words suggested a questioning of the meaning of memory. There was another kind of memory which was at work in addition to the remembering of information. "Memory" was lost, but not the joy of his faith.

"Overwhelmed with Love and Peace"

The sense of relationship with God was expressed by some in terms of love and peace. I asked Alice how she knew that she was loved by God.

> ALICE: There have been occasions when one has felt over-whelmed with love and peace when one has been praying with God or talking to others about him, or praying with them. But most of the time, it's just knowing that the longer I've lived— through all the rough times—he's never let me down . . . never . . . never.

This sense was reinforced through her conviction that God had not let her down in difficult times throughout her life. This sense of God's intervention in her life was bringing sustenance in and transformation of difficult moments.

Jill also talked about her experience of knowing peace in and about her situation:

> JILL: I think I have a kind of peace . . . which doesn't come from me. I think it comes from God.

As Alice's words had suggested, Jill felt that this peace did not originate in herself, but was dependent on the intervention of God in her life.

I began to realise the potential of understanding that, for people living in the early to moderate stages of dementia, their spiritual lives and sense of relationship with God are experienced and expressed through their feelings and emotions.

Summary

Theme 3: Knowing God in Dementia

- The experience of dementia seemed to be bringing an increased sense of the closeness of God and relationship with him. These feelings were not dependent on a cognitive "knowing." Counterintuitively, these earlier stages of dementia seemed to be bringing a growing confidence in their faith.

- A sense of knowing Jesus was central in their relationship with God and did not seem to be diminished by the advent in their lives of dementia.

- In spite of the acknowledged struggles of living with dementia, overall, feelings of God's love and peace were paramount. Awareness of God was experienced and expressed through intensity of feelings.

Theme 4: Faith in Practice

The practices of Bible reading, prayer and involvement in church activities have a prominent place in the lives of many Christians in the evangelical tradition. I wanted to understand how dementia was affecting these practices. Conversations with the research participants seemed to reveal that relationality was the key to faith practices: the individual in relation to God, and the individual in relationship with others.

In my work as a writer and editor, I have been involved in the creation of Bible and faith resources to support the faith of Christians. I was therefore particularly interested to learn more about the experience of Bible reading, prayer and church involvement for Christians with dementia.

Focus on the subordinate themes below revealed the experience of the following aspects of faith practice for the participants, and something of how these were contributing to their experience of continuing faith nurture and their well-being. There were also changes as a result of their dementias.

- Relationship, not "a doing"

     Bible reading: hearing from God
     Prayer: talking with God

- Belonging to a faith community

     Going to church
     Dependence on one another

A Relationship, Not "A Doing"

For all the participants, as previously suggested, their sense of relationship with God, was increasingly at the center of their faith, rather than practices. Alice emphasized:

> ALICE: Yes it's a relationship . . . it's not a doing, it's a relationship to someone that I love and who loves me.

The love of God and her response of loving him was the foundation of this relationship. She explained that whilst Christian practice had included activities like Bible-reading, these were not essential to her certainty of relationship with God.

> ALICE: It's very important to me but I don't think my relationship with God will stop if I didn't do it. But it's very important to me because it kind of starts and ends my day. It reminds me that that's how my life is centered, that God is the center of my life . . . but . . . it's not legalistic. If I forget, I'm not going to get worked up about it.

Bible-reading was helpful, but it was not a "legalistic" practice which oppressed her. Nevertheless, core faith practices of Bible reading and prayer, characteristic of evangelical Christian faith, were important for participants, but they happened as a result of, or within the context of relationship.

The practices of Bible reading and prayer were often described in terms of talking with, or listening to, God. Some participants were living independently and, for them, Bible engagement was primarily a solitary activity. For others who were married it was a shared activity. As I reflected on the participants' words, I noticed how these echoed the experience of Davis when he discovered it was becoming difficult to read the Bible: "The more I . . . tried to recapture the things I knew, the more they scurried away from mental recall."[33]

---

33. Davis, *My Journey into Alzheimer's Disease*, 57.

Bible Reading: Hearing from God

For the evangelical Christian, a primary way of meeting with God has traditionally been through the practice of Bible reading.[34] I was interested to hear about participants' experience of this in dementia.

"I Hear God through the Bible"

At this early stage in her experience of dementia, Bible-reading was an important aspect of Jill's interactive relationship with God.

> JILL: I read the Bible every day . . . and . . . I hear God through the Bible. . . . I think more than any other place where I hear God.

> RESEARCHER: What do you mean you "hear" God through the Bible?

> JILL: An example would be . . . I have choices to make . . . I want to know God's will over something . . . I read the Bible and pray about it . . . and I get an answer . . . not always, obviously . . . but a lot of the time I get an answer.

She felt that God was guiding her through her Bible-reading in decisions she was taking.

Jill stressed the importance of Bible reading for her faith as something through which there was a reciprocal relationship of talking and listening. I asked her, if in the light of her dementia, she thought it would continue to be important for her. Her response was emphatic:

> JILL: Oh yes . . . that would be devastating . . . if it was taken away for any reason.

For Alice, Scripture was important, not because it was a practice which was part of her Christian tradition, but because it was a resource in her loving relationship with God.

> RESEARCHER: Do you feel God is speaking to you through [the Bible]?

> ALICE: I believe he can—but sometimes he doesn't. But I believe in obedience. . . . Obedience is God's love language. And I believe that faithfully doing that is important. . . . God knows how much I love him, but it's just an act of service, if you like,

---

34. See, for example, SUIC, "Aims, Beliefs and Working Principles."

> to let him know that I really do. And . . . on occasion, does say
> these wonderful things to me. If we don't give him the opportu-
> nity then, well, we're the losers.

Alice communicated that, above all her faith was about loving God, but
that needed to be expressed in faithful action. In this way, there was a
connection between the practice of Bible reading and her sense of relationship with God. Taking time to read the Bible was providing an opportunity to hear from God.

"I Can't Read the Bible . . . Too Difficult Now to Read"

Alice has had the practice of Bible-reading instilled in her by her family
from early childhood.

> ALICE: I was in a sense . . . soaked in Scripture from a child,
> and I do forget.

However, dementia was bringing some challenges to her practice of
Bible-reading. Nevertheless, engaging with scripture in other ways was
still central to her faith practice.

> ALICE: I can't read the Bible because it's too difficult now to
> read, so I listen to it every day.

Reading the Bible was becoming difficult. But Alice had found a solution
in listening to it *being* read. CDs and web resources were making this
possible, and this was much easier than reading herself.

Scripture had always been an integral part of Rosemary's life too.
References to Bible texts peppered her responses during the interview.
At this stage in her life, the familiarity with Bible text was giving her a
language which expressed and enabled relationship with God.

> ROSEMARY: I've got texts around me everywhere.

She had deliberately placed the words of Bible texts around her home
as mnemonic resources to help her remember God, and to express her
feelings towards him. The embeddedness of Bible text was enabling her
to discover it as a resource in her present circumstances.

"WE GET FELLOWSHIP"

For some participants reading the Bible with others was easier than reading alone. I was interested that for participants who were married, this aspect of their faith life was shared.

Ron and Clare have regularly followed a routine of Bible reading and prayer together throughout their life together:

> RON: Oh yes . . . we get fellowship together actually.

Bible reading and prayer continued to be important for Jess too:

> JESS: Well I don't do much as a Christian now except going to church. I'm not very active physically in doing things. But I read the Bible every day, pray every day.

Andrew, Jess's husband, told me later that they read the Bible and pray together every day.

David didn't emphasize individual Bible-reading, but enjoyed hearing the Bible read in his "home group," where it was a group activity:

> DAVID: I tend to read it much more in home group. . . . I've never been somebody who will read daily passages, but with the home group . . . and going through the passages and while we talk about it . . . it makes it, I find it much easier.

The group interaction was making understanding and learning easier. David also talked about the role of the group in his Bible reading as his memory loss was beginning to affect him.

> DAVID: If I was doing it right now with the people involved I would remember it, but I probably wouldn't because it's a day-to-day thing, so that's quite difficult for me. . . . I've read one section of a Bible reading . . . all I've got to do is to go back and find the Bible reading.

As memory difficulties were increasing, the group event and then the physical Bible itself were resources which could trigger memory of what had been said. The interaction within his supportive group had helped David to continue to engage with the Bible.

Prayer: Talking with God

"My Whole Life is Prayer"

Whilst prayer had always been part of Alice's life experience, I wanted to understand how she felt dementia was affecting her practice of prayer.

> ALICE: Well, prayer is my whole life. I mean, all the day I pray. That's not me anymore. I can't do that . . . my prayer is more, I look out of the window and I say, "Lord I'm so grateful for this wonderful view and these flowers." So, my whole life is prayer in a sense now . . . rather just than a portion of the day.

Alice described prayer as a kind of ongoing conversation with God about all aspects of her life as she lived each day. Lack of concentration and loss of short-term memory meant that she could no longer pray deliberately at specific times, but now, she felt that her "whole life is prayer."

Rosemary's experience of prayer was also a conversation through the day:

> ROSEMARY:When I'm in my bed at night and talking to him during the day, having the talks with him when I'm just walking along with the dog and experiencing the glory all around me of his creation.

This talking with God was an intimate and interactive part of her life. Here, she highlighted that creation and "experiencing" its "glory" as natural stimulants for praise and pointers towards God as Creator.

"Without It, We Are . . . Naked"

Ron told me about the importance of prayer with Clare as part of their devotional times together:

> RON: Oh . . . the presence . . . as far as that is concerned is always there, because Clare and I often pray together. It's like everything else, without it, we are, to put it bluntly, naked. . . . Clare and I have always prayed together, so that is . . . something which is automatic-like.

Ron's use of the term "the presence" in the context of our conversation, I think, might have implied his feeling that God was always present. The word "naked" seemed to suggest that he felt that he would be vulnerable without prayer. This life of prayer was "automatic-like." It was as though it was an instinctive and natural part of his Christian life.

For Jess and Andrew, prayer is also a shared daily practice:

> JESS: But we pray every day . . . we thank God for the new day. We thank God.

Praying and Bible-reading is a simple, daily routine. Jess chose to focus on their shared thankfulness to God, expressing a positive response to God in spite of her current life situation.

"ALLOW GOD INTO SITUATIONS"

For Alice, prayer was about "allowing God into situations."

> ALICE: If we allow God into situations he can transform them . . . not necessarily by making a situation good . . . but because of the resources, the inner resources he gives us in that situation, we're able to cope with it and almost rejoice in it.

Alice felt that prayer was not about making situations good, but that, through these, God provides the inner resources to cope. Speaking out of her own situation, she concluded that prayer's transformation enables rejoicing in spite of circumstances.

Belonging to a Faith Community

I was interested to explore how the experience of belonging to a church community and relationship with other Christians was significant at this stage of the participants' lives, and to see how dementia was affecting their belonging to a local congregation.

Going to Church Services

"IT'S THE GETTING TOGETHER AND HAVING FELLOWSHIP . . . THAT MATTERS"

Living independently and having dementia had meant that Rosemary was finding it increasingly difficult to be part of a local church:

> ROSEMARY: Living in here [supported independent living] . . .
> we only have, at the moment twice a month a service, a com-
> munion service. . . . I don't like missing a time of . . . "If two or
> three are gathered together in my name I'm there in the midst."[35]
> It's the collective, the getting-together and having fellowship . . .
> and that matters I think a lot even though you're whole-hearted
> in tune, and you're with God, and with the Lord, Holy Spirit is
> filling you (as he is).

Rosemary valued meeting with other Christians, but this was difficult
in the supported living community where she was resident. Sometimes
there was a service, but practical issues made it difficult for this "getting
together" to happen regularly. It was clearly frustrating for her. However,
she felt that "fellowship" was what was most important for her about
"church." The coming together with other believers was significant in
enabling a sense of meeting with God, even though she felt personally
"in tune" with God.

Rosemary had tried to go out to a local church, but had found it
difficult:

> ROSEMARY: They said, "Well you're always welcome to come
> here." But they were very much more . . . trivial about it. . . . It
> was routine. . . . I can't at the moment join a congregation. You
> feel different when you are established here [in the supported
> living village] and you have carers coming in every day and you
> know your brain is deteriorating.

It had taken deliberate effort to go out to visit a local church. She was
clearly disappointed with the welcome from, and interaction with, regular members of that congregation. There was a sense of frustration that
she was unable to do more to be involved in church-going. Her sadness
and sense of alone-ness in this was apparent.

"It's Easy . . .
I Don't Remember What I Hear or What We Did!"

The participants who were married had a different experience of church-
going. Jess went to church regularly with Andrew, and spoke of their
involvement in church as a joint activity.

---

35. "For where two or three are gathered in my name, I am there among them"
(Matt 18:20).

> JESS: It's easy to go to church . . . I don't remember what I hear
> or what we did . . . or things like that. . . . I don't suppose many
> people recognize that I can't remember things. . . . And people
> have always been very kind to me.

Jess was continuing to be part of a local church and had good relationships with others in the church. She was finding attendance at services "easy," perhaps because the practical aspects of this were organized by Andrew, although she didn't remember what happened or what was being said. Nevertheless, she appreciated the kindness of people.

Like Jess, Ron was also finding going to church helpful for his faith, and it was, similarly, a joint activity with his wife, Clare. I asked him if the dementia had made going to church difficult.

> RON: No. . . . It hasn't done any damage at all. In fact, I would
> say it's brought me closer. . . . But why I say that is because it's
> given me a memory which I haven't got, but by going to church,
> it has . . . it's there.

Ron seemed to be saying here that, despite his memory problems, going to church allowed him to access present experience of his faith. I was aware that Ron's continued attendance at church was dependent on Clare's support.

"Too Loud, Too Noisy, Too Much"

Rosemary told me about the difficulties that dementia was bringing for attendance at church services:

> ROSEMARY: The difficulty sometimes is church itself [chuckles]. . . . I felt embarrassed having gone up to the communion rail—it was the evangelical St. P's where I was living before I came here—and . . . I would go up to the rail and take communion, but I lost my way coming back. . . . I suddenly thought, which is my pew? And there'd be people guiding me and beginning to think, "Oh this poor soul, she's forgotten where she's going." . . . I don't altogether find that people sometimes who are the church community [chuckles] are most understanding of people with dementia. It's almost as though they themselves can't quite deal with—although, of course, there's always people in that church who can give you special understanding, help and friendship. . . . Uou feel it's beginning to be too loud, too noisy,

too much. . . . You want to get out of it, go quietly home and
dwell on it and not have to socialize any more.

Rosemary's words highlighted her sense of a lack of people's understanding of dementia which was making it difficult for her to be involved in church: the difficulty in finding her seat after receiving communion; embarrassment about what others thought of her; noise and loudness. Her description also made clear the kind of inner confusion she felt as a result. Whilst she appreciated the help and understanding of some, she felt that some "can't quite deal with it." Sometimes she felt that she wanted "to get out of it" and find some quiet.

Whilst Alice was not comfortable with ritual as part of church life ("you're not going to encourage my walk with God by . . . the ritual"), she was finding clear organization of her church services helpful. The following is based on paraphrase of Alice's words from my research diary:

> Alice sometimes finds the informality and noise difficult. She sits against a wall which provides her with a better sense of security. Anything unusual happening is difficult, for example, if the service leader asks people to move around or get into groups.

> However, Alice has helped church members to understand what things are difficult for her and someone now sends her the service outline in advance so that she can be prepared for what will happen. Alice likes the old hymns, but her church mainly uses newer ones, although they always try to include an older one too.

Alice's account highlighted the importance of feeling safe in an environment. Over-stimulating noise was difficult; a sense of being physically safe was important; having a sense of order, preparation and predictability enabled her to be comfortable in a church service. She preferred older hymns, but her church mainly "uses newer ones." Alice was a naturally confident person and was therefore able to help other church members understand how dementia was affecting her, and they were looking for solutions to help with her difficulties.

I am aware that not all Christians with dementia would have the same confidence or facility in explaining their situation to their church community.

"I Do the Flowers Instead . . . They Don't Argue with You"

Jess, whilst finding going to church is "easy," nevertheless felt that her dementia was affecting how others in church see her.

> JESS: I just support him [Andrew] now because my memory loss has interfered with my being somebody or something, doing something. I do the flowers instead . . . they don't argue with you. You don't make a mistake if you're doing the flowers.

Jess's words suggested how she felt others might be assessing her when she was not seen to have a public role in her church community. She also recognized that there was loss, and that she could no longer do some things that had been part of her earlier life. Her wry "I do the flowers instead . . . they don't argue with you" suggested her own resilience and determination to continue her purposeful involvement in the community of church. But her words also hinted at a sadness, possibly revealing a sense of regret and, perhaps, a lack of felt-awareness or support from others in her wider church community.

Dependence on One Another

Participants expressed their sense of dependence on others in their communities of faith for support in their spiritual lives, especially in the light of dementia. This was both within church services, in small group meetings mid-week, or in their daily relationship with their spouse.

"People are Aware . . ."

Bill talked about the sense of support he feels which his church is providing:

> BILL: I don't have a problem in telling people that are close and or even in the church. In fact, when we had the diagnosis confirmed, Carol, during the service, said, "I just want to let you know that Bill has now had a diagnosis of early onset Alzheimer's." . . . The number of people who then came and said we're really sorry for what you're going through! And also, to Carol, because the carer is perhaps is carrying much more than the patient themselves.

And I think that was good because then people are aware that
this is what is happening.

Bill and Carol, his wife, felt part of their church community and cared for
it in a way which allowed them to share the news of Bill's diagnosis pub-
licly. The relationships were warm, and strong enough to have enabled
people to come to Bill and express their sympathy and understanding,
and their desire to support both Bill and Carol. Bill felt that telling people
about his diagnosis would help them to understand what was happening
in their lives. At this early stage in his dementia, he recognized that his
illness had difficult implications for Carol too, and his need for her support in this. I noticed that Bill by implication, referred to himself as "the
patient," assuming a medical definition of himself.

"Members of the Church . . . Very Kind"

Matthew, similar to others who were married, spoke about his involvement in his local church as being a joint involvement. He referred to his
village church life frequently throughout our conversation.

> MATTHEW: Yes . . . I think the members of the church seemed
> to . . . be very kind . . . and actually when we celebrated our fifti-
> eth wedding anniversary . . . which was last year . . . the former
> vicar and his wife both came . . . and a lot of church members
> came.

Matthew was aware of and appreciative of the kindness of others. There
was a sense that he was well-known and loved in the church community.
Its members were supportive of him in his health difficulties. His words
suggested that he felt he belonged to this community of caring Christian
people. Matthew's own attitude of thankfulness towards others suggested
mutually responsive relationships.

Relationships which were nurturing faith, apart from attendance at
church services, were important for the participants too. For Bill, "home
group" was an important expression of his church life. Bill emphasized
the relational nature of his group. They were mutually supportive and he
was already valuing that support in the early stages of his dementia.

> BILL: We pray, we pray for each other. . . . I think that the people,
> you know, that group is very supportive anyway because it's sort
> of there for you; it's there for them.

RESEARCHER: As the journey with dementia goes along, do you think there are going to be people around you, like the home group, who will support you?

BILL: They already are . . . [with feeling].

"the Spiritual Side Comes with Gail"

For the participants whose spouse was in the role of primary carer, this relationship was important for their spiritual well-being. Hellström has noted the actuality of this shared relationship and the effects of dementia on identity: "couplehood is multidimensional, constructed and shared between the spouses."[36] This seemed to be evident in their shared spiritual life.

As in earlier examples given about church involvement, married participants named their wife or husband specifically as being key for their spiritual support. For example, David said: "Well, first of all I've got Gail [laughs]. . . . That's the key one!" David saw Gail as being his primary spiritual supporter. Whilst her support was important, David also mentioned that of the wider family.

For Ron, Bible reading, prayer and going to church were done as a couple unit. The relationship with Clare was crucial for his faith practice.

RESEARCHER: Who gives you most support in your Christian life?

RON: Well, the most . . . Clare, in particular, naturally . . . but, whenever you . . . actually have fellowship with another church, or with the Baptist church . . . well that is it . . . and you're always in that situation . . . whereby you get fellowship . . . and it's mighty good!

Whilst Ron considered that Clare was most important in giving him spiritual support, the role of the wider believing community was also clearly significant for his faith sustenance and enjoyment.

This unity of spiritual support was also clear in Jess and Andrew's relationship:

---

36. Hellström, "'I'm His Wife Not His Carer!,'" 53–66.

> RESEARCHER: And as you go through this . . . time in your life do you feel that God is with you . . . or Jesus . . . or the Spirit . . . is with you?
>
> JESS: Yes, I'm sure of that. And that's why the fact that I can't remember, my memory loss, doesn't matter. And the other thing is that . . . I've got [Andrew] looking after me. And he's very good about that . . . very good at looking after me. . . . Andrew is . . . my protector, my director. And he is in charge and I just do as I'm told! And also he loves me a lot . . . which is very nice because I am safe with Andrew.
>
> RESEARCHER: Do you feel that you're safe with God?
>
> JESS: I'm totally reliant on God . . . and his relationship with Andrew as well.

Jess had a great sense of assurance of God's presence and Andrew's care. She had a sense of safety because of her relationship with Andrew. It was her trust of Andrew's relationship with God that seemed to enable her reliance on him.

This resource of a loving spouse's spiritual support was not available for the participants who were living independently.

"It's Hard for Me Living in Here"

Rosemary would like more spiritual support, but this was not regularly available. She was missing regular "fellowship" and, as expressed earlier in this analysis, church attendance outside of the care village where she lived was difficult. Being together with other Christians was very important for her.

> RESEARCHER: So, for you personally here . . . people like Alice[37] . . . and the chaplain . . . are really important in supporting you spiritually.
>
> ROSEMARY: In a spiritual way, Alice's help has been the closest thing.

Rosemary confirmed that the community's chaplain and especially the friendship of Alice had been helpful in finding support for her spiritual life.

---

37. Alice lives in the same community as Rosemary.

Whilst Alice did not have the immediate support of Christian family nearby, she coped with this by actively seeking to encourage others in their faith. For herself, she primarily seemed to find resilience to her life's circumstances through her own dependence on God:

> ALICE: I mean I know that God is always with me, because he always has been, and I know that there's nothing that can ever separate me from him.

Her own sense of being loved by God and her security in that, was enabling her to focus on the needs of others.

> ALICE: And there's always something that we can encourage people about and help them . . . and all the difficult times we go through are just to encourage us to do the same [laughs].

For Alice, her dementia seemed to be motivating her to be an encourager. In this way, she was finding spiritual sustenance in her interaction with others. The giving and receiving were a mutual experience.

Summary

Theme 4: Faith in Practice

- For the participants, being in relationship with God had precedence over the doing of faith practices.
- Faith practices such as Bible engagement, prayer and going to church services were not significant of themselves, but were important as means and expressions of relationship with God and other believers.
- Failing concentration and memory were making habitual, routine Bible-reading and prayer difficult, but these practices remained central in their ongoing relationship with God. Participants were finding other ways of using the resources of Bible and prayer.
- Attendance at church services had positive value for participants. However, their accounts also highlighted particular challenges in facilitating this in ways which expressed their mutual belonging as members of the community.

- Dependence is part of the experience of being a Christian believer.[38] The responsibility of support and care is mutual, but is especially significant for the person living with dementia.

- For those who were married, the partnership was offering significant spiritual support. For those who were living independently, there were issues to be resolved about how such support could be enabled.

Theme 5: Finding Meaning in Dementia

For all of the participants, there seemed to be a desire to find purpose in their experience of dementia in the light of their faith. MacKinlay and Trevitt's work on spiritual reminiscence in dementia has begun work in this area showing how finding meaning brings hope and transcendence.[39] Katsuno, in her research with those experiencing early dementia, also notes that recognizing purpose is part of the Christian's response: "Some participants stated that they are thankful for life given by God, including a dementing illness, because they believe that God has a purpose for everything."[40] Here, the participants in this study contributed further to understanding of this search for meaning, and bring additional insights with their perspectives from an evangelical tradition.

Individuals' stories revealed something of the experience of finding meaning through reflection in the following areas:

- Discovering purpose

- Hope and resurrection

- Time and eternity

Discovering Purpose

"My Purpose Is to Please Him"

Alice stressed her acceptance of dementia and sense of God-given calling and purpose in the experience of dementia.

---

38. Stott, "Age of Dependence."
39. MacKinlay and Trevitt, *Finding Meaning.*
40. Katsuno, "Personal Spirituality," 325.

> ALICE: I was reading the bit in the Bible where it says about if
> we take God's gift to us with enthusiasm . . . God will do good
> things with it. So I said, well this is obviously God's gift to me.
> . . . This is God's present, his gift. . . . So, if I do accept it with
> gritted teeth then nothing will happen, nothing good will come
> of it, but if I take this as God's gift with enthusiasm, he can do
> wonderful things with it.

Her sense of purpose was determined and strong.

> ALICE: And my purpose is to please him, not anybody else. And
> to please him is to, like the boy with the loaves and fishes,[41] just
> giving him the little that I have—he does great things with it.

This sense of purpose arose from Alice's desire "to please him." This conscious giving of herself in service to God seemed to be bringing great
returns. Alice's words revealed her belief in the activity of God in her own
life, working through her, for the benefit of others.

David had a driving sense of purpose too. Whereas Alice's sense
of calling was a desire to help others know God's presence in their lives,
David's goal was more broadly focused on life in this world: "People like
me can have a much better life." He was involved in medical research
and, for him, this was important for bringing a sense of meaning to life
with dementia:

> DAVID: I feel, as I say, that it's about trying to make sure that we
> can do something better for those coming behind us.

His involvement in this significant project was exciting him and giving a
sense of purpose. I wanted to know if this was related to his faith:

> DAVID: Yes I think so, because it's the faith that says to me, I can
> make a difference to other people.

It was sometimes difficult to maintain specific focus on David's faith experience rather than the medical research which he was involved with.
However, his participation in this research about his faith experience was
driven by his belief that this would also improve the lives of others. I
noticed that David's focus was life in the present, rather than his eschatological hope. In conversation outside of the interviews, Gail talked about
his sense of purpose in the medical research as: "David's mission."

41. See John 6:8–9.

"If God Has Asked Me to Have Dementia"

Jill was still getting used to the diagnosis of dementia and was adjusting her thinking about the meaning of this for her life. I asked her whether she had a sense of "calling" in this.

> JILL: [chuckles] I s'pose . . . it's a bit silly . . . being in the forefront of being a Christian as somebody who has dementia. It was quite . . . a surprise to hear that you wanted to talk to me about it . . . because I think in some ways I hadn't actually expressed my feelings about it at all . . . before.

Jill's puzzlement at the research interest in her experience of dementia as a Christian, suggested that at the moment she was not finding purpose related specifically to her situation of living with dementia. She found my suggestion of "calling" surprising and, at first, this seemed to be a new idea for her to think of living with dementia as something which might be purposeful of itself.

However, as we spoke, Jill seemed to be considering the possibility that God had allowed dementia to come into her life.

> JILL: You can learn things that people who aren't Christians can't learn, can't recognize! . . . All to do with your reaction to what God asks you to do. And if God has asked me to have dementia . . . then I know he will be there. I know that God keeps his promise. And he is there with us. . . . If we wish to acknowledge him . . . and that is the important thing. Do I wish to acknowledge that God is with me in dementia?

As we talked together, Jill was reflective. At some points, it was as if she was almost speaking to herself, and understanding more about her reaction to her illness as our conversation progressed. She seemed to feel that because of her faith she could "learn things" that those who were not Christians could not learn. Her words suggested that acknowledging God has in some way "asked her" to have dementia was important for her. She had trusted in God before her dementia. Now, it was as though she was becoming aware of the challenge of dementia, and of a choice she must make: "Do I wish to acknowledge that God is with me in dementia?" Her words reminded me of others who had spoken of the significance of *choosing* to accept the presence of this illness in their lives.[42]

---

42. Bryden, *Dancing with Dementia*, 169; Davis, *My Journey into Alzheimer's Disease*, 57.

"Jesus . . . I Would Like to Know Him Better"

I asked Jill to tell me about her sense of purpose for the future.

> JILL: I know Jesus, but I would like to know him better . . . and I long to know him more in my illness. And to some extent . . . my knowledge of Jesus is brief with regard to the illness.

As Jill was adjusting to the experience of her illness, she longed to understand more about Jesus as it progressed. She emphasized that she thought of her faith as relationship with him: she wanted to know him better. This was her expectation and ambition.

> JILL: My hope for my life would be to know God in it much more than I do now.

At this early stage in her dementia, Jill believed that her faith would continue to develop in her living with dementia in the future.

Hope and Resurrection

The finding of meaning was a consistent theme in the literature about dementia which I considered throughout this research journey. MacKinlay's model of the spiritual tasks of ageing shows how this search for meaning leads to the finding of hope, even "in the presence of loss and disability."[43] In this study, the meaning of life and purpose is found in the participants' Christian faith, and seemed to be enabling them to transcend physical and cognitive losses, and find hope.

"I'm Going to Heaven"

The hope of heaven seemed to be a source of resilience as participants considered their future life with dementia. In spite of Ron's increasing symptoms of dementia and mobility difficulties, he asserted that he was "happy" and without "worry."

> RON: Where I'm going is to heaven, and therefore, my God is up there—I know that. . . . I've got no cares in the world at all and that's what I actually find more than anything else and I am happy as the day is long. . . . We don't worry about anything. . . .

---

43. MacKinlay and Trevitt, *Finding Meaning*, 23.

> Alright, we've got a bit of difficulties, but we're all right. . . . It'll
> be right.

His contentment seemed to depend on his hope of heaven and sense of going to meet with God. His "up there" suggested that wherever heaven is, God is there, and Ron was confident that he was going to meet with him. The result was his contentment in the present because of his future hope, in spite of "difficulties."

Jess was also living her present in the light of her hope of heaven.

> RESEARCHER: So, do you have any hopes or fears about the
> future
>
> JESS: No [pause]. . . . I know I won't meet God face-to-face until
> I'm dead, but I'm not afraid of dying. Not afraid of that at all.

As other participants did, Jess asserted her lack of fear for the future, or of death. Like Ron, she spoke of meeting with God after death. As for Ron, her contentment was in the light of this future hope and sense of God's care for her in the present.

"He Has Prepared a Place for Us"

Whilst Alice was intent on living for God in ways which served others in the present, her own sense of hope was underlying her faith.

> ALICE: God is never going to desert one, he's always there and
> that he has prepared a place for us.[44]

Rosemary was also sure of her future whatever happened to her as her dementia advanced.

> ROSEMARY: I don't think God judges us on . . . our brains. . . .
> He created us like this . . . so . . . I don't have to worry about that.
> I believe in my heart and soul that just saying the name of Jesus
> or just being able to join in a hymn or sing it because I know
> it still, or try to . . . Of course, you do get to a point sometimes
> when there's absolutely . . . well maybe I won't recognize things,
> matters like that. It matters not. What does matter is that I will
> be, at the right time, with the Lord.

Rosemary's hope did not depend on her brain enabling her to express belief. She did not feel that God assessed her on this capacity. Her words

44. See John 14:1–4.

implied that, as Creator, God had allowed her brain to be affected by her illness. She had confidence that she would still be able to express her faith simply by saying the name of Jesus or joining in with a hymn which she remembered. She knew, at this stage of her illness, that it brought the prospect of not recognizing people and things. Yet, she was able to assert, "It matters not."

"There Is No Fear through Jesus"

For David, future hope was focused on the person of Jesus. I asked whether, in the light of his dementia, he had any fears for the future about his relationship with God.

> DAVID: No, I don't think there's any fear. [Pause] There is no fear through Jesus. [Pause] There isn't any fear! [Pause] I'm sure there isn't.

I noticed that David pondered the word "fear." Despite his strong faith in Jesus which he felt denied the possibility of fear, he seemed to consider this as he was thinking about the development of dementia in his temporal future.

"I Feel I Have Been Forgiven . . . "

The salvific work of Jesus was often an unspoken assumption of participants, underlying their confidence of forgiveness and heaven. Bill expressed this sense of forgiveness and future hope in this way:

> BILL: God the Father, God the Son, God the Holy Spirit—and they are here for me . . . just me. Yes, I have sinned, I have caused a lot of problems with people in the past, but all that is in the past and I just want to be a follower of you for the rest of my life, and when that life finishes I shall be with you for ever.

He asserted his resolution to follow Jesus, and his description became a prayer: "I just want to be a follower of you."

Freedom from a sense of the guilt of sin, seemed to be an important issue for these Christians as they faced the future with dementia. I asked Jess why she thought Jesus died and about her sense of forgiveness.

> JESS: For our sins . . . yeah. So that we can be sin-free. So that we don't have to sin, but we do sin . . . but when I recognize that

> and I say "Oh God, I'm sorry, I didn't mean to do that," I feel I
> have been forgiven. . . . I don't think we have to carry a burden.
> We can dump it, can't we? . . . And that's why the fact that I can't
> remember, my memory loss, doesn't matter.

Jess recognized her human sinfulness, but didn't feel this was a "burden"
because "We can dump it." She understood that the death of Jesus had
made this possible. The fact that she felt accepted by God through Jesus
enabled her to say that her memory loss "doesn't matter." She seemed to
be peaceful because of her confident belief and trust in God.

Matthew also chose to focus on God's forgiveness as he tried to explain the reason for his confidence that his faith was bringing for the future.
I had asked him if he had worries or fears about his faith as he thought
about the future with dementia, and his reasons for feeling at peace.

> MATTHEW: No . . . one of the readings I read recently was
> about the centurion who stood in the Temple and put his hand
> on his chest and said "I am a good man . . . I fast twice a week
> . . . I'm not like this tax collector." And Jesus said to his disciples,
> "Which of these two men, who do you think had the strongest
> faith?" And they said, "The one who said, 'God be merciful to
> me a sinner.'" Because whatever we do, we've all sinned in some
> way or another.[45]

Matthew, as he imagined himself in the story of the "tax collector," expressed his recognition of his own sinfulness, and implied his confidence
that he was forgiven.

"We Shall All Be Changed"

Matthew then revealed his confident hope for the future in the following way:

> RESEARCHER: Do you have any worries or fears about your
> future with God
>
> MATTHEW: [Very definite:] *No!*
>
> RESEARCHER: That's very definite.
>
> MATTHEW: I wouldn't be afraid to die . . . [Loudly and firmly:]
> if I had to!

45. See Luke 18:9–14, the parable of the Pharisee and the tax collector.

RESEARCHER: Why do you say that so firmly?

MATTHEW: [Long pause, struggling with tears:] Because . . . Jesus went up to Calvary . . . and on the third day . . . he [voice breaking] he rose . . . "And we shall all be changed"[46] [voice breaking with tears].

RESEARCHER: "From glory into glory" [referring, unintentionally, to a different verse].[47]

MATTHEW: Yes.

[Matthew is tearful. Researcher reaches out her hand to Matthew. He responds, holding onto Researcher's hand very firmly.]

Matthew was definite in his response that he was not afraid of the future because of his dementia. This assertion was grounded in his hope of resurrection. He drew on words from 1 Corinthians 15:50–57. His hope was firm because he believed in the death and resurrection of Jesus. In the context of our conversation about his dementia, this seemed to be giving him hope that his own physical condition would be transformed. The importance of this for him brought him to the edge of tears. His strong emotion was expressed through facial expression and through his physical grasp of the researcher's hand.

For Matthew, for whom symptoms of dementia were becoming more troublesome, I was moved by how he expressed himself through his whole embodied self. Instinctively, as researcher, I responded physically in an empathic way. Methodologically, this mutual physical response resonates with Finlay's "constantly evolving, negotiated, dynamic, co-created relational process" and is resonant with the care for one another caught up in the Heideggerian notion of *sorge*.[48]

In response to Matthew's reference to the Bible verses, I asked him if I could read this passage to him. Matthew agreed and at the end of the reading, he was looking and sounding moved. His words surprised me.

---

46. "Listen, I will tell you a mystery! We will not all die, but we will all be changed" (1 Cor 15:51).

47. "And all of us, with unveiled faces, seeing the glory of the Lord as though reflected in a mirror, are being transformed into the same image from one degree of glory to another; for this comes from the Lord, the Spirit" (2 Cor 3:18).

48. Finlay, *Phenomenology for Therapists*, 166; Heidegger, *Being and Time*, xx.

> MATTHEW: I know where it comes from! . . . "The Dream of Gerontius."[49]
>
> RESEARCHER: Why do you think those words are so important for you as a Christian?
>
> MATTHEW: Those words are wonderful!
>
> RESEARCHER: Why do they give you such comfort and strength?
>
> MATTHEW: Does it matter? Because, I can look at a bird. What will I do in heaven? I might see a bird first thing . . . before I see the Lord.

A former, keen choral singer, the Bible text reminded him of words he had sung from Elgar's "Dream of Gerontius" which is based on the prayer of a dying man. It was clear that the memory of the music and the words we had read from Scripture, brought thoughts of resurrection and transformation. They clearly brought him great comfort.

I was interested that Matthew foresaw the certainty of heaven as an embodied experience ("I can look"; "I see the Lord"). He seemed to find my question "Why do they . . . ?" irrelevant ("Does it matter?"). He was unconcerned about understanding *how* things will happen. His question suggested that he was content to trust God. The confidence of his belief expressed through his faltering speech was deeply moving for both of us. As researcher I was mindful of these words: "No matter what the condition of any human being, his or her personhood in God requires that pastor and care giver come before that person in reverence."[50]

Time and Eternity

A striking aspect of all the conversations was the participants' faith assumption that the "now" of time was within the context of eternity with God.

---

49. Matthew is referring to "The Dream of Gerontius" (1900), by Edward Elgar, a work for orchestra and voices, which uses the text of a poem by John Henry Newman (1890), the prayer of a dying man.

50. Shamy, *Guide to the Spiritual Dimension of Care*, 129.

"God . . . Has Prepared a Place for Us"

Alice saw her present experience of dementia in the context of her awareness of eternal "time":

> ALICE: Whatsoever things are good and pure and beautiful and
> . . . think on these things,[51] so whenever things are in turmoil,
> we replace that with the good things, things which are of eternal
> peace and eternal significance.

Amidst the turmoil of life with dementia, the perspective of the eternal
home God had prepared for her was providing stability and peace.

Time and eternity seemed to be brought together in the ideas of
forgetting and remembering. Rosemary also expressed her dependence
on God's memory of her:

> ROSEMARY: I just know that if I forget God, he's not forgotten
> me. . . . God . . . if he's the God . . . and I know he is . . . the God
> who I trust and believe in . . . and it's here [indicates inner self]
> . . . I can speak from experience not from some theory.

Here, the two dimensions of physical, earthly life and timeless eternal
life seemed to encroach on one another in Rosemary's awareness of reality. She knew that her cognitive capacity was declining, yet she asserted
that she believed she would not forget God. In doing so, she implied that
remembering God was not just a function of brain cells. Outside of the
physical reality, God's remembering of her is eternal. Rosemary's certainty
of future with God was based on her trust and belief in him. Her use of the
word "experience" ("not . . . some theory") suggested that she was trusting
her sense of relationship with God rather than cognitive belief.

"I Know Where I'm Going . . ."

For all participants the certainty of their faith gave a sense of security
which was equipping them with resilience for the present and hope for
the future. Bill expressed it like this:

> BILL: I think in a sense, this side of heaven that is going to be
> part of my journey. The other side of heaven. . . . Well that's dealt
> with then! [Chuckles.]

---

51. See Phil 4:8.

His belief in a continuing life after death in heaven, put his dementia in the present context of time into eternal perspective. It was "going to be part of my journey." He did not believe that dementia in the temporal world was the end of his story. For him, his hope of heaven resolved the difficulties of dementia in the present.

For some participants who had been living with dementia for a number of years there was a sense of calm in the present, in the light of their hope of heaven. Ron expressed this feeling of confident contentment in the following ways:

> RON: I know where I'm going to . . . and I will always partici-
> pate in one thing and one thing only. . . . If we know where
> we're going we cannot help but feel contented. . . . Therefore,
> by me knowing where I'm going, I've never ever bothered to
> be so worried about this or worried about that. . . . Everything
> falls in its place.

For Ron, it was almost as though the situation of the present time was unimportant in the light of his eternal destiny. His certainty was enabling him not to worry. His confidence in a future with God meant that "everything falls in its place." In the disorientating time that dementia was bringing to him, he was finding meaning because of his sense of eternal purpose found in his faith in God.

Rosemary was also able to make sense of the present confusing experiences brought by her dementia because of her belief in a future with God.

> ROSEMARY: What does matter is that I will be, at the right
> time, with the Lord. That will just be glory we can't begin to
> imagine. [pause] Amen.

Time was, in a sense, unimportant for Rosemary's earthly life. Yet the "right time" suggested a sense of God's control over her life. She expected one day to be "with the Lord" and she imagined with confidence that the "glory" of that experience would be beyond earthly imagination.

"I Have Now"

Prompted by our interview about the experience of faith as a Christian living with dementia, Jess wrote the following poem[52] together with her husband:

> Everybody is in a rush
>
> But I have all the time in the world—
>   I have now.
>
> I have to fit into other people's
>   "Rush-Push-Busy" world
>
> But I have all the time in the world—
>   I have now.
>
> I only have Now—that's all I have
>   all the time
>
> Lost past No Tomorrow
>   ONLY NOW.
>
> What a privilege because
>   Now is the accepted time
>
> Today is the Day of Salvation.

In their poem, Jess expressed the positive qualities which living in the present moment were bringing to her life. She saw this as liberating within the confining busy-ness of the world's pressured-time focus. Jess reflected on the freedom which declining memory of the recent past was bringing. As an older person living with dementia she had no expectations of time on earth. Her faith was bringing a liberty and an awareness of "now" being a privileged time for which she was thankful. The words "Today is the Day of Salvation" are a reference to the words of 2 Corinthians 6:2, and affirmed her sense of the importance and the significance of the present moment for life and relationship with God, and trust in his promise of help.[53] This moment of "now" described thus, transcends

---

52. "Everybody Is in a Rush." The authors of this poem were participants in this research study and have asserted their rights to anonymity.

53. "For he says, 'At an acceptable time I have listened to you, and on a day of salvation I have helped you.' See, now is the acceptable time; see, now is the day of salvation!" (2 Cor 6:2).

chronological time and puts life in the context of eternal significance and God's *Kairos* time.

Summary

Theme 5: Finding Meaning in Dementia

- Faith was enabling the participants to find meaning and a strong sense of purpose in their experience of dementia. They felt that their illness was within the care and control of God.

- The participants' hope of faith was centered on the work of Christ on the cross and his resurrection, giving them assurance of forgiveness and hope of continuing embodied life with God.

- Belief in eternal time was putting the events and struggles of earthly time in fresh perspective, and bringing a sense of calm and contentment in the present.

- Belief in God's eternal remembering of individuals was providing a sense of safety in the face of their present forgetfulness.

- The sense of God's eternal "now," experienced through faith, was enabling transcendence of the temporal present.

- Faith is mysterious. Yet, even though such mysteries can't be explained, the effects of faith were bringing transformation to the lives of these people who were living with dementia.

Chapter Conclusion

This hermeneutic phenomenological account of the lived experience prompts the theological reflections of the following chapters. These aim to reveal deeper insights into the issue of the experience of faith in dementia and to raise further questions about this experience. The reflections will include consideration of: the identity of the Christian who lives with dementia; the experience of walking through the "shadows" of dementia as a follower of Christ; the ways in which memory and faith intertwine, bringing growth in the light of the believer's hope in Christ.

Introduction to
Theological Reflections

"Even though I walk through the valley of the shadow
... I will fear no evil" (Ps 23:4 ESVUK)

IN CHAPTERS 7–9, I reflect theologically on issues which have emerged in light of the literature and the lived experience of the participants. The reflections are structured using a model of orientation, disorientation and reorientation. This model draws on Brueggemann's "scheme" which he used in his exploration of the psalms.[1] Whilst his focus is the psalms, he also suggests a wider application which is reflected in the life of Jesus and in the life of the church.[2] Here, I use it as a framework for theological reflection on the faith experience of my participants as they were living through the experience of dementia.

I will use a Gadamerian approach which moves back-and-forth between the lived experience of the research participants and the other conversation partners of this book.[3] Through this means, a "fusion of horizons" brings new perspectives, new emphases and insights to deepen understanding of the experience and practice of Christians who are

---

1. Brueggemann, *Praying the Psalms*, 3; *Spirituality of the*, viii.

2. Brueggemann, *Spirituality of the Psalms*, x, xi; Phil 2:5–11.

3. Gadamer, *Truth and Method*, 291.

living with early to moderate dementia. In doing this, the reflections aim to contribute to faithful practice in the life of the church.

Mindful of Hauerwas's biblical agenda (as discussed in chapter 1), these reflections assume a context of the scriptural narrative from Creation, through Christology to Eschatology.[4] In keeping with objectives set out in chapter 1, they will look for perspectives brought by Scripture to redescribe the phenomenon under investigation, the experience of Christian faith for those who are living with dementia.[5]

In light of the methodology of Practical Theology, these reflections take a critical correlational approach in which theology and experience are brought together in mutually critical dialogue.[6] In doing so, these chapters begin to fulfil the interpretive and normative tasks of Osmer's practical theology.[7]

The Structure of the Reflections

The structure of the reflections, reminiscent of Brueggemann's model, envisages the faith experience of my participants as one which moves between these three different dimensions. Into the stability of their "settled orientation" of faith, has come the new, disorienting challenge of living with dementia.[8] In this changed situation, the experience of participants discovers the surprising light of Christ—"a man of sorrows . . . acquainted with grief" (Isa 53:3).[9] Living with the shadows of dementia, their experience reveals that they were finding transformation and new orientation, in the light of the hope of the gospel.

These three elements do not represent a linear progression, but are dimensions of the participants' experience of faith, which inform one another continuously.

4. See Hauerwas, *Peaceable Kingdom*, 98.

5. Brueggemann, *Redescribing Reality*, 5–6; Swinton, *Dementia*, 19–21.

6. Browning, "Pastoral Theology in a Pluralistic Age," 93; Pattison: "Some Straw for the Bricks," 139–41.

7. Osmer, *Practical Theology*, 4.

8. Brueggemann, *Spirituality of the Psalms*, 9.

9. Brueggemann, *Spirituality of the Psalms*, 27–28.

Orientation: Knowing Who I Am

In chapter 7, I reflect on the foundations of the participants' sense of identity and stability in their living with dementia. I use the theological lenses of being created by God in his image, being found in Christ, and belonging to the community of faith gathered by the Holy Spirit. I will briefly acknowledge eschatological hope as part of this orientation, and consider this in further detail in chapter 9.

Disorientation: Walking through Shadow

Chapter 8 reflects on the impact—sometimes unseen—of this particular kind of suffering on the faith experience and practice of these Christians who are living with dementia.

Reorientation: Transforming Faith

In chapter 9 I seek a deeper understanding of what was enabling reorientation in the participants' experience of faith. I will consider how memory was funding their faith, and how this in turn was resourcing their perception of God's purpose, trust in God, and endurance of the challenges which dementia was bringing. Lastly, I consider the transforming impact of eschatological hope in the participants' experience of faith as they live with dementia.

7

Orientation

Knowing Who I Am

"I am loved by God" (Alice)

Introduction

THE COMING OF DEMENTIA begins to interrogate the meaning of what it is to be human. For the believer, even in its earlier stages, the illness begins to question theological understanding of what it means to be human, and, in consequence, their identity as being in relationship with God in Christ. This is not only of relevance to those who are in the advanced stages of their illness. It is relevant to those who are newly diagnosed, or in the early years of their journey with the disease, and who are beginning, to struggle with loss of words, concentration and short-term memory. In this first reflection, I explore the theological underpinnings of the participants' certainty of who they are in relationship with God.

Throughout the research conversations, the participants' assertions of their sense of identity in the light of their experience of dementia suggested their consciousness of the questions which dementia was bringing to others' perceptions of "who I am." In response, their words expressed their felt certainty of having enduring identity as people loved by God ("I am loved by God," Alice). Typical of Christians of an evangelical tradition, the participants' sense of who they were was founded in their transcendent sense of being in relationship with God in Christ: "It's a relationship" (Alice); "I know Jesus" (David); "Nothing . . . can ever separate me from him"[1] (Alice). It was this sense of knowing who they were in Christ that was framing their experience of dementia.

Nevertheless, the certainty found in their experience of faith asks questions of the traditional theological paradigms of what it means to be human, created in God's image, and also, as cognitive capacity fades, the soteriological certainty of identity in Christ. Bryden's question, asked out of her own early experience of dementia, resonates with the faith-filled certainty of my participants ("Where does this journey begin, and at what stage can you deny me my self-hood and my spirituality?").[2] It also prompts the new questions that dementia brings to theology of the evangelical tradition.

What does it mean for the Christian to be formed in the image of God in Christ when memory and other capacities are beginning to fail? The answers to such questions have significance, not only for theology, but for Christians living with dementia and their loved-ones. For them, their prognoses and the first signs of stigmatizing behaviors from others begin to ask: Who are you? (I will consider participants' experiences of this in the following reflection.)

In this reflection, seeking further understanding of the orientation of the participants' lives, I consider theological and biblical perspectives which inform their certainty of identity as disciples of Jesus. Such perspectives have profound importance for the ways in which my participants perceive themselves, and also for the ways in which the body of Christ responds to them as fellow Christians. First, I consider the significance of being created by God in his image; second, I will reflect on the significance of being in Christ; third, I explore the context of my participants' experience, found in their participation in the ongoing narrative of God's story, as his people in the body of Christ.

Created by God

Traditionally, for the Christian believer, being created in the image of God provides the starting place for biblical and theological understanding of what it means to be human, including those who live with dementia.[3]

---

1. See Rom 8:38–39.
2. Bryden and MacKinlay, "Dementia: A Spiritual Journey," 71.
3. Anderson, *On Being Human*, 70.

Whilst the phrase "image of God" (*imago Dei*) appears in Scripture only a few times,[4] it provides foundation for theological understanding of the Christian faith, setting a purposeful trajectory through Scripture: we are creatures of God, loved by him, and made with a purpose, "to glorify God, and to enjoy him forever."[5] This notion of identity is presumed in Christian faith and assumed and embedded in the participants' phenomenological accounts. Their God was sovereign and the Creator. For example, Alice expressed her purpose being "to please him"; Bill thought of God as "the Boss"; Rosemary spoke deliberately of worshipping "Creator God."

Theological understanding of the *imago Dei* relentlessly leads us forward to the image found in Christ and to the discovery of the Christian's identity, whatever their capacities, as being "in him" (see Col 1:15). With such an identity, the Scriptural account, points inevitably to eschatological hope of resurrection and the state of being-with-God for ever (1 Cor 15).[6] It is this foundational understanding of the pre-eminence of God and his purposes which permeated the words of the participants and was giving them sustaining hope ("I know where I'm going," Ron).

The Rational/Relational Tension

As discussed in the literature review (chapter 3), understandings in our contemporary western context of what it means to be "me," have been shaped by perspectives from philosophy and psychology, often depending on rational or relational criteria. Yet, both of these, eventually, might seem to threaten the identity of those living with dementia. This tension has also been reflected in Christian tradition and is, therefore, important for understanding the nature of faith experience in dementia.

From Aquinas through to modern theologians such as Henry and Clark,[7] the criteria for the reflected image of God have included reason as pre-eminent: "In the rational creature alone we find a likeness of image."[8] Protestant thinking has been more closely associated with Augustine's

---

4. Brueggemann, *Unsettling God*, 59.

5. Westminster Assembly, "Westminster Shorter Catechism."

6. Grenz, "Social God and the Relational Self," 83.

7. See Anderson's discussion of the perspective of a conservative evangelical orientation in *On Being Human*, 225.

8. Aquinas, *Summa Theologica* Ia, q.93, a.6.

focus on human orientation towards God and the relational.[9] Yet Augustine also argues that to be made in God's image ultimately depends on rationality: the defining characteristic is "a rational soul, which raises him above the beasts in the field."[10] Modern evangelical theology has lived with an uncomfortable tension between its style of rational, linear, propositional thinking,[11] developed in response to Enlightenment thinking, and the relational aspect of faith response found in Augustine, protestant reformers such as Luther, and modern scholars such as Buber and Barth. Whilst Christians have emphasized the relational as an essential part of being created in the *imago Dei*, still, eventually, some scholars suggest an ultimate dependence on rational capacity, which leads us back to the rational criteria of Aquinas.

Evangelical theology brings emphasis on personal relationship with Christ, dependent on God's gift of salvation which is freely given.[12] Confidence in their sense of such a relationship with God was evident in my participants' accounts. However, some sections of evangelicalism have also portrayed ongoing soteriological status as dependent on verbal and cognitive assent to the central tenets of Christian faith, drawing on Bible verses such as Romans 10:9-10.[13] Such an understanding would seem eventually to risk excluding those suffering with advancing dementia from relationship with God. Dementia reveals inconsistency in this position. Perhaps, unwittingly, some evangelicals have implied limits on the grace of God for *some* human beings.

Such tensions are deeply embedded in the evangelical tradition. I was struck by the response of one of the participants (David) whose words hinted at this. I had asked him in what ways he felt that declining cognitive understanding affects faith. Certain of his own relationship with Jesus ("I know Jesus"), I noticed that he pondered over this issue:

> DAVID: The trouble is . . . when people have got dementia and it's much further on . . . they wouldn't be able to know, because

9. Anderson, *On Being Human*, 74–75.

10. Augustine, *On Genesis*, 186. See also Reinders, *Receiving the Gift of Friendship*, 228–29.

11. For example, Reasonable Faith (www.reasonablefaith.org)

12. Zahl, "Reformation Pessimism," 82; "It is the gift of God" (Eph 2:8).

13. "If you declare with your mouth, 'Jesus is Lord,' and believe in your heart that God raised him from the dead, you will be saved. For it is with your heart that you believe and are justified, and it is with your mouth that you profess your faith and are saved" (Rom 10:9–10 NIVUK).

> if they didn't already know, because they wouldn't be able to
> understand it . . . in much later stages . . . but that faith I would
> hope will continue with me.

David was sure of his own faith as he imagined his future with dementia. Yet, he struggled with the question of the possibility of having faith without "knowing."

Traditional understandings of what it means to be a human, created in the image of God with its reason-relational dimensions, do not provide easy solutions for the Christian with dementia who knows that his cognitive capacity is diminishing. For those living in the early to moderate stages of dementia, still able to envisage the future, they may understandably feel that a "hypercognitive society" threatens not only their identity but also the security of their faith.[14]

However, such conclusions might seem to distance us untruthfully from those who live with the increasing consequences of cognitive impairment, and, in particular, the voices of those we have heard in this study. Speaking of her certainty of enduring relationship with God, Alice said: "but now, even when my brain falls apart . . . it doesn't matter." For her, and the other participants in the research, their certainty of being in a two-way relationship with God has pre-eminence: "It's a relationship to someone that I love and who loves me" (Alice).

As I have listened to the voices of the participants in this research, and to the voices of theology, two subsequent questions arise. From a biblical perspective, what then is the nature of being human (including the Christian living with developing dementia), created by God? What is the nature of God the Creator?

Being Human

"Then the LORD God formed a man from the dust of the
ground and breathed into his nostrils the breath of life,
and the man became a living being" (Gen 2:7)

The biblical story of creation begins with the will and intention of the Creator: "In the beginning God" (Gen 1:1 NIVUK). In Christian thought, unlike the perspectives of secular western society, the human creature

---

14. Post, *Moral Challenge of Alzheimer Disease*, 5.

is not an autonomous being who can find fulfilment in self alone.[15] The biblical creation account makes clear: "We are not the authors of our own stories."[16] Rather, God is sovereign: he is the one who creates and gives "the breath of life," so that the human becomes "a living being," sustained by, and dependent on, God the Creator. The participants' words reflected this sense of the who is God in charge of their lives ("If God has asked me to have dementia," Jill).

Body-and-Soul

The creation story gives a holistic sense of what it is to be human. *Together*, the "dust" and "breath" form the "living being."[17] The Hebrew word *nephesh*, often translated as "soul," indicates God's "breath of life." Anderson in his exploration of the nature of being human speaks of "ensouled body and embodied soul." This understanding concurs with the Old Testament Hebraic understanding.[18] However, Christian tradition, influenced by dualist Greek thought, has over the centuries separated the physical and spiritual, and this dualism has persisted into twenty-first-century thinking. I noticed that David's words implied an uncertainty about this as he imagined his own future of living with advancing dementia: "Maybe the dementia gets worse, but that part of me will belong to Jesus."

In the New Testament, Pauline writing sometimes appears to be ambivalent about this issue, for example: "Set your minds on things above, not on earthly things. . . . Put to death, therefore, whatever belongs to your earthly nature" (Col 3:2–5 NIVUK). Gooder notes that, through Augustine, elements of platonic thinking have become interwoven with Protestant understanding.[19] However, she highlights that the word *psuche* (the New Testament Greek word often translated as "soul") is not precise, but is used in a variety of ways by Paul. Gooder asserts that in keeping with his Hebrew heritage, Paul's use of this word

---

15. For example, Giddens, *Modernity and Self Identity*, 70–108.

16. Swinton, *Dementia*, 164.

17. *Terra animate*, as Augustine describes the human being. See Augustine, *City of God* 20.20.

18. Anderson, *On Being Human*, 38, 210.

19. Gooder, *Body*, 22–23.

incorporates the body, pushing us to recognize that for Paul both the words "body" and "soul" are neutral and describe who we are as people—bodies animated by a vital life force.[20]

Even a subtle ignoring of the wholeness of what it means to be created in the image of God, may result in damaging stigmatization which participants in the research were already beginning to experience. In contrast, a unified body-and-soul understanding of what it means to be human brings reassurance, both for the person living with dementia and their loved-ones.

Contrary to the fragmented understanding of personhood where cognitive capacity is definitive, the *imago Dei* understanding is of the *whole* person—body, mind and soul—the integrated self, expressed through the unity of body and soul.[21] This understanding is of significance for those who *know* that their cognitive capacities are diminishing. In biblical terms, the living, breathing human being, whatever their incapacities, is made in the image of God, holy and worthy of honor. One participant (Alice) emphasized her completeness in this way:

> ALICE: Our worth and value doesn't depend on . . . what our health is like or the state of our bodies. . . . He just loves us for who we are . . . so we are complete in him.

In these understandings of who we are as human beings there is hope for those living with developing cognitive incapacity. In keeping with this theological understanding, the participants in this study expressed that they know themselves to be "more than a diseased brain."[22]

Made for Relationship

There is another important aspect to notice which is consequent on the understanding that human beings are created by God. In the beginning, God said: "Let us make mankind in our image, in our likeness" (Gen 1:26 NIVUK). In using the first person plural pronoun, God's words suggest the inherent relationality of what it means to be human. Anderson expounds the Creation accounts, proposing that the "*imago* is not totally present in the form of individual humanity but more completely

20. Gooder, *Body*, 41.

21. Swinton, *Dementia*, 166–67.

22. Bryden, *Dancing with Dementia*, 152.

as co-humanity";[23] "in the image of God . . . male and female he created them" (Gen 1:27).

Human beings are made for relationship, not only with God, but with one another: "It is not good that the man should be alone" (Gen 2:18). One of the participants (Jess) expressed her identity as a person embedded in social relationships: "Just because you can't remember things . . . you're still a human, you're still a parent, wife . . . husband." Drawing on Buber's relational "I-Thou" concept[24] with its three-way, interactive relationship, Anderson proposes that "it is in relationship with other persons as well as with God that the divine image is expressed."[25] From the beginning, in the Garden of Eden, God himself actively seeks and initiates relationship, and ordains it as an inherent characteristic of human being (see Gen 2:18, 20b–24; 3:8, 9).

The reciprocal, relational nature of the *imago* is caught up through Scripture in the command to love God who "so loved the world" (John 3:16) with its *sequitur*, "love your neighbor as yourself" (Luke 10:27 NIVUK).[26] It is reflected in the community of God's people through the Old Testament story, and then in the New Testament in the community of believers who are *together* the body of Christ (1 Cor 3:16; 12:12–31 NLT).

From a theological perspective, relationality is not a criterion for personhood which can be in doubt, but arises out of being made in the image of God.[27] Whilst this being-in-relationship with God is inherent in being human, relationship with others brings increasing challenge for those who live with dementia ("They don't understand," Rosemary).

What Sort of God in Dementia?

In asking the above question, Kevern recognizes that living in this freshly acknowledged context of dementia has potential to prompt new perspectives on our understanding of God.[28] This God is relational and loving and, in spite of their developing dementia, this is the God of whom the participants speak: I am "loved by God, no matter what" (Alice).

23. Anderson, *On Being Human*, 73.

24. See Buber, *I and Thou*.

25. Anderson, *Spiritual Caregiving*, 33.

26. Williams, "Knowing God in Dementia," 6.

27. Swinton, *Dementia*, 159.

28. Kevern, "What Sort of a God?" 174.

The Relationality of God

Theologically, from Augustine to Moltmann to Zizioulas and others of the Christian tradition, God is understood to be inherently relational in his trinitarian nature. This notion has been understood in a variety of ways. Kilby, in her discussion of the Trinity, suggests that a definitive definition is, in the end, unimportant; rather, the three-in-oneness of God provides a kind of grammar for understanding Scripture and vocabulary for Christian faith.[29] I would propose that, in consequence, it must also provide an underlying grammar for understanding the experience of faith in dementia. One participant (Bill) expressed his understanding in in this way: "There are three bosses I suppose: Boss 1: Father; Boss 2: Jesus; Boss 3: Spirit . . . and they're all working together on our behalf."

Augustine's emphasis on the one-ness of God has perhaps contributed to the individualism of Protestantism, and that of evangelicalism.[30] Together with his stress on the capacity of reason, this may leave the person with developing dementia increasingly isolated.[31] Moltmann's seminal work *The Trinity and The Kingdom* insists instead on the prior relational nature of the Trinity.[32] Swinton finds hope in Moltmann's concept of *perichoresis* for understanding of the kind of God to be found in dementia:

> God who is a Trinity of persons . . . is a perichoretic community of love constituted by the relationships of the three persons of the Trinity: God the Father, God the Son, and God the Holy Spirit; each person is inextricably interlinked in an eternal community of loving relationship.[33]

This trinitarian model might suggest hopeful analogy with human relationality and the security of each person within the diverse community of the body of Christ. However, Kilby and Kevern both warn of the danger of projecting a social model of Trinity as the ideal of human community, suggesting that it can lead to an understanding of God *in imagine hominis.*[34] To see the relationality of the Trinity as a social model for human

---

29. Kilby, "Perichoresis and Projection," 443–44.

30. Kilby, "Perichoresis and Projection," 433–35.

31. Augustine, *On Genesis*, 186. See note 12 above.

32. Moltmann, *Trinity and the Kingdom*, 174–76; Kilby, "Perichoresis and Projection," 440.

33. Swinton, *Dementia*, 158.

34. Kevern, "What Sort of a God?" 179; Swinton, *Dementia*, 159n10.

interaction, is deficient as response to the needs of the person living with dementia, who may be, or may become, socially isolated. Swinton contends that understanding the relational nature of God is not about providing a model for human relationship. Rather, God-as-Trinity provides new possibilities for thinking about the person with dementia, who is both part of the human family *and* in relationship with God.[35]

Being as Communion

Orthodox theologian Zizioulas's discussion of the Trinity in *Being as Communion* provides further perspective for thinking about this quality of relationality and its potential for illuminating what it is to be a Christian believer living with dementia. He makes the point that relationship isn't primarily about the human ability to *respond* to God and others, rather our human relationality is an inherent, ontological quality.[36] Zizioulas asserts that this relational God, this God who exists as communion, creates and draws his creatures into loving communion both with himself and with each other.[37]

Swinton's reflection on our understanding of God in the light of dementia and this discussion of Trinity, focusses on this essential characteristic of the relational nature of God. The three-personed-community of the godhead, move together in a perfect unity, "of loving relationship."[38] Williams argues that it is within the context of this relationship that human dignity and sacredness, no matter what an individual's attributes, are found:

> Human dignity, the unconditional requirement that we attend
> with reverence to one another, rests firmly on that conviction
> that the other is already related to something that isn't me.[39]

Drawing on Zizioulas, Hudson elicits the idea that because our human-ness is so bound up in God the Trinity, "we know one another as persons only through the intimate, personal relationships of the Trinity."[40]

35. Swinton, *Dementia*, 158–59.

36. Zizioulas, *Being as Communion*, 17–18.

37. Zizioulas, *Communion and Otherness*, 43. See also John 17:22, "That they may be one, as we are one."

38. Swinton, *Dementia*, 158.

39. Williams, "Person and the Individual."

40. Hudson, "God's Faithfulness and Dementia," 53.

All are invited "in the person of Jesus Christ, by the personal power of the Holy Spirit . . . into the Son's personal communion with the Father." Jesus' prayer for his disciples expresses this: "That they may be one, as we are one" (John 17:22). This inherent relationality is hope-ful for those who live with declining cognitive capacity. One participant (Rosemary) spoke of the mystery of her relationship with God in this way:

> ROSEMARY: "God, Jesus his Son, and the Holy Spirit who in-dwells[41] . . . all . . . to me are a mystery"; "the Spirit of God is always in me. Now I am always conscious of that, even if it's really bad.

At the heart of this relational Trinity, experienced by the Christians in this study, is the creative and redeeming impetus of God's love-in-rela-tionship ("God . . . loves me," Alice).[42]

"God Is Love"

Amidst complex doctrinal issues, there is the profound, practical and theological quality of love, demonstrated in God's gift of Jesus (see John 3:16). Reflecting out of my evangelical tradition, biblically, God's inten-tional love brought humankind into existence; God's sacrificial love ex-pressed through his Son enables human beings to find relationship with him; the Holy Spirit sustains that loving relationship with God in Christ. As one participant (Bill) said:

> BILL: God the Father, God the Son, God the Holy Spirit—and they are here for me . . . just me. Yes, I have sinned . . . but all that is in the past and I just want to be a follower of you.

The participants' certainty of their identity and their experience of God's love as Christians ("He loves me . . . that's it . . . yeah," David), is underwritten by New Testament understanding of being "in Christ," the true image of God (Col 1:15). Here, is the key to the identity of the Chris-tian who is living with dementia. In the light of participants' experience and Scripture what does it mean for the Christian living with developing dementia to be "in Christ"?

---

41. For example, "Do you not know that your bodies are temples of the Holy Spirit, who is in you?" (1 Cor 6:19 NIVUK).

42. See 1 John 4:16.

Being in Christ

The biblical account of our identity and our relationship with God centers on Christ who, as Pauline writing asserts, *is* the image of God (Col 1:15). In his discussion of human identity, Grenz places this Christological revelation of God's image as pivotal in the overarching metanarrative of God's story.[43] Moving forward from "the creatio-centric" perception of humanity and the tragedy of the Fall in Genesis 1–3, the Scriptures (as Jesus himself confirmed) sustain this Christo-centric theme, showing how that in Christ the true image of God is found (Luke 24:44).

Christ's coming is the catalyst for a new creation: "In the beginning was the Word, and the Word was with God, and the Word was God. . . . The Word became flesh and made his dwelling among us" (John 1:1, 14 NIVUK). The writings of St. Paul, develop this theme. Jesus Christ *is* the divine image, the second Adam, who makes peace between creature and Creator (1 Cor 15:20–22; Rom 5:12–17).[44] For the Christian believer this is significant. In spite of failing bodies, our identity "in Christ" "finds its *telos* in the new creation," going from the past, and beyond the present into hopeful future (see Heb 1:1–4).[45] Therefore, out of his frailty, Matthew is instinctively able to voice St. Paul's words as his own: "We shall all be changed."[46]

New Testament imagery of being found "in Christ" (1 Cor 15:22) begins to disclose its significance for the person living in the earlier stages of dementia, bringing confidence in the security of knowing who they are and their salvation. This notion, brings together two ideas which are of utmost importance for the Christian. The ideas of *identity* and *salvation* are fused in the participants' "intrinsic faith" in Christ, and, thereby, begin to respond to questions raised by Keck about loss of personhood and faith in those with dementia.[47]

Imagining their future with dementia, the participants were confident in the security of their faith in Christ. Drawing on Barth, Swinton

43. Grenz, "Social God and the Relational Self," 80.

44. Grenz, "Social God and the Relational Self," 80.

45. Grenz, "Social God and the Relational Self," 82.

46. "Listen, I will tell you a mystery! We will not all die, but we will all be changed" (1 Cor 15:51).

47. Keck, *Forgetting Whose We Are*, 14, 15. See also the discussion of this in Swinton, *Dementia*, 9.

asserts that for the person living with dementia, soteriological status is secure in Christ's salvific work:

> Through Christ we are included in Christ. When we come to realize that all that needs to be done has been done in Christ, we come to realize that all that we are and all that we can be is who we are *in Christ*.[48]

Where faith is core to identity, this biblical understanding and assurance of being "in Christ" is key for the person of faith in the light of developing dementia.[49] It enables peace in the present: "There is no fear through Jesus" (David).

A New Identity in Christ

The participants' phenomenological accounts revealed aspects of their individual human identities (for example: a policeman, a mother, a teacher). Yet, the essence of who they felt themselves to be was caught up in this understanding of being in Christ: "I am born again" (Ron); "loved by God" and "a child of God" (Alice); "the core is knowing Jesus" (David). Having Christian faith was not merely a useful resource for them, it was who they were. Their transformative experience of Christ had precedence over their experience of dementia. Their illness had happened to them as people who were finding their identity in Christ. Barth's comments illuminate this:

> To be a Christian is *per definitionem* to be in Christ. The place of the community as such, the theatre of their history, the ground on which they stand, the air that they breathe, and therefore the standard of what they do and do not do, is indicated by this expression. Being in Christ is the *a priori* of all the instruction that Paul gives his churches, all the comfort and exhortation he addresses to them.[50]

In the Gospel narratives we see that the lives of the disciples were transformed by their meeting with the risen Jesus on Easter Day. For them, the resurrection signalled the beginning of the new creation. The

---

48. Swinton, *Becoming Friends of Time*, 187.

49. For example, MacKinlay and Trevitt, *Finding Meaning in the Experience of Dementia*, 22.

50. Barth, *Church Dogmatics*, 4/2:277.

Day of Pentecost saw the coming of God the Spirit into the world, and the apostles' lives were changed.

In a variety of ways, the participants spoke of the significance of their life-changing encounters with God which had established their orientation of faith ("When I was about fifteen I had a vision. And it changed me completely," Jess). This transformation didn't arise from information acquired so that it could be lived out, but was the result of God-initiated inner transformation. Like the early disciples, they were *given*, as Anderson comments, "assurance of their own shared destiny with him as an indwelling spirit of hope."[51] The new identity in Christ was sealed with God's gift of the indwelling Spirit: "The Holy Spirit is filling you (as he is)" (Rosemary) (Eph 1:13, 14). This assurance of identity and destiny had not been diminished by the advent of dementia.

Being "Saved"

In spite of evangelicalism's emphasis on grace, as discussed earlier, some have suggested an additional hermeneutic of dependence on cognitive response to Christ, accompanied by a declaration of propositional truths.[52] Interpretations of scripture, shaped by "Enlightenment understandings of knowledge" may appear to demand cognitive work: for example, ongoing understanding of the salvific significance of the cross; ability to recall and recognize personal sin, repent and receive God's forgiveness (see Rom 10:9, 10).[53] Yet, such "knowing," situated in cognitive activity, is becoming increasingly difficult for the Christian with dementia, even before the effects of more advanced dementias. If it is subtly assumed as an essential element of being "in Christ" then the person living with early-moderate stage dementia may be appropriately concerned about the future security of their faith in Christ. However, as Swinton reminds his readers, whilst doctrine is important for the community of faith, it is not this factual knowledge which saves us.[54] As cognitive abilities begin to diminish ("I thought . . . I was quite clever!," Alice) the participants'

---

51. Anderson, *Spiritual Caregiving*, 152.

52. Greggs, "Beyond the Binary," 154–55. See, for example, Barrier, "Five Things You Have to Believe."

53. Greggs, "Beyond the Binary," 164; Williams, "Knowing God in Dementia," 6.

54. Swinton, *Becoming Friends of Time*, 106.

words demonstrate that their experience of faith is increasingly dependent on God, "But now I realise everything that happens is of God."

In the gospel narratives we see Jesus recognizing embodied, or "tacit," faith expressed through individuals' enacted dependence on him (Mark 5:25–34).[55] For example, Jesus' response to the woman healed of her bleeding, "your faith has made you well," includes the New Testament Greek word *sozo* (made well). This word, sometimes used to mean "saved," encompasses Christ's gift of wholeness which embraces the person in every aspect of their self. Again, Christ's promise of paradise to the repentant, dying thief (Luke 23:40–43) suggests that a dependent trust and turning to Jesus were all that was required for his soteriological security. For the first disciples, as Swinton suggests, "propositional knowledge was something that emerged from the experience of trusting in Jesus rather than the other way around."[56] For those whose ability to think clearly is fading, this understanding brings reassurance. One participant (Rosemary) speaking of her intrinsic certainty of God's enduring presence with, and in, her said:

> ROSEMARY: He will be with me . . . right to the end! Even if my . . . because my feelings are still as strong, if not stronger, as my mind becomes less intellectualized and able to . . . I shall be more filled with the feeling of the love of God. . . . It's here [indicates inner self]. . . . I can speak from experience not from some theory.

Safe in Christ

St. Paul's writing makes it clear that it is through the incarnation of Christ and his redemptive work that it has been made possible for Christians to understand themselves as being "in Christ" (Rom 6:11). Security of relationship with God is dependent on this; there can be no separation from God "in Christ" (Rom 8:38–39). Swinton writes:

> I am who I am in Christ alone . . . "We were therefore buried with him through baptism into death in order that, just as Christ

---

55. See the discussion of tacit knowledge in Kontos and Naglie, "Tacit Knowledge of Caring and Embodied Selfhood," 688–704.

56. Swinton, *Becoming Friends of Time*, 104.

was raised from the dead through the glory of the Father, we too may live a new life" (Rom 6:4).[57]

In his focus on those with cognitive incapacity, Swinton argues that see-ing ourselves "in Christ" changes the hermeneutic that we use to inter-pret our experience:

> To see ourselves as we truly are: *creatures who know ourselves only in relation to Jesus.* There was therefore *never* a time when who we were was determined by the particular neurological configuration of our brains. We may have thought there was, but we were quite wrong. Who we are is who we are in Christ, and, crucially, *that is hidden.*[58]

The Christian's story is not a solitary one.

Belonging in the Community of Faith

Being Part of God's Story

The participants in this research, living with early to moderate stages of dementia, were intensely aware of their individual relationship with Christ, yet, as they talked about God's will for their lives, there was awareness of being caught up in the purposeful narrative of God's people stretching from Creation to the Eschaton. Their phenomenological ac-counts revealed their understanding that they were part of God's fam-ily (see Rom 8:14–17), for example: they sought "fellowship" with other believers, and listened to God's Word together in their "home groups."

The biblical narrative has given the Christian believer a community story which is inherently caught up in the time-transcendent purposes of God himself.[59] Hauerwas speaks of this community of believers as "formed by the story witnessed to by scripture."[60] Allusions to Bible text are threaded through participants' contributions to this research. It is in this—the transcending, ongoing story narrated through Scripture—which the participants situated themselves, shaping their autobiographi-cal accounts and discovering meaning for their present experiences in its light. Hauerwas reminds us that "the story and its people" need a

57. Swinton, *Becoming Friends of Time*, 188–89. See Col 3:1–4.

58. Swinton, *Becoming Friends of Time*, 189.

59. Keck, *Forgetting Whose We Are*, 45.

60. Hauerwas, *Community of Character*, 15.

community for its remembering, telling and hearing."[61] Without community, the story cannot be remembered, recalled, lived out in the present or bring hope for the future.[62] This activity of remembering is becoming especially significant for my participants.

Yet, their lived experience brings questions to the church's understanding about such an account of collective memory. The experience of one participant (Rosemary) was already making this difficult. Speaking of her frustrating attempts of trying to be part of a local church, she concluded: "I can't at the moment join a congregation." How might the church of today be one which enables those who live with dementia to participate in such remembering?[63]

A Member of the Body of Christ

Following the resurrection of Christ, his ascension and Pentecost, understanding of the Church as the body of Christ is developed in the New Testament, especially in the writings of St. Paul: "So we, who are many, are one body in Christ, and individually we are members one of another" (Rom 12:5; see also 1 Cor 11:23–26). The Scriptures are clear, whoever we are as individuals, as followers of Jesus, all are "in the one Spirit we were all baptized into one body" (1 Cor 12:13). In this way, knowing who we are is found not only in our individual relationship with God in Christ; it is found in the community of faith. The Spirit's distribution of diverse gifts to the "members" of Christ's body does not respect status or capacity:

> Now there are varieties of gifts, but the same Spirit; and there are varieties of services, but the same Lord; and there are varieties of activities, but it is the same God who activates all of them in everyone. To each is given the manifestation of the Spirit for the common good. (1 Cor 12:4–7)

St. Paul further emphasizes in his letter to the Corinthian Christians that all parts of the body are of equal value; without one part, the whole is damaged and incomplete (1 Cor 12:21–26). Each person is only part of the whole because of the grace of God. Christ himself invites us to serve those we regard as "least" as though we were serving Christ himself (Matt 25:37–40). I was conscious of my participants' desire to serve Jesus

61. Hauerwas, *Peaceable Kingdom*, 98.

62. Hauerwas, *Community of Character*, 15.

63. Crowther's work begins to respond to this in Crowther, *Sustaining Persons*.

and others as they lived with dementia ("like the boy with the loaves and fishes [John 6:8–9], just giving him the little that I have," Alice).

Resonating with this understanding of the community of faith as the body of Christ, Grenz emphasizes that "the image of God . . . is found in the relationality of persons in community."[64] This is not a human social reflection of a relational Trinity, as referred to earlier, rather it is an incorporation by the Spirit "into the dynamic of divine life."[65] Reminding us that St. Paul describes the children of God as "joint heirs with Christ" (Rom 8:17), Grenz finds the *imago Dei* in those who "participate together in the Jesus-narrative."[66] Understood in this way, the identity and faith of the person living with dementia is assured within the body of Christ and, as such, is included in the expression of the image of God.

Yet, the lived experience of dementia begins to interrogate Scripture and those of us who are part of today's church. It is not merely a question of inclusion. There is a difference between including and belonging. Well-meaning expressions of compassion may make others simply the object of our charity.[67] Hudson draws out how such a view of the beneficent self disempowers those who appear to be weaker, reminding us:

> In this body the weaker members are accorded due respect and dignity, not because of strong members' benevolence or sympathy, but only because the body is made whole by Jesus Christ the head.[68]

If those living with this disease are equally recipients of God's grace and calling, how are we treating them with "special honor" (1 Cor 12:23 NIVUK)? What does it mean in embodied practice that these Christians *belong* to the body of Christ?

The work of Gaventa and Eastman explores biblical perspectives which bring theological insight for this issue.[69] Gaventa points out that included in the Pauline notion of belief (*pistis*) is the sense of God's faithfulness and his initiating prior action.[70] It is God's love which "has been

---

64. Grenz, "Social God and the Relational Self," 89.

65. Grenz, "Social God and the Relational Self," 91.

66. Grenz, "Social God and the Relational Self," 92

67. Swinton, *Dementia*, 278.

68. Hudson, "God's Faithfulness and Dementia," 60.

69. See my discussion of this in Williams, "Knowing God in Dementia," 12–14.

70. Gaventa, "Which Human?" 57.

poured into our hearts through the Holy Spirit" (Rom 5:5).[71] In contrast to a vulnerable, individualized, "me-and-Jesus"[72] understanding of personal faith, Gaventa elucidates that differentiated experience happens within the reality of being in the body of Christ.[73] Eastman additionally brings enlightenment through her exploration of the use of the pronouns "we" and "you" (second person plural) in St. Paul's writing to the Romans.[74] Her careful exposition reveals the hope that corporate knowing of God brings for the individual person with diminishing cognitive capacity, for example, nothing "will be able to separate *us* from the love of God that is in Christ Jesus our Lord" (Rom 8:39).

The phenomenological accounts of the participants revealed diverse experiences of being part of the Body in their communities of faith. One participant (Bill), at the beginning of his experience of dementia, spoke warmly of his church home group: "The people . . . that group is very supportive anyway because it's sort of there for you." Jess, who is further on in her journey with this illness, and is supported by her husband, said wryly: "It's easy to go to church. . . . I don't remember what I hear or what we did . . . or things like that." Rosemary, referred to earlier, was living independently, and was beginning to find involvement in a local church difficult. I will reflect further on the difficulties of being part of church in the following chapter. Here—even in its earlier stages—dementia was bringing challenge to the local church.

In the light of developing dementia, theological understanding asks questions of how this body-life can be expressed in practice. Despite the acknowledged theoretical unity in Christ, living with dementia might seem to undermine this in practice.

Hope-ful Orientation

However, for the participants in this study—whatever their particular experience of a local church community—their sense of who they were was being shaped by their hope in Christ. In him, they are part of the church eternal—the communion of saints which transcends time and space. This

---

71. Gaventa, "Which Human?" 58.

72. Grenz, "Social God and the Relational Self," 84.

73. Gaventa, "Which Human?" 60.

74. Eastman, "Double Participation," 93–110.

understanding of being part of the eschatological communion was a pre-eminent aspect of the participants' experience and orientation.[75]

An Eschatological Orientation

In Scripture, God's purposeful narrative leads humans from the Garden of Eden to the Garden of Gethsemane, to resurrection and eschatological hope of a new creation.[76] Following the resurrection of Christ, God's Spirit comes, giving the disciples assurance and indwelling hope of their shared destiny with Jesus.[77] Such confidence was evident in the phenomenological accounts of the participants ("I am going to heaven," Ron).

Grenz highlights this eschatological orientation which is discovered through the scriptural narrative and in the notion of being in Christ as the image of God: "the biblical narrative of the *imago dei* does not end with Christology." God's people found in local congregations are part of the church eternal and are destined for new creation.[78] This "divinely given destiny" is the hope which permeates the experience of those who participate in Christ, and the experience of the participants: "He has prepared a place for us" (Alice); "That will just be glory!" (Rosemary).[79]

The participants' sense of being members of the church eternal discloses the great importance of this doctrine for the building and sustaining of hope for the person living with dementia. The local expression of church is able to contribute to this when it reminds believers of their hope in Christ as members of the eschatological communion of saints. A local creaturely community of faith may sometimes disappoint in its practical expressions of care and understanding of those who live with dementia, but the assurance of being part of the church eternal is bringing transforming hope.[80]

This will be considered further in the final section of these theological reflections (chapter 9). It is the participants' sure hope (Heb 11:1) in Christ which was sustaining them as they began to experience the

75. Grenz, "Social God and the Relational Self," 82–83. See also chapter 6.

76. Grenz, "Social God and the Relational Self," 83.

77. Anderson, *Spiritual Caregiving*, 152.

78. Grenz, "Social God and the Relational Self," 82.

79. Grenz, "Social God and the Relational Self," 83.

80. "And we boast in our hope of sharing the glory of God . . . and hope does not disappoint us, because God's love has been poured into our hearts through the Holy Spirit that has been given to us" (Rom 5:1–5).

disorientation of dementia, and was also a dimension of their faith experience which was enabling a reorientation.[81]

Conclusion

In this first reflection I have considered the important question of knowing who you are in the advent of developing dementia. My participants' orientation is found in knowing that they are creatures of a sovereign God; their identity is in Christ, the image of God, their *telos* is in the shared narrative of God's story, within the community of faith. The participants' certainty of being in relationship with God and their identity as Christians lays the foundations which resource them for the disorientation of dementia. In the following chapter, I focus more closely on difficult aspects of the their lived experience of faith which result from the impact of their illness.

81. See also chapter 9, 234–238.

8

Disorientation

Walking through Shadow

"Like the sun that's gone behind the clouds" (Rosemary)

Introduction

WHILST THE PARTICIPANTS' ORIENTATION of faith is confidently expressed, the coming of dementia inevitably brings disorientation. As I have sought understanding of their experience through the analysis and theological reflection arising from our conversations, the hidden-ness of some aspects of this became evident.

I was aware that in the interviews my participants gave positive accounts of their faith experience in dementia, despite the tragedy of their illness and experience of difficulties. Their honesty and courage were apparent in their words, as was their trust in God. It was as though the struggle of living with dementia was assumed and accepted, whilst their faith experience provided their pre-eminent sense of being.

From my own context of evangelical faith, I was conscious of a danger of colluding with the participants' positivity in their desire to affirm the faithfulness of God. I became aware of the danger of an apparently triumphalist perspective, which was not acknowledging the hidden pain of living with the darkness of dementia. Yet, their nuanced allusions to struggle, frustration, and alienation prompted further questioning of this experience of faith as they walked through the shadows of dementia:

What is it like as a committed Christian to experience these moments of anguish in the context of relationship with God, even in the earlier stages of dementia? Why might it be that these Christians seemed unconcerned to speak of their own pain? Why did they, in some senses, seem even to be "rejoicing" in their suffering?

Here, seeking the dialogical interplay of Gadamer's ever-changing horizons with Heidegger's concept of *poiesis*, different perspectives are unveiled.[1] In the light of these, I reflect theologically on the experience of the suffering brought by dementia revealed in subtle ways in the phenomenological accounts. In this hermeneutical journey of the book, I look for theological understanding and pastoral response to the nature of the participants' faith experience and moments of darkness. In spite of their positivity, these were disclosed in their words and through our embodied encounters.[2]

Seeking resolution to this conundrum of the experiences of joyful faith in the midst of darkness, I bring these into conversation with Scripture, theological and pastoral literature, looking especially to the writings of Brueggemann, Hauerwas and Weil. Swinton has spoken of Practical Theology's art of perception, in which he highlights the difference between "the act of *looking*" and "the act of accurate *perceiving*."[3] Such perceiving, in which we seek to look from God's perspective and through the lens of the cross, has the potential to transform our understanding in ways which might enable the spiritual flourishing of those most directly affected by the disorientation which dementia brings.

In this reflection, I begin by considering contextual questions which are shaping response to the issue of their particular kind of suffering, considering perspectives from theological discussion, and the normative insights which the Scriptures bring to our understanding. In the light of these, the reflection then focuses on the darkness of the experiences of my participants who are living with dementia as disciples of Christ.

---

1. Gadamer, *Truth and Method*, 301–6; Heidegger, *Introduction to Metaphysics*; Pippo, "Concept of Poiesis," 3, 22. For my discussion of this approach, see chapter 4.

2. Manen, *Researching Lived Experience*, 130–31.

3. Swinton, "Reforming, Revisionist, Refounding," 5.

Responding to Adversity

"He is my strength, my rock . . . my salvation"[4]
(Rosemary)

A Pastoral Theology of Suffering

Human adversity of any kind provokes two kinds of questions which have been debated through the centuries of Christendom: the theodical question of evil; and the distinct theological pastoral question of how to understand and respond to suffering within the context of Christian faith. Whilst the first might suggest doubt and denial of a sovereign God (see Job 1:9–11), the second arises out of belief and expresses trust, in spite of suffering.

A biblical model of response to suffering is found in the story of Job. In the midst of his anguish and loss, and in spite of his friends' unhelpful words and unanswerable questions, he declares, "I know that my Redeemer lives" (Job 19:25). In the end, he didn't seek answers from God, but simply asserted his trust in God (Job 42:2). In the light of the lived experience of the participants in this research, it is my intention to focus primarily on this second question, seeking understanding of their experience of faith which dementia brings within the context of trust in God in a fallen world.

The Wrong Question

The confusion between the two questions has potential to bring deep frustration and further pain to people of faith who are beginning to live with dementia. For example, one participant in the research (Alice) recounted how fellow Christians insisted that she must be "blaming" God for the advent of her dementia:

> ALICE: So they said, "So are you blaming God for all this?" I said "No I'm not!" [They said,] "Aren't you angry with God?" I said, "No, I'm not!" So they didn't believe me! [Laughs.] . . . And they said, "Well, you've obviously forgotten because of your dementia. You can't remember that you're cross with God." I said, "I've never been cross with God!" [Frustrated laughter.] . . . It doesn't help. . . . [Quietly:] It doesn't help.

4. Rosemary was referring here to verses from the Psalms (e.g., Ps 18:2).

Another participant (Jill) also used the word "blame," in this instance out of concern that others might think that her own failures had in some way brought this suffering on herself. In both cases, the questions being asked of their illness resonate with the dialogue between Job and his friends: either, Job might reasonably deny God who had allowed such undeserved suffering; or it was Job's evil actions which had brought punishment from God. In both cases, it was the questions of others which had potential to bring additional suffering through the expression of their own uncertainties. Hauerwas notes that whilst such questions may be of speculative interest, "rather we are torn apart by what is happening to real people, to those we know and love."[5] Practically, my book concerns how God's people respond to the experience of dementia, and the nature of and reasons for such response.

It is interesting that the word "blame" used by participants assumed fault: in one case, disbelief ("Are you blaming God for all this?" Alice); in the other, sin ("as if it's my fault," Jill). This inclination to focus on sin in the context of suffering is evident in the Gospel accounts of Jesus' miraculous healings. For example, in the case of the man born blind, the disciples wanted to know whose sin had caused his condition (John 9:2). Taking Job as an example, Reinders has pointed to the difficulty of such assumptions of a divinely controlled "moral geometry": often those who are apparently deserving of punishment go free, whilst those who are innocent are deeply affected by adversity.[6] The falseness of this geometry is clearly shown to be faulty in Job's story where the righteous man suffers great loss. Yet, as Reinders notes, at the end of Job's conversation with God, he recognizes his own unworthiness, apart from any specific wrongdoing. In spite of his suffering, he ceases to question God about his personal condition and affirms his trust in God (Job 42:1–6).[7] The implied question of one of the participants, "Why not me?" (Jill), seems to be a more appropriate one from the perspective of faith. Again, this question points to the primacy of the pastoral issue of the nature of response to the experience of suffering.

5. Hauerwas, *Naming the Silences*, 1–2.

6. Reinders, *Disability, Providence, and Ethics*, 1–15.

7. Reinders, *Disability, Providence, and Ethics*, 121.

The Relationship between Evil and Suffering

Whilst theological discussion has linked evil and suffering, for the purposes of this reflection, I will focus mainly on the participants' experience of suffering in dementia. However, Christian tradition and scholars have wrestled with this underlying question of evil throughout the centuries. For example, Swinton frames his broader discussion of pastoral response to suffering within the context of the questions about evil.[8] He notes that Augustine, in his investigation into the nature of evil, seems to conclude that evil has no being in a creation which God himself declared "good":

> For the Omnipotent God, whom even the heathen acknowledge as the Supreme Power over all, would not allow any evil in his works, unless in his omnipotence and goodness, as the Supreme Good, he is able to bring forth good out of evil.[9]

Swinton derives from this that it is the turning away from God which is evil.[10] Hauerwas, echoing Augustine, asserts that evil does not exist as a distinct entity.[11] Barth declared the non-existence of Satan, stating that his existence is only "as the ordained object of denial."[12] Aside here from biblical debate around the personification of evil as Satan (Job 1:6–12; Luke 4:1–13), Barth's theological conclusion, also echoing Augustine, that evil arises from denial of God, has potential for illumination of the positive experience of faith through a time of suffering. In the participants' accounts of living with dementia, their deliberate commitment to God was the context for the suffering they were facing.

Whilst the nature of evil, apart from human transgression, is difficult to define, it raises the pastoral question of sin and the possibility of forgiveness for those living with dementia. Keck, with controversial choice of words, raises the difficulty of repentance for the "de-subjected patient."[13] Yet, as I have suggested elsewhere, there are ways, apart from the cognitive, in which those living with dementia might be supported

---

8. Swinton, *Raging with Compassion.*

9. Swinton, *Raging with Compassion,* 22; Augustine, *Enchiridion* 3.11.

10. Swinton, *Raging with Compassion,* 22; Augustine, *City of God* 11.9.

11. Hauerwas, "Seeing Darkness," 38.

12. Hauerwas, "Seeing Darkness," 36. Hauerwas is drawing here on Jenson's discussion of Barth. See Jenson, "Nihilism," 4; Barth, *Church Dogmatics,* 3/3:519–31.

13. Keck, *Forgetting Whose We Are,* 166. I discussed the problem of de-personification raised by Keck's work above, see chapter 3.

in acknowledging sin, troublesome guilt and receiving Christ's forgiveness.[14] However, in the experience of the participants in this study, whilst sadness and struggle are discernible, these are the result of their illness, not their sin. Sin is not mentioned by them apart from implication in allusion to their assurance of forgiveness ("I feel I have been forgiven. . . . I don't think we have to carry a burden," Jess). In their experience, as the data testifies, within the suffering of dementia, they confidently affirmed their growing sense of trust in God ("Faith is growing more," David).

Cultural Context

It is important to acknowledge the cultural context within which the participants encounter the sadness and suffering brought by dementia. Swinton has noted that before the Enlightenment reservations about the apparent inconsistency of belief in a good God alongside the experience of suffering were not considered.[15] It was with the coming of post-Enlightenment Western culture, that the questions of theodicy became apparent.

As Bosch has explored, modern culture was one in which "reason supplanted faith as point of departure"; "human planning took the place of trust in God."[16] The post-Enlightenment culture has, in consequence, de-throned God, becoming, "thoroughly anthropocentric." The difficulties which Enlightenment brought for Christian faith of the evangelical tradition have been evident in its emphasis on individualism seen in pietism and the attempts to rationalise Christian faith. Bosch speaks of the "new theological discipline . . . Christian apologetics," which emerged in the era of post-Enlightenment.[17] Arising from this post-Enlightenment framework, Hauerwas points to the logical question to ask in response to the suffering of illness: "Why does a good god allow bad things to happen to good people?"[18] If we accept the metanarrative of Enlightenment reason and autonomous human beings, the questions of "theodicy" are, in fact, wrongly addressed to God. Why, after all, does medicine not cure all illness and its associated suffering?[19] Theodicy, if it involves doubt of

14. Williams, "Knowing God in Dementia," 8–9.

15. Swinton, *Raging with Compassion*, 34.

16. Bosch, *Transforming Mission*, 269–71.

17. Bosch, *Transforming Mission*, 268.

18. Hauerwas, "Seeing Darkness," 37.

19. Bosch, *Transforming Mission*, 266.

God, suggests denial of God. Consequently human beings are left alone to face the tragedy of human suffering. Such questions, if they are allowed to stand unchallenged, bring deep discomfort to those living with dementia.

Yet, this is not the position of God's people who, as discussed earlier, inhabit the biblical narrative in which God is sovereign. In Brueggemann's reflection on suffering and hope in the experience of the Israelites, he asserts that amnesia leads to despair.[20] Yet, remembrance of God brings hope. So it might be concluded from this that whilst denial of God in the lived experience of dementia brings anguish, trust in him—as demonstrated in the lives of my participants—transforms their experience of suffering, bringing hope. As pastoral theologians are discovering, the experience of suffering for the Christian believer does not of itself result in "a crisis of faith."[21] Hauerwas rebuts the unbelieving tendency to ask theodical questions, and re-directs us to the biblical account of suffering:

> The realism of the Psalms and the book of Job depends on the presumption that God is God and we are not. When Christians think theodical justifications are needed to justify the ways of God at the bar of a justice determined by us, you can be sure that the god Christians now worship is not the God of Israel and Jesus Christ.[22]

This biblical metanarrative is the one within which the participants locate their own experience. It is within this cultural context that response to the question of suffering, in relation to their faith, must be sought.

The New Testament Norm

Hauerwas has pointed out that for New Testament Christians, suffering did not require explanation:

> For the early Christians, suffering and evil, which for present purposes I do not need to distinguish, did not have to be "explained." Rather, what was required was the means to go on even if the evil could not be "explained."[23]

20. Brueggemann, "Suffering Produces Hope," 97.
21. Swinton, *Raging with Compassion*, 111.
22. Hauerwas, "Seeing Darkness," 36–37.
23. Hauerwas, *Naming the Silences*, 49.

St. Peter's expectation of suffering is conveyed in his first letter: "In this you rejoice, even if now for a little while you have had to suffer various trials" (1 Pet 1:6); St. Paul also assumes the presence of suffering: "We also glory in our sufferings" (Rom 5:3 NIVUK).

Of course, the fundamental thread through the Gospels and the epistles is the Christ who chose the life of the suffering servant, who "made himself nothing," and bore our *suffering* on the cross (Phil 2:6–8 NIVUK; Isa 53:4). His call to take up your cross and follow him (Matt 16:24), suggests that believers should not be overwhelmed by the advent of suffering. Hauerwas writes: "Any truthful account of the Christian life cannot exclude suffering as integral to that life."[24]

As those called to follow Jesus, the participants' focus was on him and their hope found in the resurrection. It is this christological orientation which provided the perspective for understanding their suffering. In spite of the losses being brought by dementia, their faith orientation resonated with Job's affirmation of trust in God. No matter what their physical and material circumstances, this was their faith. Into this comes the particular disorientation of dementia. In the lives of Christians who live with dementia, this is where theory meets lived experience in the "now" of temporal, corporeal existence.

The Biblical Agenda

From the perspective in which scripture sets the agenda and boundaries, a faith response to the questions dementia raises keeps in view the whole sweep of the biblical narrative.[25] Theologically, God's good creation was spoilt in the Garden of Eden when humankind chose their own will rather than God's, resulting in human suffering throughout time ("this broken world," Alice*)*. Yet, always, within this human temporal history, there has been the possibility of response to God's love and relationship with him in Christ. From the beginning, God's plan of redemption was in motion (for example, Gen 3:15). St. Paul reminds his readers: "Just as sin reigned in death, so also grace might reign through righteousness to bring eternal life through Jesus Christ our Lord" (Rom 5:21 NIVUK). Throughout Scripture, the story of God's people is focused towards its christological and eschatological orientation.

24. Hauerwas, *Naming the Silences*, 85.
25. Hauerwas, *Peaceable Kingdom*, 98.

The sufferings of God's people, recorded in the letter to Hebrews, illumine the experience of suffering as well as the significance of memory. God's people were strangers living in a foreign land, enslaved, abandoned and despised, exiled from their homeland and outcasts (Heb 11–12:3). Yet, the litany of human suffering culminates in the suffering of Christ and the ultimate hope that this brings (Heb 12:2). Biblically, suffering and hope are not mutually exclusive; in fact, biblically, it seems that they are mutually conducive.[26] Throughout the biblical narrative (as illustrated by the writer of Hebrews) the suffering of God's people leads to hope in Christ by way of the Cross and resurrection (Heb 12:1–3).[27]

Experiencing Shadow

Affliction

Knowing the theological and biblical theory of response to suffering is different from the experience of living in shadow or knowing the sadness of dementia as it affects one's own life.

In her exploration of suffering, Weil thoughtfully and movingly refines the anonymous questions of suffering with her use of the word "affliction" to suggest specific, embodied particularity.[28] It is a word which refers to the experience of enduring pain, not a passing physical pain, but one which engulfs the whole person.[29] It is, she suggests, "an uprooting of life" which affects every part of life, "social, psychological and physical." Barclay, drawing on Weil, takes this word "affliction" and uses it to explore the experience of living with Alzheimer's.[30]

The affliction of dementia becomes "an inescapable part of existence."[31] At times, its darkness might even make the believer *feel* God is absent.[32] One participant (Rosemary) questioned her experience in this way: "Is it like the sun that's gone behind the clouds?" However, Weil places the transforming love of God alongside the experience of

26. See Brueggemann, "Suffering Produces Hope," 95–99.

27. For further discussion of this, see chapter 9.

28. Weil, *Waiting on God*, 63–78.

29. Weil, *Waiting on God*, 63–64.

30. Barclay, "Psalm 88," 96–98.

31. Barclay, "Psalm 88," 96.

32. Barclay, "Psalm 88," 96; Weil, *Waiting on God*, 66; Davis, *My Journey into Alzheimer's Disease*, 53–54.

affliction, available for all who turn their gaze toward him: "It rests with them to keep or not to keep their eyes turned towards God through all the jolting."[33] Whilst the discovering of this illness in their lives was unavoidably affecting every part of the participants' existence ("completely engulfed" [Ps 88:17 NIVUK]), yet they expressed unfaltering trust in God's presence with them in their experience of dementia.

The moment of diagnosis brought the shock of sudden shift of self-perception, and of grief, as revealed in David's words: "I was quite staggered by this . . . I was really quite shocked." Bryden also recalls the sense of shock of diagnosis and the immediate change that dementia signified for the whole of her life: "The day before my diagnosis I was a busy and successful single mother. . . . The day after I was a label—Person with Dementia."[34] Jess's words echo this: "When I was *labelled* 'memory loss.'" Weil speaks of the fear of the changes which affliction brings, not only in one's self-perceptions, but in those of others.[35]

Like St. Paul who lived with the affliction of his "thorn . . . in the flesh" (2 Cor 12:7–10), the participants in the research, mentioned the realities of their suffering in passing ("It's a very minor thing," Rosemary); yet these were present reality in their lived experience. In the following I reflect on glimpses of the struggle and darkness they experienced within themselves, and the frustrations of disempowering stigma directed at them from others. In each circumstance, these were always expressed in their felt context of "Even though . . . you are with me" (Ps 23:4). There was an unfailing recognition of Christ's presence with them in the confusion of their developing dementia.

The Naming of Grief

There is a strange reticence in naming the nature of this suffering. Goldsmith, for example, refers to the "process of denial and collusion" through which friends and loved-ones might seek to protect, but which, in fact, might remove the possibility of preparation for the further development of the disease.[36] In his exploration of the psalms of disorientation, Brueggemann points to a deeper reason for this reticence. He suggests

33. Weil, *Waiting on God*, 69.
34. Bryden, *Dancing with Dementia*, 156.
35. Weil, *Waiting on God*, 64.
36. Goldsmith, "Through a Glass Darkly," 129.

that for some Christians there is "a mismatch between our life experience of disorientation and our faith speech of orientation."[37] He notes, "It is a curious fact that the church has ... continued to sing songs of orientation in a world increasingly experienced as disoriented." Whilst the "Yet I will rejoice in the LORD"[38] of Habakkuk is an expression of faithfulness to God in spite of tragic and terrifying events, the observer might conclude that such declarations arise from "wishful optimism," perhaps, even a refusal to contemplate the suffering which some endure.[39] The acknowledgement of the disease and its disorientating influences is attested to in this research by evident grieving, frustration or sadness of participants, and that of their loved ones. However, they did not choose to dwell on the difficulties of dementia. Perhaps, our faith culture resists the embrace of negativity, as though, as Brueggemann suggests, to do so "was somehow an act of unfaith."[40]

Yet, as Brueggemann points out, it is strange that a Bible-reading focused faith community should often not pay more attention to the psalms of lament. The psalmist, who is overwhelmed with his troubles ("my soul is full of troubles" [Ps 88:3]) declares his grief, and the exiles sit down together and weep far from home (Ps 137:1). Jesus himself legitimates the activity of lament as he quotes from Psalm 22 in the extremity of his agony on the Cross: "My God, my God why have you forsaken me?" (Matt 27:46; Ps 22:1). Such lament is not to deny God, or his power and control. Rather, as Brueggemann contends, it is "an act of bold faith."[41] The one in anguish continues to address God in searching for solution. The laments of the Psalms are conversations which take place within the arena of faith, within a community which trusts in God.

Goldsmith, reflecting on dementia as a time of disempowerment, asks whether it is not acceptable at times to rage in response to the losses dementia is bringing, even though such raging may be difficult for others. Lament in this context is a necessary part of the wrestling with God which leads to perceiving of the light, reorientation and celebration of his sovereignty ("they shall ... proclaim his righteousness to a people yet

---

37. Brueggemann, *Spirituality of the Psalms*, 25.

38. "Though the fig-tree does not blossom ... the produce of the olive fails ... the fields yield no food ... yet I will rejoice in the LORD" (Hab 3:17–18).

39. Brueggemann, *Spirituality of the Psalms*, 26; Barclay, "Psalm 88," 89.

40. Brueggemann, *Spirituality of the Psalms*, 26.

41. Brueggemann, *Spirituality of the Psalms*, 27.

unborn, that he has done it" [Ps 22:31 ESV; see also Ps 22:27–31]). In a sense, these research conversations were expressions of lament.

Disclosing Shadows

In this section, I focus more precisely on the particular difficulties that my participants were experiencing. I will look at three aspects of this which were revealed in the phenomenological accounts: becoming strangers; unseen struggles; challenges to faith practices.

Becoming Strangers

Bryden has suggested that there are "two burdens from our disease . . . the struggle with the illness itself" and the "disease of society" which, perhaps unconsciously, stigmatizes and disempowers.[42] Barclay, in her reflection on Psalm 88, powerfully evokes the isolation and exclusion of those living with dementia: "You have taken from me friend and neighbor—darkness is my closest friend" (Ps 88:18 NIVUK).[43] These shadows of exclusion, and struggle with darkness, are present in the lives of those who are living in the early to moderate stages of dementia. Even in the earlier stages, anguish results from the perceived reactions of others to their illness which begin to distance them from their wider communities. Unseen by others, such struggles bring moments of darkness.

The sense of stigma affecting those who feel labelled "dementia" is recognized, as discussed in chapter 3, by Kitwood as "malignant social psychology," and by Sabat as "malignant social positioning." Reinders, in his exploration of disability, highlights this disabling problem: "Many would say that they feel neither wronged nor harmed by their disability, but by how other people treat them."[44] Weil challenges the community of faith with this statement: "Except for those whose whole soul is inhabited by Christ, everybody despises the afflicted to some extent, although practically no one is conscious of it."[45]

Illustrated in the participants' words, in spite of their positive outlook, there was awareness of being in some senses "despised," and of becoming

---

42. Bryden, *Dancing with Dementia*, 142.

43. Barclay, "Psalm 88," 93.

44. Reinders, *Disability, Providence, and Ethics*, 7.

45. Weil, *Waiting on God*, 40.

"strangers" to others.[46] For example, Jill spoke of her concern for others that her dementia might be an embarrassment to them; Jess said of her role in church: "my memory loss has interfered with my being somebody or something." For Jess, with her difficult childhood memories of her grandmother's treatment in an "asylum," any sense of stigma may also in part have resulted from the historical negative views of mental health disorders.[47] Goffman, one of the earliest researchers to consider the effects of stigma, recognized this hidden perspective, that the image of self is confronted by the image of themselves which others reflect back to them.[48]

Perhaps, even more significant for the Christian is the insidious *spiritual malpositioning* discerned by Barclay, and described in this way by Swinton.[49] This might suggest doubt of a person's faith which therefore threatens separation from God. So, one participant (Alice) spoke indignantly of fellow Christians who questioned her relationship with God because of her increasingly apparent illness ("They nullify my Christian walk!"). Swinton has noted: "Those who come proclaiming that the standard ways of relating to God might not apply to them will inevitably create a dissonance that is at best disorienting and at worst offensive."[50] How can the experiences of such "stigma" be understood theologically? The community of the biblical story of exile, both in the Old and New Testaments, offer illumination for a faith understanding of this experience.

This "becoming-a-stranger" resonates with the believer's participation in the continuing biblical story of faith. Brueggemann draws on the experience of the loss and chaos in Jerusalem which preceded the people's journey into exile.[51] Goldsmith, also looks for understanding of the experience of living with dementia in this image of the exiled Israelites.[52] Their homeland in ruins, displaced as exiles, how could they sing the Lord's song in a foreign land?[53] The imagery persists into the New Testament: the writer to Hebrews reminds the readers of the pattern of living as strangers. Swinton extends the notion, drawing out St. Peter's analogy

46. Barclay, "Psalm 88," 93; Swinton, *Dementia*, 258–59.

47. Kitwood, *Dementia Reconsidered*, 42–45.

48. Goffman, *Stigma*,154.

49. Barclay, "Psalm 88," 90. In her use of the phrase "malignant spiritual positioning," Barclay is citing from a personal conversation with John Swinton.

50. Swinton, *Dementia*, 269.

51. Brueggemann, "Suffering Produces Hope."

52. Goldsmith, "Dementia," 125–35.

53. Goldsmith, "Dementia," 127–28.

with the church: the community of faith are "aliens and strangers" (1 Pet 2:11 NASB).[54] From a biblical perspective, all believers, whatever their capacities, live as "strangers" in this world.

Being a stranger ultimately resonates with participation in Christ's own suffering. As referred to in the analysis of the lived experience, I noticed Jess's awareness of the sacrificial *living* of Christ ("the sacrifice of being a human"). Rejected by the Jewish leaders, Jesus became the supreme outcast, accursed by his death on the cross.[55] The prophet Isaiah's surprising picture of the coming Christ shows him as "despised and rejected by others; a man of suffering, and acquainted with infirmity" (Isa 53:3). Jesus identified himself as the outcast, and as being in allegiance with those who suffer: "For I was hungry and you gave me food, I was thirsty and you gave me something to drink, I was a stranger and you welcomed me" (Matt 25:35).[56] This is the Christ who disciples are called to follow and serve.

Unseen Struggle

In his biography, Davis wrote of his early experience of darkness in his living with dementia:

> Now I discovered the cruelest blow of all. This personal and tender relationship that I had with the Lord was no longer there. . . .
> There were no longer any feelings of peace and joy. . . . I could only cry out bitterly to the Lord, "Why, God, why?" . . . Why have you made my sunlight turn into moonlight?"[57]

Later, as he worked through this new situation, he finds resolution as he comes to acceptance and peace.[58]

In the experience of the participants in this research, their accounts also disclosed moments of private darkness and struggle. They recognized their encroaching memory loss. For example Ron said: "I had a memory then, I haven't one now. . . . It's not funny." Throughout our conversation, his hesitant (and sometimes misplaced words) suggested the

---

54. Swinton, *Dementia*, 274–76.

55. "Christ redeemed us from the curse of the Law by becoming a curse for us" (Gal 3:13).

56. Swinton, *Dementia*, 276.

57. Davis, *My Journey into Alzheimer's Disease*, 47.

58. Davis, *My Journey into Alzheimer's Disease*, 55–56.

frustration he was feeling.[59] At this point on the journey with dementia, he was realizing some of the implications of his memory loss. Rosemary also talked about overwhelming experiences resulting from her failing memory: "I just . . . crumpled underneath it." The conversations themselves also disclosed the frustrations of words going missing and slowness of thought during our exchanges (for example, in the conversations with Ron, Matthew, Rosemary). Spiritual experience was being affected too. Rosemary described her sense of loss of self and distance from God, "Oh God, where are you?" recognizing such moments as a "dark night of the soul." On several occasions, participants were close to tears as they described the experience of dementia. For example, as Matthew spoke of Christ's crucifixion and resurrection ("I wouldn't be afraid to die . . . because . . . Jesus went up to Calvary . . . and on the third day . . . he rose").

Despite, the participants' inclination to dismiss these signs of struggle (for example, "they're not dominating my life. My life is dominated by the Lord," Rosemary), nevertheless they are part of the unseen, inner experience of faith which requires response in the present moment.

Challenges to Faith Practice

The awareness of loss bring implications for faith practices too which are the outworking of participants' relationship with God. This was particularly the experience of those who did not have the support of a spouse. Practices such as Bible engagement, prayer and participation in church services were beginning to be affected in a variety of ways—lack of concentration and short-term memory—brought to light in the research conversations.[60] For example, for Jill in the early stages of her dementia, it would be "devastating" if Bible-reading became impossible. Alice can no longer easily read Scriptures, but has found solution to this in web resources and in using CDs: "I listen to it every day." Specific, personal prayer-times were also difficult ("That's not me anymore," Alice). Rosemary talked about the difficulties of being involved in church services:

> ROSEMARY: [I] felt embarrassed. . . . I would go up to the rail and take communion, but I lost my way coming back. . . . I don't altogether find that people . . . who are the church community are most understanding of people with dementia.

59. MacKinlay, "Listening to People with Dementia," 101, 104.
60. See, for example, chapter 6.

Whilst participants were adapting practices in the light of their dementia, it is an area where the support and understanding of the fellowship of Christ is essential.

Such adversity brings the one afflicted, as Weil writes, to "the foot of the Cross."[61] In Luther's pastoral theology of the cross, in spite of his ambivalence about the role of evil in suffering, he considers the experience of disability as one through which God leads the sufferer to the cross.[62] This divine solidarity with human experience provides metaphor for these participants who are living in the light of the cross, in spite of the shadows.[63]

The Shadow of the Cross

As St. Paul explores, Christ, the image of God in humankind, becomes the suffering servant, who in obedience to his Father lays down his life for others (Phil 2:6–8). The Gospel accounts reveal the incarnated image of God being with those who suffer and are rejected. The very nature of God-in-Christ is revealed as the one who stands with the stranger.

During one of the research conversations Bill intentionally showed me a wooden cross. He had hammered nails into this, and found in this, as he began to live with dementia, an expression of his confidence that Christ was, and would be, with him in the uncertainties of his illness. Bonhoeffer[64] puts the suffering of believers into perspective alongside the suffering of Christ on the Cross in this way: "In the hour of the cruellest torture they bear for his sake, they are made partakers in the perfect joy and bliss of fellowship with him." Barclay, reflecting on the darkness of the Cross, highlights revelation in this serendipity: those who are afflicted share in Christ's own desolation on the Cross.[65] This seems to be Bill's experience as he adjusts to the experience of dementia.

Christ on the Cross

Keck and Kevern have each reflected specifically on the experience of dementia in the light of the cross. Keck finds identification and hope for

61. Weil, *Waiting on God*, 69.
62. Heuser, "Human Condition," 184–215, esp. 188.
63. Explored further in Moltmann, *Crucified God*.
64. Bonhoeffer, *Cost of Discipleship*, 81.
65. Barclay, "Psalm 88," 97.

those living with dementia and caregivers in the "brokenness of God on ˏ
Calvary" which, transfigures human brokenness. The crucified Christ,
suffering and despised, allows those walking in the shadow of dementia
to see Christ as fellow sufferer: "The tangles and plaques in the brain of
the Alzheimer's patient can be seen in the matted hair and blood-stained
garments of Christ. Both this disease and the Cross are prolonged experiences of death."[66]

Keck's exploration, addressed principally to caregivers, sets this anguish as the scene for apocalyptic desire and resolution, "Let it be over."
Kevern, in response to this position, insists that Christ's suffering on the
Cross has profound relevance to the lived experience of the person living
with dementia in the temporal, corporeal moment.[67] If the apocalyptic
is the only focus for comfort, then God is placed outside the experience
of living with dementia amidst the change and physical deterioration of
the present. Kevern's point is relevant to those with mild to moderate
dementia, who need assurance of Christ's presence with them *now* and
as they imagine the future progress of their illness. Christ's suffering is
pivotal in human understanding of the story of redemption: he is able to
redeem us because, "he is subject to all the weaknesses and contingencies
inherent in being human."[68]

Hauerwas directs us deeper into the suffering of Jesus himself. The
cry from the Cross "My God, my God" was not simply an acknowledgement of pain and coming death, but a cry in response to abandonment
by his Father.[69] Christ's experience of darkness is the extremity of suffering, unknowable by humankind. Christ's separation from God, "is the
Father's deliberately giving his Christ over to a deadly destiny so that our
destiny would not be determined by death." Theologically, this takes us
to the mystery (and hope) of the self-giving love of the trinitarian God,
discussed in chapter 7. Even in the extremity of affliction, Christ, as part
of the Trinity, is held within the loving communion of God. The being
"in Christ," discussed in the first reflection, envisages the one living with
dementia caught up in this mystery of the bond of love.[70] Perceptively

---

66. Keck, *Forgetting Whose We Are*, 171–72.
67. Kevern, "Sharing the Mind of Christ," 411–12.
68. Kevern, "Sharing the Mind of Christ," 417–18.
69. Hauerwas, *Cross-Shattered Christ*, 59–66.
70. Weil, *Waiting on God*, 70–71.

and movingly, Weil writes that "those who persevere in love" hear its note even in the lowest depths.[71]

Comfort in Darkness

In their experience of struggling with dementia, the participants were not at the time of the interviews suffering the extremities of the symptoms that advanced dementia brings. Yet, in these early to moderate stages, they needed to struggle with the difficulties they were experiencing. They were also living each day with the knowledge of the future development of their illness. For a people embedded in God's story, there is the comfort of his words and presence: "For just as we share abundantly in the sufferings of Christ, so also our comfort abounds through Christ" (2 Cor 1:5 NIVUK).

Conclusion

Interweaving with the sadness and losses, dementia brings a shifting of perception of the journey of faith. In some ways, its advent brings disorientation. Yet, for the participants in this study, inherent in knowing themselves as being "in Christ," the finding of purpose and hope was possible in the light of his resurrection. Reorientation seemed to be happening as these disciples of Christ kept their gaze fixed on him.[72]

In the following chapter, I consider the participants' experience of reorientation in their new context of dementia. Seeking illumination, I will explore the notion of memory as a resource for faith. Then, drawing on St. Paul's writing about the Christian's response to suffering, I reflect on what it was that enabled the participants' experience of growing faith as they were living with dementia.

---

71. Weil, *Waiting on God*, 68–69.
72. Weil, *Waiting on God*, 69.

9

Reorientation

Transforming Faith

"And we shall all be changed"[1] (Matthew)

Introduction

IN THE MIDST OF the uninvited experience of dementia, the participants in this study appeared to be finding transformation and reorientation. In his exploration of the psalms, Brueggemann reflects on this movement of God's people "from plea to praise," "from wretchedness to joy."[2] There is no going back, but mysteriously, the participants in the research, like God's people in the psalms, seemed to be finding resolution in their experience of faith in the light of their hope in Christ.

One might have expected that the "sacred canopy" of belief would be in jeopardy within the experience of dementia.[3] Yet, the phenomenological accounts of this research, have suggested that this was not the case for these particular Christians.[4] Surprisingly, their experience revealed paradox. Memory was funding faith despite the loss of memory.

1. Matthew is referring to 1 Cor 15:51, "Listen, I will tell you a mystery! We will not all die, but we will all be changed."

2. Brueggemann, *Spirituality of the Psalms*, 47–49.

3. Brueggemann, *Spirituality of the Psalms*, 47.

4. See, for example, Beuscher and Grando, "Using Spirituality to Cope," 584–85; Katsuno, "Personal Spirituality," 315–35.

In spite of the sadness and struggles of living with dementia: there was purpose, not meaninglessness; closeness to God, not distance; hope, not despair. Encapsulating it all, is the paradox of God himself who is *Emmanuel*, accompanying his people through the valley of their shadows. The disorientation of dementia was inevitably bringing a reorientation. The believing individual and their community, often find themselves, as Brueggemann comments, "surprised by grace."[5]

Such "newness" may seem inexplicable, apart from perceptions of a sovereign and loving God.[6] Paradoxically, these two characteristics are the opposite of the troubling questions which theodicy brings to God's omnipotence and love. Swinton notes that Christians, enabled by the hopefulness of the gospel narrative, suffer differently."[7] It is this different context of suffering that I will now focus on.

In the following, building on the discussion of the first two themes, I reflect on key aspects of this ongoing reorientation which bring understanding to the participants' present experience of dementia. Each happens within the context of God's love and that of the community of faith. In the first section of this reflection, I explore aspects of underlying memory which were interweaving with participants' present faith experience. These were resourcing their faith as they responded to the incipient difficulties of dementia. Then, in the second section of the reflection, arising out of this memory funded faith, I seek further understanding of the nature of the participants' response to their loss and struggle, in the light of St. Paul's pastoral words to the church about response to suffering.[8] Here, bringing experience together with scripture, the fresh perspectives disclosed suggest the ways in which the participants' reorientation is enabled through a transforming faith.

Through this lens I envisage a reframing of the Christian's encounter with the challenges brought by dementia. I consider their reorientation arising from the perception of God's purpose, their trust in God and their endurance. In the light of their eschatological hope (or imagination), it seemed that these aspects of their faith were bringing transformational spiritual growth.

5. Brueggemann, *Spirituality of the Psalms*, 47.

6. Brueggemann, *Spirituality of the Psalms*, 48.

7. Swinton, *Raging with Compassion*, 111.

8. "Not only that, but we rejoice in our sufferings, knowing that suffering produces endurance, and endurance produces character, and character produces hope" (Rom 5:3–4 ESV).

First, I reflect on how memory is funding my participants' faith.

Memory Funding Faith

Remembering Faith

Dementia questions the nature of memory, and consequently, the meaning of faith for Christians who live with dementia. Yet Brueggemann has written intriguingly that memory is an essential ingredient of faith in times of loss: "The primary ingredient, the primary resource of faith that is indispensable in a season of loss is *active, determined, concrete, resilient memory*."[9] If this is true, how then can faith be understood, or continue, for those living with developing loss of memory? If, as discussed in the literature review (chapter 3), memory is considered simply as functions of cognitive recall or ordered autobiographical memory, then the possibility of experiencing faith in later dementia is in doubt ("They wouldn't be able to know," David).[10]

However, the lived experience of faith in dementia highlights this paradox. Whilst some aspects of memory were certainly fading, it seemed that, in other ways, the participants' "memory" of God was becoming stronger. The participants recognized their "memory loss." Yet their words expressed undiminished, even strengthening, experience of faith. Ron's words about memory referred to his confidence in his faith despite memory loss ("that is dementia . . . a memory is there and it's not there"). An exchange with Jess about her sense of God's presence with her, similarly expressed this:

RESEARCHER: Do you feel that God is with you?

JESS: Yes, I'm sure of that. And that's why the fact that I can't remember, my memory loss, doesn't matter.

Whilst the participants acknowledged that their illness was increasingly affecting their short-term, factual re-call, there was certainty of their "memory" of faith, and the present experience of this bringing them "closer" to God.

As discussed in chapter 3, there are different ways of perceiving memory. These perspectives offer potential for understanding the faith

9. Brueggemann, "Suffering Produces Hope," 96.
10. See chapter 7, 179–180.

experience and practice of those who are living with dementia. For example, the writing of Brockmeier, Schacter, and Merleau-Ponty brings focus not on factual, autobiographical recall, but instead on meaning, and on implicit and embodied memory. Tallis additionally highlights that memory has a temporal fluidity: whilst our memories are tethered to past experience, they become present experience as they are remembered.[11] The meaning of memories and how these are embedded in the whole person suggest potential for understanding the relationship between memory and faith in those who are living with dementia.

For the Christian believer there is the further spiritual dimension. For my participants it is found in their assertion of transcendent relationship with God: "A relationship to someone that I love and who loves me" (Alice). The memories of relationship with God were clearly important for participants' experience in the present.

Encounters with God

Their remembered experiences of God have had transformational impact for the participants' lives in the present. They were eager to speak of these. Some examples from their phenomenological accounts illustrate this. Bill recalled how as a teenager "dead words" became "living words" and he "believed in Jesus as being my Saviour"; Ron recounts how, as a young adult, he was "born again." He reflected on the impact of his conversion in his present experience: "it is something that doesn't leave you." Rosemary described an experience of encounter with God more recently which has transformed her life and understanding of God. She also recounted how, in moments of darkness, she sings praise to God, remembering words from the past, which were bringing a transforming sense of God's peace and joy in the present: "you've learnt them and they come back to you."

Practical theologian Root, draws similar conclusions through discussion of his own experience: encounter with Christ has informed his living in the present.[12] Participants' memories of their "awakenings" of faith and of divine-human interaction had changed their perspectives on their lives, and were significant in helping them to live with dementia in the present.

11. Tallis, *Aping Mankind*, 125, 271.
12. Root, *Christopraxis*, 3–17.

Memory and Faith Interweaving

During the research conversations, I became aware that my prompts to remember God, were having *present* impact. For example, Rosemary's irrepressible expression of her faith in God as she was speaking to me concluded with a firm "Amen"; Bill's description of his experience became a prayer ("I just want to be a follower of you"); Jill paused midsentence to remind herself that God would keep her in his peace in future trauma ("He keeps his word . . . his promises. . . . [Quietly to self:] He keeps his promise").

In his discussion of memory and faith in dementia, resonating with this, Keck notes that at times to remember God, seems to be synonymous with belief.[13] It is as though the experience and its memory, are "interwoven in all aspects of our relationship with God."[14] He also suggests that to remember God results in behavior which "resembles an experience of faith," that "remembering the divine" is not "a neutral, dispassionate epistemological process," but combines "both cognitive and affective elements."[15]

The words of the participants were not so much about recalled events on a linear timeline, but about a state of being which was encompassing and making sense of their faith experience in the present moment. Memory and faith interweave, undermining the specificity of autobiographical time. Dalby, Sperlinger, and Boddington's research about the effects of Alzheimer's Disease on spirituality revealed a similar interweaving: "Their spiritual life was not separate from life. In this way, the experience of spirituality seemed to be woven into the fabric of their life, part of them, and therefore dependable and sure."[16] Such interweaving of memory and faith seemed to be funding participants' personal experience of relationship with God, both in the present, and in imaginative anticipation and preparation for future living with their illness. It was this "intrinsic faith" which was providing "an interpretative framework" for the participants in their present experience of living with dementia.[17]

13. Keck, *Forgetting Whose We Are*, 48–49.
14. Keck, *Forgetting Whose We Are*, 52.
15. Keck, *Forgetting Whose We Are*, 48–49.
16. Dalby et al., "Lived Experience," 82.
17. Swinton, *Spirituality and Mental Health Care*, 31.

Biblical Perspectives: Heart and Memory

The participants' memories of divine-human interaction and God's Word were engrained in who they were as people. Rosemary's words reflected this: "I love the Lord God with all my heart and all my soul."[18] Her words recalled scripture, suggested her intentional present experience, and resonated with biblical understandings of memory. These understandings shape the language of faith. Biblical perspectives on the meanings of memory have potential to illuminate the experience of believers who live with dementia.

Old Testament Perspectives

In the following I draw on Childs's seminal exploration of memory (*zkr*) in the Old Testament. He highlights the dynamic connections between the Hebraic concepts of memory (*zkr*) and the "heart" (*leb*).[19] The Hebraic word *leb* is variously translated as meaning the "inner man, mind, will, heart," signifying the core of what it is to be human.[20] Earlier, I reflected on this Hebraic understanding of the wholeness of the person in the context of identity. This concept also has implications for the Hebrew words for "memory" and "heart." *Zkr* signifies not merely a cognitive activity of the brain enabling recall. Rather, it too is associated with the *whole* person—body, soul and mind. The Israelites' remembering of God at significant points in their history brought renewed trust in God, and hope for the future in the midst of loss, resulting in changed living.[21] This scriptural remembering of God always involves an intentional turning towards him of the whole person, and results in transformation.

This kind of heart remembering, growing out of the Old Testament law, is affirmed in the teaching of Jesus. To live in harmonious relationship with the divine (and others) is summed up in this call to *remember* God in loving him with heart, soul and mind, as recalled in Rosemary's words (see Matt 22:37; Deut 6:5). As God's people remember him in this essential way in the face of new circumstances, there is inevitably a radical

18. See, for example, Mark 12:30.

19. Childs, *Memory and Tradition*, 17–19.

20. Strong, "3820 *Leb*."

21. Brueggemann, "Suffering Produces Hope," 96–99. See also, for example, the resolution to rededicate themselves to God during King Josiah's reign (2 Chr 34; 35).

re-directing of life and purpose.[22] The participants' words, in the light of their dementia, suggested this deliberate re-framing of their lives in the light of dementia: "this side of heaven that [dementia] is going to be part of my journey" (Bill).

New Testament Perspectives

In Pauline writing, the Greek word for heart (*kardia*) still carries the sense of the core of inner being with its will and affectivity. But here, the heart is also the place where Christ dwells through the Spirit. St. Paul writes:

> I pray that, according to the riches of his glory, he may grant that you may be strengthened in your inner being with power through his Spirit, and that Christ may dwell in your hearts through faith, as you are being rooted and grounded in love. (Eph 3:16–17)

New Testament scholar N. T. Wright argues that Paul's designation of the heart, *kardia*, as the locus of the Spirit's work, is not made to differentiate it from the rest of the person, but as "the place from which life and energy go out to the whole of the rest of the person, body and mind included."[23] In participants' experience their rootedness in Christ brings transformed living to the whole person, and to their impact on others (see Eph 3:14–21).

Keck's discussion of memory in the New Testament intriguingly suggests connection between the sense of the Hebrew understanding of memory with "the New Testament emphasis on belief and conversion."[24] As with *zkr*, conversion entails an intentional turning of the whole person towards Christ. Participant in this process is God the Holy Spirit, through whom the believer is born into God's family and, as St. Paul reminds Timothy, is crucial in the believer's inhabiting of this collective memory: "Guard the good deposit . . . with the help of the Holy Spirit who lives in us" (2 Tim 1:14 NIVUK).

22. For example, in Ezra 8–9 the biblical narrative recalls the re-commitment of the Israelites to God after their return from Exile.

23. Wright, "Mind, Spirit, Soul and Body."

24. Keck, *Forgetting Whose We Are*, 50.

Memory of the Word

For my participants, God's Word plays a significant part in their relationship with God and growth as disciples of Jesus: "I hear God through the
Bible . . . I think more than any other place where I hear God" (Jill). Their
accounts were scattered with references to the words of Scripture which
inform their lives and present experience:

> ROSEMARY: I've got [Bible] texts around me everywhere. . . .
> They will come into my head and I'll say them: "You are my
> strength and my joy . . . you are my rock and my salvation"
> Goodness me, if you say those words and don't get anything
> from it . . . even in the midst of difficulty . . . yes![25]

The story, the words and meaning of Scripture permeated their phenomenological accounts.

Lennon's consideration of heart and memory resonates with evangelicalism's focus on God's Word.[26] The Bible itself, Lennon proposes, is a
store of vital, "radical and dangerous memory" which provides "memory-
sight" and transforms our lives "because it invites us to faith."[27] To keep
God's word "in your heart" means in your memory," re-forming and
in-forming the mind and heart. The stored memory of Scripture, written
"on the tablet of your heart," means that "we become empowered . . . by
our memories," in the present, to see as God sees. Lennon's exploration
echoes Brueggemann, who has likened it to a "compost pile" which is full
of "generative material."[28] Whilst the traditional practice of daily, sequen-
tial Scripture reading is becoming more difficult for the participants, the
Word is funding their ongoing remembrance of God and bringing growth.

Such understandings of the interplay between heart and memory
resonate with the participants' accounts of their encounters with God,
and these were bringing persistent transformation to their experience in
the present. The relationship between memory and faith was having increasing significance for participants' reorientation of their faith in God
in the new context of living with dementia.

---

25. Rosemary is to referring to verses from the Psalms (e.g., Ps 27:1; 95:1).

26. Lennon, *Eyes of the Heart*, 84.

27. Lennon, *Eyes of the Heart*, 89.

28. Brueggemann, *Texts Under Negotiation*, 61.

Transforming Faith in Dementia

In New Testament writing, as discussed in chapter 8, suffering and difficulties are expected as a normal part of the life of faith. The challenges of dementia are of a particularly tragic kind, but still it seems, that spiritual growth is possible. In the lives of the research participants they affirmed a growing sense of relationship with God (for example, "Closer to God. 'Nearer My God to Thee,'"[29] Rosemary).

In the following, I reflect on the participants' experience of their growing faith in the light of dementia. I look for insight from Pauline writing from his letter to the early Roman Christians, which suggests this movement from disorientation of suffering to the reorientation of joyful hope in Christ:

> We boast in our hope of sharing the glory of God. And not only that, but we also boast in our sufferings, knowing that suffering produces endurance, and endurance produces character, and character produces hope, and hope does not disappoint us, because God's love has been poured into our hearts through the Holy Spirit that has been given to us. (Rom 5:2–5)

I will bring the participants' experience of faith into dialogue with the words of St. Paul, and reflect on key aspects of their response to dementia. Using this lens, I consider the nature of their growing experience of God which seemed to be sustained by faith's trajectory of hope in Christ.

Perception of God's Purpose

Meaning or Purpose?

In MacKinlay and Trevitt's consideration of the experience of dementia, finding meaning is a key goal which enables transcendence of loss and disabilities.[30] Their work resonates with other models of spiritual growth, such as that of Erikson's psychosocial stages of ageing, which shows the possibility that transcendence leads to hope.[31] Whilst they are writing

---

29. Rosemary is referring to the hymn "Nearer My God to Thee" (1841), lyrics by Sarah Flower Adams.

30. MacKinlay and Trevitt, *Finding Meaning*, 86.

31. MacKinlay and Trevitt, *Finding Meaning*, 86, 87.

about a broader area of spirituality than the specific focus of this book, their work suggests that the experiencing of dementia may be "the starting point for spiritual growth" which enables a deeper sense of relationship with God.[32]

MacKinlay and Trevitt's model might seem to mirror what is happening for the participants in this research. However, in the case of these Christians living with dementia, the research discloses that the finding of meaning, or the failure to do so, is not at stake. Their faith places them firmly in the context of God's story within the body of Christ, not their own. The theological question here is about *understanding* of God's purpose; the pastoral question concerns *acceptance* of this, enabling transcendence of despair and the envisioning of hope.

Made for a Purpose

It might seem surprising that the participants in this study had a strong sense that dementia had purpose in their lives, or that its advent had meaning which they wanted to understand. Yet, the seeking of ultimate meaning is generally regarded as fundamental to human growth.[33] As committed Christians, the participants' sense of seeking *purpose*, even whilst living through the disorientation of dementia, was congruent with their belief in being created by God with a purpose: "If God has asked me to have dementia . . . then I know he will be there" (Jill).[34]

Whatever the changes dementia was bringing to their lives, the participants' sense of acceptance of their illness was caught up in this sense of being involved in God's hopeful purposes for their lives. In the creation accounts (Gen 1; 2), Adam is set in a working relationship with God, within the boundaries God provided (Gen 2:15 NIVUK). In the New Testament, the disciples were sent out by Jesus to partner with God in his mission to the world (see Matt 28:19–20). For the research participants, their unwelcome illness is part of the bigger story and plan of God's will and purposes. Participants seemed to have no doubt about this in their experience of developing dementia: "faith says to me, I can make a difference to other

32. MacKinlay and Trevitt, *Finding Meaning*, 86.

33. For example, Frankl, *Man's Search for Meaning*; MacKinlay and Trevitt, *Finding Meaning*, 15, 20–24.

34. Westminster Assembly, "Westminster Shorter Catechism." See chapter 7.

people." Alice's words reflected the broader orientation of her faith life: "My purpose is to please him, not anybody else" (Alice).

Choosing to Accept

In Gethsemane, Jesus faced the climactic moment of acceptance of his Father's will. Kevern, in the context of dementia, notes that this acceptance re-iterated Jesus' commitment to the enacting of his Father's purposes, which involved the way to the Cross.[35] Christ was not searching for meaning, but was identifying with, and accepting, God's purpose for his life. It is the participants' identification with and "in Christ" which enables their own crucial step of acceptance.

Both Bryden and Davis, in their accounts of their experience of dementia, describe how choosing to accept God's purpose was transformational.[36] Davis speaks of his new understanding of the words, "Thy will be done," which had enabled him to find peace in his life as he trusts in Christ.

St. Paul's encouragement to the suffering church—"All things work together . . . according to his purpose" (Rom 8:28)—is no triumphalist assertion, but a costly and courageous statement of trust: "I choose . . . instead of raging wildly at the things I have lost. I must thank God."[37] The transcendence of suffering, following from acceptance of God's will and purpose, was reflected in the participants' accounts of their experience. Alice was able to assert out of her own lived knowledge of dementia:

> ALICE: Lord, this is your gift for here. . . . Therefore, I will accept it as this gift and with your help I will do what I can in order to reflect your glory in it.

Re-Framing Purpose

The advent of dementia in the life of a Christian unavoidably shifts perception of one's own place in God's purposes. God's story and God's faithful covenantal love have set the grand narrative for the believer.

---

35. Kevern, "Sharing the Mind of Christ," 419.

36. Bryden, *Dancing with Dementia,*169–70; Davis, *My Journey into Alzheimer's Disease,* 56–58.

37. Davis, *My Journey into Alzheimer's Disease,* 57.

The immediate contextual question which underlies the participants' responses is not, therefore, "Why would a loving God allow this to happen to me?" Rather, it is "What is God's purpose for my life in this new context?" This implicit sense of the participants' experience of dementia is within God's loving hold on their lives, and is evident in their words (Rosemary: "What will be, will be . . . when it comes, in your time Lord and your will"). It is not, as Swinton notes, "that God is indifferent to the suffering that dementia brings." Rather, it has purpose both for the person living with dementia and others: "a mystery which is firmly rooted in God's creative and redemptive actions in and for the world."[38] This energizing new sense of purpose was reflected in the encounters with participants and their words. Whatever happens in this stage of her life, Rosemary asserts that she just wants "to bring glory to him."

It is into this arena of acceptance of God's purpose that the transformative phenomenon of trust in God's faithfulness is disclosed.

Trust in God

Trusting in God's Faithful Love

The faith experience of believers living with dementia, is perhaps better understood as a relational trust: "The God who I trust and believe in," (Rosemary); "God is with me" (David). As the symptoms of dementia advance, Swinton suggests that this word "trust" has potential as providing a way of understanding the faith of those who are living with cognitive incapacity.[39] The dependence involved in trust in God, not propositional truth, becomes the primary ingredient of faith which is a simple reliance on God's relating to us.[40] Rosemary said:

> ROSEMARY: I can accept it [dementia] through God being with me . . . as my mind becomes less intellectualized and able to . . . I shall be more filled with the feeling of the love of God."

Concurring with Hauerwas, Swinton asserts that to be a disciple of Jesus means a relinquishing of any trust in our own abilities or significance.[41] In the participants' experience, their illness was resulting in

38. Swinton, *Dementia*, 184.

39. Swinton, *Becoming Friends of Time*, 100–109.

40. Swinton, *Becoming Friends of Time*, 102–3.

41. Hauerwas, *Peaceable Kingdom*, 86.

this increasing sense of trustful dependence on him: "I am closer to God because there's less of me" (Alice).

The pattern of suffering which impels believers to discover themselves closer to God is a familiar biblical one. Trust in God's faithful memory is underwritten by its foundation in the biblical account of the covenantal relationship between God and his people. In extremity, the Israelites found themselves recalled to God. For example, In the exile of Babylon, as they remembered God, their tears mixed with songs. Brueggemann points to their trust in the covenant faithfulness and steadfast love of God with his people: "Know therefore that the Lord your God is God, the faithful God who maintains covenant loyalty with those who love him and keep his commandments, to a thousand generations" (Deut 7:9).[42] It might seem, as we observe the anguish and sadness brought by dementia, that in the face of human pain and struggle, God's sovereignty is in tension with his fidelity to his people.[43] However, in our fallen, broken world, Brueggemann asserts that God's sovereignty insists on a committed, engaging of his covenant partners in a long-term perspective on *his* purposes ("He allows things in this broken world," Alice). He draws out that it is in the midst of trouble that something miraculous and transformative happens. Such trust, brings assurance, that "God is doing something new that is congruent with God's past actions."[44]

Memories of God's past faithfulness in participants' own individual lives were funding their faith in the present, and bringing assurance for an unseen future: "He's never deserted me. He keeps his word . . . his promises" (Jill); "He loves me" (Alice) The writer to the Hebrews sums up the continuing promise of God to his people: "I will never leave you or forsake you" (Heb 13:5).

The participants' perception of purpose and trust in God were enabling their endurance, in the light of the hope of Christ (see Rom 5:2).

Endurance under Pressure

"Endurance" in St. Paul's understanding (sometimes translated "perseverance") is a key word which informs our understanding of the suffering and the believer's response to it (e.g., Rom 5:2 NIVUK). Stott brings

---

42. Brueggemann, "Suffering Produces Hope," 95–103.

43. Brueggemann, *Unsettling God*, 63.

44. Brueggemann, "Suffering Produces Hope," 98.

insight to the New Testament Greek word for this (*hypomone*) which has the sense of endurance whilst living under pressure.[45] Of course, diagnosis of dementia acknowledges a chronic illness which is not a passing interlude. Bryden writes out of her own experience: "dementia is not just an end stage, it is a journey . . . and there are many steps along the way."[46] The journey requires endurance, and this requires the support of others in Christ's Body, and this is assumed in St. Paul's words written to a community.

The participants' experience of dementia is characterized by joy and growth towards hope. Rosemary's words revealed this endurance in the face of her dementia: "Maybe I won't recognize things. . . . It matters not. What does matter is that I will be, at the right time, with the Lord."

Rejoicing in Suffering

The words recorded during the research, sometimes bittersweet, were marked by "rejoicing" (Rom 5:2 ESV) and thankfulness. Some examples from the data encapsulate this:

> DAVID: I might forget who they were [laughs] . . . I'm sure that Jesus must have laughed.

> RON: I'll never lose that joy, but I have lost my memory.

> ROSEMARY: I'm so grateful for what God's offered me and given me that I can relax and just say, "What will be, will be . . . in your time Lord and your will."[47]

Goldsmith has pointed to this apparent paradox of connection between suffering and thankfulness. He suggests that it is "as though the very experience of suffering helps us to appreciate other things so much more."[48] Katsuno's research resonates with this study. Noting that thankfulness is part of the Christian's response to dementia, she reflects that rejoicing is possible because of the sense that God has a plan, and the individual

---

45. Stott, *Message of Romans*, 141–42. The same New Testament Greek word is used for "endurance" in 2 Cor 1:6 NIVUK. See also Scripture4All, "Romans 5"; "2Corinthians"; Cranfield, *Romans*, 103–6; Dunn, *Romans 1–8*, 264–65; Fitzmyer, *Romans*, 395–98.

46. Bryden, *Dancing with Dementia*, 40, 48.

47. See also chapter 6.

48. Goldsmith, "Tracing Rainbows," 132.

has security within this.[49] Stott's comments on Romans 8:17 also bring biblical insight to the reason for this joyful endurance: "The recognition that there is a divine rationale behind suffering. . . . We are co-heirs with Christ, if indeed we share in his sufferings in order that we may also share in his glory."[50] The participants' joy and thankfulness resonate with Brueggmann's account of reorientation in the psalms where praise results from acknowledging and accepting the will of a sovereign God, and from the affirmation of trust in his faithfulness to them. This movement to acceptance and thankfulness was illustrated in the words of Alice: "Thank you Lord, this is your gift for here. . . . Therefore . . . I will do what I can in order to reflect your glory in it."

Brueggemann draws his understanding of new orientation into the New Testament. Recognizing that Jesus' central proclamation in the New Testament was about the coming Kingdom of God, he suggests that Jesus' ministry was "a living out of the liturgical assertion of these psalms."[51] In a way, such a living out is reflected in the lives of the participants: "We may have a bit of difficulty," Ron acknowledges, but this is in the context of his sure faith, "I know where I'm going."

Before hope is fully realized, St. Paul's model suggests a further characteristic of endurance of sufferings. The word "character" following "endurance" suggests a maturing towards this hope of faith: "Endurance produces character, and character produces hope" (Rom 5:4). If this is the biblical expectation, how can this spiritual growth be happening in dementia?

Spiritual Growth

To speak of those who are living with dementia, growing spiritually (see, e.g., Rom 8:29) might seem difficult to envisage, even inappropriate. However, it did not seem unimaginable for the participants in the study. They felt their faith was "growing . . . much more of a closeness" (David); and that their lives were increasingly being aligned with his purposes, "If God had not willed me" (Rosemary).

Even as cognitive awareness is diminishing, the participants' experience resonates with St. Paul's words about the work of the Spirit in the

49. Katsuno, "Personal Spirituality," 325.
50. Stott, *Message of Romans*, 141.
51. Brueggemann, *Psalms*, 54.

believer's life—"in your inner being"—strengthening the awareness of Christ and his love (Eph 3:16, 17). Scripture points to the evidence of love, joy and peace arising from the presence of the Holy Spirit within the believer; the participants' words and embodied expression resonate with this (Gal 5:22–23). Scripture suggests that it is in these fragile, human "jars of clay" that the life of Jesus is revealed (2 Cor 4:7–12).

The idea that spiritual growth is possible within dementia, has until recently been little studied. MacKinlay and Trevitt, discussed above, framed their research into finding meaning in the experience of dementia, as being one of the spiritual tasks of ageing.[52] They proposed that the trajectory of spiritual growth can lead to self-transcendence which, even in the tragedy of dementia, brings spiritual growth and enables hopefulness.[53] In contrast to the typical narrative of the progression of dementia as one of "decline and loss," Kevern has also highlighted that living with dementia provides opportunity for spiritual growth. Faith is not only "a pragmatic coping strategy."[54]

Resonating with this thesis, Dunlop has suggested that "early dementia may provide a renewed opportunity to trust and rest in God."[55] He focuses on recognition of the ways in which the fruit of the Spirit are being developed in the lives of those who live with this illness, and the transformation of its struggles in ways which honor God. These aspects of growth, together with their sense of purpose in serving God through their dementia, were characteristic of the participants in this research. Their faith poses questions to the community of Christ. How will the church continue to support them in their spiritual growth? So that together, as the body of Christ, we might be "rooted and built up in him and established in the faith, just as you were taught, abounding in thanksgiving" (Col 2:7). My own "dwelling" with the lived experience of the participants over the period of this study, has reinforced my questions.[56] In the here-and-now of living with dementia, what is it that enables these followers of Jesus to endure and live positively with their dementia?

52. MacKinlay and Trevitt, *Finding Meaning*, 23.
53. MacKinlay and Trevitt, *Finding Meaning*,166.
54. Kevern, "Dementia and Spirituality."
55. Dunlop, *Finding Grace*, 162.
56. Finlay, *Phenomenology for Therapists*, 228.

Enabling Endurance

THE PRESENCE OF THE HOLY SPIRIT

As revealed in the phenomenological accounts of the participants, sense of relationship with God ("a relationship, not a doing," Alice) is preeminent in their experience of dementia, as well as being characteristic of their evangelical tradition. The participants expressed their sense of God being with them in different ways ("Oh . . . the presence . . . is always there," Ron).

In St. Paul's understanding of suffering, its endurance, sustained by hope, is enabled by God's love, and mediated through the indwelling Spirit: "God's love has been poured into our hearts through the Holy Spirit" (Rom 5:5–6). In his exploration of Romans 5:1–11, Stott draws out two reasons for the believer's awareness of God's love: the presence of the Holy Spirit, and the knowledge that God has demonstrated his love in giving his Son. Stott emphasizes that the sense of God's presence is dependent on his loving intervention: "It is God's love for us, not ours for him, which is in mind . . . what the Holy Spirit does is to make us deeply and refreshingly aware that God loves us."[57] Particularly relevant in considering the developing characteristics of dementia, is Stott's emphasis that this is the love *of God for* the believer; it is not dependent on our ability to love him. The sense of being loved *by* God and experiencing resulting peace was expressed on several occasions in participants' words: "overwhelmed with love" (Alice); "I have a kind of peace . . . which doesn't come from me. I think it comes from God," (Jill).

This feeling of confident dependence on God, expressed by the participants, emerges from the roots of their faith. Theologically, it is the Holy Spirit who was enabling their transcendent sense of relationship with God:

> But you have received a spirit of adoption. When we cry, 'Abba! Father!' it is that very Spirit bearing witness with our spirit that we are children of God, and if children, then heirs, heirs of God and joint heirs with Christ. (Rom 8:15–17)

In St. John's Gospel, Jesus assured his disciples of the Spirit's presence as the ultimate reminder of God and his words.

---

57. Stott, *Message of Romans*, 143.

> The Advocate, the Holy Spirit . . . will teach you everything, and
> remind you of all that I have said to you. Peace I leave with you;
> my peace I give to you. (John 14:26, 27; cf. Luke 12:12)

When words are difficult to find, St. Paul reminds believers that the Spirit searches our hearts and helps us in our weakness: "We do not know how to pray as we ought, but that very Spirit intercedes with sighs too deep for words" (Rom 8:26, 27). In this intimate work, there is comfort for those who are beginning to lose the language of words because of their dementia. There is also a reminder here of the mysteries of how the Spirit of God might be at work in those whose ability to remember is diminishing. Participant Ron's words "I haven't got a memory, but I have . . ." suggest this paradox of cognitive decline alongside his remembering of God. As dementia progresses, knowing *about* God may become more difficult, but the Spirit within the believer reminds them of God's attentive presence and his knowing of them.

THE REMEMBERING COMMUNITY OF FAITH

Importantly, endurance in New Testament writing is within and enabled by the supporting remembering community of faith, the Spirit-indwelt body of Christ.[58] Hauerwas, orienting our focus on those who live with adversity, notes that those who suffered in the New Testament "had a community of care that has made it possible for them."[59] Swinton expands:

> Response to the . . . existence of suffering was not to question
> God's goodness, love, and power, but rather to develop faithful
> forms of community within which the impact of . . . suffering
> could be absorbed, resisted, and transformed as they waited for
> God's return.[60]

The word "absorbed" suggests not only a serving of one another, but an integration in which the weight of the suffering is mutually carried. As Crowther notes, "the communal aspect of suffering cannot be overlooked."[61]

---

58. Hauerwas, *Peaceable Kingdom*, 98.
59. Hauerwas, *Naming the Silences*, 53.
60. Swinton, *Raging with Compassion*, 35.
61. Crowther, *Sustaining Persons*, 167. See also 1 Cor 12:26a.

Even though the research participants knew that their memory and concentration were beginning to cause them difficulties, yet they spoke of the importance of being with other believers. This was expressed in terms of appreciation for the kindness of others in their church (Matthew), supportiveness of a small group (Bill, David) and simply being part of the church community: It's the collective, the getting-together and having fellowship . . . that matters (Rosemary). Jess spoke of the importance of going to church services even if she couldn't remember details later. Ron's words, "it's given me a memory which I haven't got, but by going to church, it has," hint at the moments of faith experience brought by his continued involvement in church. Participants who were married spoke of their spouse's spiritual support ("We get fellowship together," Ron).

The experience of those living with dementia highlights the importance of the corporate nature of the community of faith. Where evangelicalism has prized "individual privatized commitment over corporate participation," those living with dementia challenge the church to find new orientation, in its awareness of being-as-community, the body of Christ.[62] Bryden, who was facing her own present and future with dementia, wrote: "As I travel towards the dissolution of my self, my personality, my very 'essence,' my relationship with God needs increasing support from you, my other in the body of Christ. . . . I need you to minister to me, to sing with me, pray with me, to be my memory for me."[63] One of the participants (Alice) similarly stressed her need to be reminded by fellow believers: "They have to remind me."[64]

However, as attendance at church services and conversation with others becomes more difficult, the local church itself may, unintentionally, become deeply forgetful of its members who live with dementia.[65] Difficulties in this area were reflected in the phenomenological accounts, particularly of those who were living independently. Their voices and experience are reminders that this time of early to moderate dementia is a special moment of opportunity for the church.[66] Christians living with dementia are able, in some measure, to express their present needs, to prepare for, and to anticipate what might be helpful in their ongoing

62. Kent, "Embodied Evangelicalism," 108.

63. Bryden and MacKinlay, "Dementia: A Spiritual Journey," 74.

64. See chapter 6.

65. Mast, *Second Forgetting*, 105.

66. For example, Bute, "My Glorious Opportunity," 23.

experience of trust in God. Crowther, in her exploration of spiritual care for those living with dementia, speaks of the necessity of the local church's solidarity with those living with dementia.[67]

The questions raised by the shadows of dementia, as Hauerwas suggests, can find response in and through a community.[68] Within the body of Christ, with its mutual reverence and sharing of one another's burdens, there is the potential to enable perseverance in faith "until he comes" (1 Cor 11:26).

Eschatological Hope

A powerful and key factor in enabling a new orientation for Christians who live with dementia is the trajectory of God's story characterized by eschatological hope: "In this hope we were saved" (Rom 8:24 NIVUK). As St. Paul's words in Romans make clear, this "hope of . . . glory" (Rom 5:1-5) founded in Christ and mediated through the Holy Spirit, is the reason why these believers can respond positively to suffering. The participants' certainty of their future with God, was liberating them to pursue God's purpose in this new situation, and enabling them to feel peaceful, even joyful, in the present. Keck's exploration of this hope in the lived experience of dementia recognizes its importance, proposing that apocalyptic themes "radically transform" the Christian understanding of suffering in the present: "Our hope amid despair is real because of the life and work of Christ."[69]

Christian Hope Is Different

Hopefulness is generally acknowledged as an important aspect of well-being, but there has been little research into the subjective experience of the impact of the hope of faith on those live with dementia.[70] MacKinlay and Trevitt's work has begun to focus on this in their work on finding spiritual meaning in the experience of dementia. In their model, hope is the *outcome* of persons finding meaning.[71] However, the nature of the

---

67. Crowther, *Sustaining Persons*, 167.

68. Hauerwas, *Naming the Silences*, 53.

69. Keck, *Forgetting Whose We Are*, 173.

70. Herth, "Fostering Hope," 1250–59; Wolverson et al., "Remaining Hopeful," 457.

71. MacKinlay and Trevitt, *Finding Meaning*, 154–58.

hope of these participants, which begins from a biblical faith perspective, is particular and distinctive. Theologically, hope *originates* with God, and its experience is enabled by the Holy Spirit in the believer ("poured into our hearts" [Rom 5:5]), drawing them into the divine life (as I have discussed in chapter 7). For my participants, as Christians from an evangelical tradition, eschatological hope wasn't merely a theological precept; rather, it encompassed and permeated their lived experience, and was motivating them within the temporal context. This is the transforming christological hope of resurrection and eternal security given by God.

The Hope of "Heaven"

Ron's assertion "I'm going to heaven" was an expression of his trust and hope in God, which was enabling him to be "contented" in the present. However, as Wright notes, this word "heaven" is not simply indicating the *ultimate* destination."[72] Neither is it only a re-assuring (but, perhaps, convenient) way for those who observe the pain of others to avoid their struggles in the present. Writing about faith's understanding of dementia, Goldsmith's "Remembered by God" model might appear to be similarly comforting, suggesting, as some have interpreted, that "God will make everything all right in the end."[73] But, as Kevern reminds us, such an understanding of eschatological hope is inadequate for those who are aware of their needs and increasing frailties in the present if it gives no assurance of God's continuing presence with the person as they journey through dementia.[74] The participants in the research were not sustained by a vague hope of a distant "heaven," but by the sense of relationship with Christ which is transforming their experience in the present, and continues into and through eternity.

Living in the Story

As considered earlier, my participants' strong sense of identity was situated in God's hopeful story. This "counterdrama" was providing foundation for their dynamic and transcendent hope.[75] Brueggemann reminds

72. Wright, *Surprised by Hope*, 25–26.
73. Goldsmith, "Dementia," 129–31.
74. Kevern, "What Sort of a God?" 176.
75. Brueggemann, *Texts Under Negotiation*, 57–91.

us of the difference which the evangelical infrastructure (that is, the text of the Bible) brings to our understanding of our human lives.[76] The Bible, perceived as redescription of the way in which we see the world, challenges and brings new perspectives.

The writer of Hebrews uses the Scriptural narrative to affirm the certain hope of believers ("Faith is the assurance of things hoped for, the conviction of things not seen" [Heb 11:1]), reminding them of their part in God's story. In Hebrews 11—12:3 the writer recalls the suffering of Old Testament heroes which led to the suffering of Jesus, to his resurrection, and to the hope of Christ's reign. Counterintuitively, the experience of suffering, throughout the drama of scriptural faith, leads to hope.[77] It is in the light of this particular kind of hope that he encourages the endurance of fellow believers:

> Run with perseverance the race that is set before us, looking to
> Jesus . . . who for the sake of the joy that was set before him he
> endured he cross . . . and has taken his seat at the right hand of
> the throne of God. (Heb 12:1–3)

Repeatedly throughout the biblical narrative, it is loss and brokenness which evoke memory of the faithfulness of God and lead to hopefulness.[78] Within this counterdrama, God's redemptive movement through history means that the present is always informed, as Swinton notes, by "eschatological rhythms and echoes."[79]

Present-Not-Yet

From a biblical perspective, the drama of God's story is ongoing through the liminal era of the church. Suffering and sadness, including that of dementia, are part of temporal life. Yet, God's promises of hope—being with him—made possible through the saving death and resurrection of Christ, were transforming the lives of the Christians in this study as they were living with dementia in the present moment of today ("If we know where we're going we cannot help but feel contented," Ron).

---

76. Brueggemann, *Texts Under* Negotiation, 27, 28.

77. Brueggemann, "Suffering Produces Hope," 97–98.

78. Brueggemann, "Suffering Produces Hope," 97–99.

79. Swinton, *Raging with Compassion*, 55.

St. Paul's "endurance" of present suffering is framed in the light of this hope in Christ, and it is this which enables transcendence (Rom 5:1–5 ESV). The future beyond temporal life is a theological mystery. In our conversations, Matthew dismissed my question about what he was expecting of eternity: "Does it matter?" The details, of course, *are* a mystery. However, the well-rehearsed story of faith and its immanence, mediated through Christ's Spirit, was bringing to participants an evident calm, even joyful confidence. Their hope arising from their trust in God brings peace in the present and gives confident assurance of eternal security with God. Matthew, one of the frailest of the participants, struggled with tears as he spoke of this hope in the light of recollection of Jesus' death and resurrection: "We will all be changed" (1 Cor 15:51).

Crowther, in her pastoral writing, helpfully highlights this tension between the "present and not yet" aspect of the experience of faith in dementia. Christ's reign of love is both "present and a foretaste" of his ultimate victory over suffering. More than this, through the assurance of relationship with Christ and in "solidarity" with the community of faith, this hope becomes "a present and personal hopefulness as it is received objectively."[80] This concept resonates with the experience of my research participants, and begins to explain their insistent, hopeful positivity in the present. Just as the memory of God's past faithfulness has informed and funded present experience of God; just as the Kingdom of God is both present and not yet (Luke 17:20–21); so too the participants' trust in God's promises for the future fund their eschatological hope, and bring transformation to their *present* lived experience. In some transcendent, mysterious way, the hope of the future is actualized in my participants' experience in the present moment of now. Greggs captures this future-present mode of being:

> God makes his way from his future into our present, allowing the church through the Holy Spirit to anticipate proleptically the coming of his Kingdom as his eschaton impinges on our time.[81]

Jess's poem powerfully expressed her own sense of this as well: "I only have Now. . . . Today is the Day of Salvation."

Brueggemann speaks of a "very pastoral eschatology" which "cedes one's life over to the purpose and power of God."[82] In the light of the

---

80. Crowther, *Sustaining Persons*, 169.

81. Greggs, *New Perspectives for Evangelical Theology*, 4.

82. Brueggemann, *Texts Under Negotiation*, 41.

lived experience of my participants, such an eschatology was bringing transformation to these disciples of Jesus who were living with dementia in the present.

Conclusion

In his exploration of the movement of God's people from disorientation to new orientation, Brueggemann suggests that, whilst we "can narrate, recite and testify [to]" the lived experience of God's people, how this newness happens cannot be explained. It's as mysterious as how a "leper is cleansed, or how a blind person can see (Luke 7:22)."[83] Yet, in the lived experience of my participants, there are clues to how their reorientation was happening. Their faith, funded by memory, disclosed through the expression of their trustful hope in God, was bringing spiritual growth as they walked through the shadows of dementia. Their eschatological hope and its imagining reframes the experience of dementia and sustains its endurance in transformative ways in the present. Brueggemann suggests that such "hope in the midst of loss . . . is not a psychological trick. It is a massive theological act . . . a statement about the fidelity of God who is the key player in the past and in the future."[84]

In the reflections of chapters 7, 8, and 9, I have explored the participants' experience of faith using the structure of orientation, disorientation and reorientation.[85] The coming of dementia has intruded on the participants' clear sense of knowing who they were in Christ. Their illness was inevitably bringing disorientation into participants' lives and, at the time of our research conversations, had begun to bring changes to their perspectives. Although their positive outlook tended to conceal it, their words also revealed aspects of struggle which their illness was causing. Resonant with Heideggerian concepts, the phenomenological accounts began to "unconceal" the nature of this shadow.[86] Rather than crisis of faith, their new situation has brought reorientation with renewed trust in God. Being "in Christ" with these hopeful out-workings are a mystery.[87] Yet, the transformative effects of their faith could be seen in the lives of

---

83. Brueggemann, *Spirituality of the Psalms*, 47–48.

84. Brueggemann, "Suffering Produces Hope," 99.

85. Brueggemann, *Praying the Psalms*, 3.

86. Heidegger, *Being and Time*, 187.

87. "Listen, I will tell you a mystery" (1 Cor 15:51).

these individuals in their confident, joyful, sense of security with God as they faced challenging futures with developing dementia.

In the final chapter, the conversation of the book moves towards the closure of the hermeneutical circle, considering the implications of the research, and leading to recommendations which, it is hoped, may contribute to transforming pastoral practice. In the light of their lived experience and these theological reflections, how can the body of Christ live "in solidarity" with these fellow disciples of Jesus?[88]

88. Crowther, *Sustaining Persons*, 167.

10

Towards Faithful Practice

Introduction

IN THIS BOOK I have set out to explore and deepen understanding of the faith experience and practice of Christians from the evangelical tradition who live with early to moderate stage dementia. This chapter points to ways in which this work has begun to fulfil the goals outlined in the Introduction. In the following, I seek to show how the findings of this particular study—in its qualitative research and through the theological reflections—bring original insight and fresh understanding to the area. I will then consider implications for ministry and theology and suggest strategies towards the hoped-for outcomes outlined in the Introduction. In closing, I suggest further research possibilities in which implications of this study might be further tested.

The Journey of the Research

At the start of my research journey, I was aware of Christian believers within the evangelical faith tradition who were beginning to experience the impact and disorientation of early to moderate dementia symptoms. The review of literature confirmed a gap in the research regarding exploration and understanding of this faith experience of Christians, particularly those from an evangelical tradition.

I selected a hermeneutical phenomenological approach to the qualitative research because I believed it would facilitate the unique contribution of these committed Christians who were living with dementia. In
consequence, this book brings original understanding about their specific faith experience. In particular, this study has provided an opportunity
to hear the voices of those who were living in the early to moderate stages
of dementia.[1] Their experience was then brought into conversation with
theological and pastoral perspectives.

It became clear, during the research, that the participants' faith was
of fundamental importance to them both in the present, and as they *prepared* for an envisaged future with the consequences of their developing
illness. The courageous voices of the participants in this study, resonated
with the small numbers of others who have appealed to fellow Christian believers to support them spiritually: "I need you . . . as I travel this
journey of dementia, I will rely on others increasingly to support my
spirituality."[2] Like, Bryden, participants in this research also acknowledged their dependence on relationship with others in helping them to
know God's presence with them.

This research resonates with calls from other writing to recognize
the potential of this stage of dementia. Robinson has written compellingly of the unique insights which those who are beginning to live in
the "fuzzy and confused world" of dementia can bring to our understanding.[3] Alice, in this study, also asserted her insider perspective: "it's
a privilege to understand dementia from the inside . . . very different than
from the outside." The research has responded in particular to the opportunity which this stage of dementia offers for learning about the faith
experience of Christian believers of an evangelical tradition.

In keeping with the transformative goals of Practical Theology's pastoral cycle, implications for practice and theology have arisen from this
study. At this stage of the book, in this "clearing,"[4] there is a fusion of the
horizons[5] of the different perspectives: the voices of the lived experience,
the theological reflections, resonance with other pastoral and theological

1. Robinson, "Should People with Alzheimer's," 104.
2. Bryden, *Dancing with Dementia*, 153.
3. Robinson, "Should People with Alzheimer's," 104.
4. Heidegger, *Being and Time*, 167.
5. Gadamer, *Truth and Method*, 301–6.

writing on this subject, Scripture, and my own intuitive response to what has been learnt.

An ongoing concern throughout has been to seek the redescription brought about through a biblical perspective.[6] My own voice as researcher is part of the critical conversation of Practical Theology. I acknowledge that other researchers may bring different interpretations to the data presented in this study, but these have been brought with the aim of bringing deeper understanding to an ongoing conversation, towards transformative practice.

The Experience and Practice of Faith in Dementia

A surprising aspect of this study has been the positive nature of the participants' experience of their illness in light of their faith. This was enabling them to see dementia differently from expectations which the researcher might have brought to this study. The study revealed, perhaps counterintuitively at first, that the experience of dementia was bringing these participants an increasing sense of closeness to God and relationship with him. This resonates with the limited research available.[7] Although there may be moments of darkness and struggle, an underlying assurance of trust in God remained and was sustaining them in their faith.

Key Aspects of the Participants' Faith Experience and Practice

- *Faith and its sense of relationship with God* remained central to identity ("The core is . . . knowing Jesus," David). The sense of being-in-relationship with God had precedence over the doing of faith practices. As other pastoral literature has suggested, and as confirmed in this research, feelings were becoming more significant as the illness was progressing.[8]

- *Faith in practice.* Traditional approaches to Bible engagement, prayer, participation in worship and other activities were becoming more difficult as a result of the ongoing development of their dementia.[9]

6. Brueggemann, *Redescribing Reality*, 4–6, 26–29; Swinton, *Dementia*, 19–21.

7. See, for example, Beuscher and Grando, "Using Spirituality to Cope," 591–92.

8. McFadden et al., "Actions, Feelings, and Values," 76–78.

9. Davis, *My Journey into Alzheimer's Disease*, 57.

However, these practices remained central and significant as means of sustaining faith and expressing relationship with God and other believers.[10] Participants were recognizing these difficulties and finding other ways of using these resources of faith.

• *Belonging in the community of faith*

— *The identity* of Christians living with dementia is highlighted by the nature of their participation in the body of Christ. As attendance at church activities becomes more challenging, dementia asks questions about how their belonging is expressed in the local congregation, and also how their giftedness is recognized.

— *Stigmatization.* The research has posed questions about how the person living with dementia is regarded (perhaps by implication), or treated within their community of faith. In some conversations, the effects of subtle stigmatization were revealed. Resonating with other literature, Christians with dementia may experience stigmatizing responses to the symptoms of their illness within their local faith community—even, spiritual stigmatizing which communicates a doubt of their faith.[11] Sometimes, as participants' comments disclosed, it was not always easy for them to feel welcome in a local congregation. In spite of this, conversations with some participants revealed that the support of their local churches was deeply appreciated.

— *Naming dementia.* As the phenomenological accounts and the subsequent theological reflections have disclosed, Christians living with dementia may find it difficult to acknowledge its impact in their lives. Other believers may not notice, understand, or wish to recognize the struggles and sadness that it is bringing.

— *Relationships with others.* These were clearly important in the faith activities in which participants were involved, and were a means of providing mutual support, for example: church services and other activities, "home groups" for prayer and Bible engagement. In this research, for those who were married, the partnership was providing significant spiritual support. For those who lived alone, there were issues to be resolved about how the support of the community of faith could be enabled.

10. Hoggarth, *Seed and the* Soil, 145–47.
11. Barclay, "Psalm 88," 90.

- *Faith memory* was an important resource for funding faith, shaping participants' experience of faith in the present moment of their lives, and bringing hopefulness for the future. Experiences of God's past faithfulness were important for the present experience of God's dependability and love for them.

- *Spiritual growth* was evident in the lives of the participants within the context of dementia. It is also demonstrated in biographical writing, such as that of Bryden and Davis, and in the unique experience described in this research.[12] Some pastoral writing has begun to address this issue, for example, that of Collicutt, Crowther and Dunlop.[13]

- *Disorientation to reorientation.* Whilst the accounts of lived experience revealed the strong faith commitment and experience of the participants, these also disclosed the struggles and darkness that dementia was bringing to their lives. Their transforming faith was being enabled and characterized through the resources of their faith memory, through perception and acceptance of God's purpose, and trust in him, in the light of eschatological imagination. Their new orientation was being enabled by a sense of God's presence and within the context of the community of faith.

- *Re-framing of purpose*, rather than search for meaning, was evident in the lives of the research participants. It has also been shown to be significant for spiritual well-being in other writing, such as that of Bryden and Bute.[14] The participants' involvement in this study had been motivated by their desire to bring their unique insights towards transforming practice in the service of God and others. Their discovery of purpose in living with dementia questions the understanding and recognition of this within the community of faith.

- *Being hopeful.* A distinctive quality of these participants' experience of dementia was their hopefulness. Such hope is founded in the theological understandings of their Christ-centered faith. For the participants it was bringing assurance of forgiveness and hope of continuing life with God. Counterintuitively, this hopefulness was

12. Bryden, *Dancing with Dementia*; Davis, *My Journey into Alzheimer's Disease*.

13. Collicutt, *Thinking of You*; Crowther, *Sustaining Persons*; Dunlop, *Finding Grace*.

14. For example, as discussed earlier, Bryden and MacKinlay, "Dementia: A Journey Inwards," 134–44; Bute, "My Glorious Opportunity."

evident in their accounts, and was sustaining faith and transforming the lived experience of dementia in the present. In some ways, this resonates with MacKinlay and Trevitt's finding of hope in dementia.[15] However, this study has built on this further through its specifc focus on lived experience of committed Christians and theological exploration of faith in the evangelical tradition.

In concluding this section, I recognize that the experience of faith— and faith in dementia—is mysterious. Yet, even though it can't be explained, its effects were evident and bringing transformation to the lives of these people who were living with dementia. Their lived experience together with the theological reflections brings both insight and implications for how pastoral and ministerial practice, and theology might find re-orientation in the light of dementia.

Orienting to the Task

In the light of this research, Osmer's fourth task of Practical Theology now asks: How might we respond practically to the findings of this research?[16] What might it mean for the church to "participate faithfully in God's mission" in order to serve and bring Christ's love to Christians who are living with dementia?[17]

In the following, I focus on three areas highlighted at the beginning of the book (chapter 1) in the hoped-for outcomes of this research. The deeper understanding of the experience of Christians living with dementia through this study has brought new perspectives and challenge for practice and theology. In the following, I consider the implications and of this research and make suggestions for response in three areas: the church's response to those who live with dementia; challenge concerning their pastoral care and spiritual nurture; the potential for fresh theological understanding in the light of dementia. The following suggestions and recommendations arise out of the experience of this journey. My hope is that these will contribute to the response of God's people to this area of ministry.

---

15. MacKinlay and Trevitt, *Finding Meaning*, 151–70.
16. Osmer, *Practical Theology*, 4.
17. Swinton and Mowat, *Practical Theology*, 27.

The Response of the Church

St. Paul writes to the Corinthian church: "If one member suffers, all suffer together with it" (1 Cor 12:26a). Crowther, reflecting on this, speaks of the necessity of solidarity with one another as we suffer: "If our Christian convictions are to mean anything in suffering, it will be as they help us to see our lives, our narratives, located in God's narrative and community."[18] Whilst such solidarity was apparent in the experience of some of the participants, yet all of their accounts revealed, in different ways, incipient difficulties resulting from their dementia in some areas of the shared life of faith ("They don't understand," Rosemary). How, then, might the church respond to their members who live with early to moderate dementia?[19]

Recommendations: The Local Church

The qualitative research and the theological reflections have highlighted the need for the re-framing and re-orientating of practice within the community of faith, in the light of dementia. As the issues of dementia are increasingly recognized, I propose that the "climate" of believing communities, which may unintentionally stigmatise, objectify and exclude, be challenged. This might be achieved in some of the following ways.

- *Training and education* about faith in dementia, encouraging a positive perception of those living with this illness, and seeking ways of recognizing and enabling the expression of the gifts which they bring to the life of the church.

- *Advocacy* by those who live with dementia. In these early to moderate stages of dementia, some are willing and able to tell their stories (as participants in this research have done, and as seen in the work of Bryden and Bute).[20] This can bring understanding, affirm those who are living with dementia in a community of faith, and motivate loving, responsive action.

  Whilst participants in this particular study were positive about their faith experience in living with dementia, I am aware that there

---

18. Crowther, *Sustaining Persons*, 167.

19. Adams also begins to address this issue in *Developing Dementia-Friendly Churches*.

20. Bryden, *Dancing with Dementia*; Bute, "My Glorious Opportunity."

is a need to find ways of hearing the voices of those for whom their illness is bringing doubt in faith.

- *Practical theological engagement* in local churches with focus on: the nature of being a Christian who lives with dementia; being a community of faith to which those with dementia belong. How does a community's theology work out in practice?

- *Recognition of the sadness and struggle* that dementia is bringing to some members of a local congregation. Learning to name and express this grief, and to lament as a community "in solidarity" with the person with dementia and their families.

- *Addressing specific practical difficulties* which are affecting individuals' active participation in various ways. For example, not remembering where you were sitting after going to the front for communion (for example, Rosemary); arranging transport for someone who lives independently but still wants to come to a church service (for example, Alice can no longer drive); remembering those who are increasingly affected by issues of dementia, and whose absence from church activities may not be noticed.[21] There will be context-specific issues for which imaginative thinking and awareness can find solutions.

Recommendations: *The Wider Community of Faith, Denominational and Other Faith Organizations*

- *Ministerial and leadership training* which brings attention to the issue of spiritual care for those who are living with dementia, and enables development of strategies towards this end.

Faith Nurture in the Context of Dementia

St. Peter's injunction to the early believers—to keep on growing "in the grace and knowledge of our Lord and Saviour Jesus Christ" (2 Pet 3:18)—brings a double-edged challenge to the church. First, in the context of this book, there is the question of the ongoing faith growth for believers who

---

21. Mast, *Second Forgetting*, 105.

live with dementia ("I know Jesus, but . . . I long to know him more in my illness," Jill); second, there is challenge to other members of the church about their own growth in faith as the community learns to walk with those who live with dementia.

Bryden's work has highlighted the need for this mutuality of care which enables the spiritual growth of those living with dementia. A passionate advocate of growing faith throughout her journey with dementia, she has recognized her dependence on others in the body of Christ ("I need you to minister to me").[22] Crowther also makes an important point about such spiritual companionship: it is about "care partnerships rather than care being done to the person."[23] Such a view helps us to see what it might mean, in practice, that all parts of the body of Christ should have equal concern for one another (1 Cor 12:25).

In the light of the discussion of this book—my own experience, the lived experience, the theological reflections, and Scripture—how might the church disciple believers who live with dementia and nurture their continuing spiritual growth? Imaginative, empathic and creative response might enable the following.

Recommendations: In the Local Church/Faith Communities

- *Loving, purposeful accompaniment of individuals* who are encountering the disorientation of dementia. For example: through deliberate friendship (as illustrated in the co-working of MacKinlay and Bryden);[24] spiritual mentoring may also be a means of spiritual growth for those who are beginning this journey. This would enable, for example, a working through of the issues of reorientation, as discussed in chapter 9.

- *Bible-reading and prayer* with those who are living with dementia and no longer finding these practices easy to do individually. The development of the *Being with God* books were an attempt to provide a resource to encourage and enable this.[25]

---

22. Bryden and MacKinlay, "Dementia: A Spiritual Journey," 74.

23. Crowther, *Sustaining Persons*, 182.

24. Bryden and MacKinlay, "Dementia: A Journey Inwards," 134–44.

25. See Williams, *Words of Faith*; *Words of Hope*; *Words of Peace*.

- *Development of creative ways of using and building memories* as a resource for faith in the present, and in preparation for the future. For example, intentionally encouraging Scripture engagement, singing of Christian songs and hymns which bring into the present moment Christian teaching and experience (for example, "Music, songs . . . brings you into that peaceful sense of joy and happiness," Rosemary).

- *Being hope-ful* was characteristic of the participants' faith in dementia. Enabling expressions of this hope-ful faith can bring, and strengthen, faith experience in the present moment.

- *Encouragement and recording of the telling of faith stories* and experience, both as a resource for the person living with dementia, and as a resource for encouraging fellow believers in their own faith and in the ongoing support they are seeking to give.

- *Development of discipleship groups* in churches (or in a local area) which intentionally welcome those living with dementia. These would give opportunity for sharing of faith experiences, enable Bible engagement and prayer for one another, and mutual learning. These would contribute to the journey of reorientation discussed in chapter 9.

Recommendations: *The Wider Community of Faith, Denominational and Other Faith Organizations, Chaplaincy Teams in Care Homes and Hospitals*

- *Development of pastoral expertise* which understands and can focus on the particular needs of Christians who are beginning to live with dementia in a local community of faith. This might be achieved through ministerial, church leadership, and chaplaincy training.

- *Ongoing development of Bible, prayer and faith resources* which aim to enable the person living with dementia to continue to spend intentional time with God.[26] As well as resources aimed at facilitating individual devotional practice, development of group faith resources would enable the participation of those living with dementia in corporate faith activities. Recognition of this ministerial need requires

---

26. For example, Williams, *Words of Faith; Words of Hope; Words of Peace.*

ongoing commitment of Christian publishers and organizations to develop, and to find ways to fund such projects.[27]

New Perspectives for Theology

Alongside the pastoral concerns, the lived experience and reflections have also illuminated significant theological issues and questions. As Root has suggested, in "the lived nature of practical theology" *praxis* cannot be separated from theology.[28] There is a dialogical interplay between the two.

As stated in the Introduction, one of the outcomes envisaged at the beginning of my study was that it would bring further understanding to the theological issues raised by dementia. In particular, I have been concerned to show how this illness questions theological (and cultural) issues within the evangelical tradition. Addressing the theological implications is significant because theological assumptions inform our practice. Yet, this study has been exploring a *new* context within the community of faith. Lack of fresh theological engagement with these arising questions has potential to cause pain and bring discouragement to those facing the challenges of living with dementia (both the person with the illness and their loved-ones).

Building on the work of other theologians of dementia,[29] I contend that committed exploration of the theology of dementia, arising from the lived experience of this disease, can contribute to the faith experience of those living with this illness, and also that of their communities of faith. These issues are not only relevant to the spiritual support of those who live with dementia, but have wider significance for how the evangelical community understands its faith. Whether or not an individual lives with dementia, what is the nature of our faith and discipleship?

Arising from this study, I suggest that more focus is needed within the evangelical tradition towards biblical and theological understanding of the faith experience and practice of Christians who live with dementia. In the light of dementia, how can transformative, new theological understanding be brought to the church?

---

27. See my summary of the goals and outcomes for this research in chapter 1.

28. Root, *Christopraxis*, 34.

29. Such as Keck, *Forgetting Whose We Are*; Swinton, *Dementia*.

Recommendations

- *Development of practical theological expertise* pertaining to the new insights into faith brought by dementia, for example, through ministerial training and university research.

- *Development of theological education and training* which responds to the profound theological questions which dementia asks of evangelical theology, and of its resulting practice. *In the light of dementia*:

  — What does it means to be human, created by a loving and sovereign God?

  — What is the nature of "saving faith" and the Christian believer's reason for assurance of this?

  — What does it mean to be a disciple of Christ, whatever my particular capacities?

  — What does it mean to be a participant in the body of Christ?

  — What are the implications of collective memory of Scripture for the community of faith and its practices?

  — What is the nature of the Christian believer's hope and its impact in the present?

- *Development of ministerial and leadership training* to enable practical thinking about the above theological questions, in the light of the experience of dementia.

- *Provision of accessible theological education* at a local level for the community of faith (for example, through cross-city initiatives). Dialogical approaches to learning (for example, small group study and workshops) have potential to bring theological and biblical understanding of these questions.

  A contention of this book is that further understanding of these theological issues, deliberately pursued in the light of dementia has potential to affect pastoral practice in ways which will be significant for those who are living with dementia, and their communities of faith.

Limitations Deepening Focus

This book has sought to make a contribution to the area of inquiry. In light of the approach of hermeneutic phenomenology, the aim has been to further *understanding* of the faith experience of Christians living with dementia, "rather than to *explain* the experience."[30] As I have discussed in the methodological chapters, whilst the timescale and scope of a research project such as this brings some limitations, these have enabled the deepening of focus brought by this research, towards the outcomes discussed above.

My own situated-ness arising from my evangelical tradition has been an essential strength.[31] It has facilitated my empathic understanding of the participants' faith, a mutual sense of co-operation, and a shared sense of purpose. The purposeful sampling has allowed a strong focus on the book's topic through analysis of the participants' experience, and the arising theological reflections. In addition, this study has enabled reflection on the theology and practices of the evangelical tradition, relevant to the task of this book.

Towards transferability, I have looked for senses of identification and resonance with others experiencing and reflecting on similar situations. In line with the goals of Practical Theology highlighted by Swinton and Mowat, this book has raised issues and offered insight beyond the particularities of the situation investigated. In doing so, it "creates a resonance with people outside of the immediate situation who are experiencing phenomena which are not identical, but hold enough similarity to create a potentially *transformative resonance*."[32]

Further Research Possibilities

Patton suggests that "whilst one cannot generalize from . . . very small samples, one can learn a great deal, often opening up new territory for further research from them."[33] It is hoped that this book and its research have achieved this, opening up possibilities for further investigation in the following areas of practice and theology.

---

30. Swinton and Mowat, *Practical Theology*, 121.

31. Gadamer, *Truth and Method*, 303

32. Swinton and Mowat, *Practical Theology*, 47.

33. Patton, *Qualitative Research*, 46.

The Experience of Evangelical Christian Faith in Dementia

- Further investigation of the implications of this study for evangelical theology and biblical hermeneutics.

- Development of a strategy which would enable research with Christians for whom dementia has had a negative impact on their faith.

- Investigation of the difference "couplehood" brings to the faith experience for Christian believers who live with dementia, in comparison with those who are living alone.[34]

- Further development of pastoral practices and faith resources which can support the spiritual lives of Christians living with dementia. For example, the testing of new approaches to Bible engagement and prayer, the development of spiritual mentoring of those in early to moderate stages of dementia.

- Development of strategies which enable the Christian living with early to moderate dementia to be prepared and resourced spiritually for the more advanced stages of their illness.

- Exploration of mutual, dialogical learning between the evangelical faith tradition and Christians of other faith traditions with regard to this issue.

Research Related to the Experience of Other Faiths

- Exploration of the resonance between the spiritual experience of other faiths and that of the Christian faith whilst living with dementia. What mutual learning is possible through such resonance?

Broader Relevance to Societal Needs

- Investigation into how the significance of the spiritual dimension for those living with dementia is acknowledged in public policy and professional practice documents.

---

34. Hellström, "'I'm His Wife Not His Carer!,'" 53–66.

Closing

In this final chapter of the book, the hermeneutical circle of this conversation comes to a close. I have sought to show the ways in which the study has brought fresh insights into the experience and practice of Christians from the evangelical tradition who are living with early to moderate symptoms of dementia. I have also suggested strategies for how the community of faith might respond to its findings.

My own understanding has been challenged and developed as I have listened to those living with dementia, and dwelt with their lived experience in a variety of ways over the period of thesis- and book-writing. This investigation into the nature and experience of faith in dementia has questioned my own pre-suppositions about what it means to have faith as a Christian from the evangelical tradition. It has confirmed for me the crucial importance of being attentive to the faith experience of those who live with dementia, and has inspired my own search for ways in which to nurture faith and receive the gifts of faith which they are bringing to the church.

This book has sought to bring fresh perspectives regarding the significance of the spiritual lives of Christians living with dementia. It has raised significant questions of theological and biblical understanding for evangelical faith. It brings challenge to the evangelical community of faith to consider appropriate ministerial, pastoral and theological response in this new context of living with dementia.

Now, at the end of this writing process, the book leads to the further task and challenge of practical theology: to find "lived-out" ways of responding to its hoped-for outcomes, in ways which have potential to bring transformation to the practice of the community of faith, as it participates in the loving and purposeful mission of God. In concluding this book, I am challenged and moved as I recollect words from Jess's poem which she composed with Andrew's help:

> I only have Now . . . Lost past, No tomorrow, ONLY NOW. . . .
> What a privilege because . . . Today is the day of salvation.

Bibliography

Adams, Trevor. *Developing Dementia-Friendly Churches*. Cambridge: Grove, 2018.

Alzheimer's Research UK. "Facts and Stats." Online. http://www.alzheimersresearchuk. org/about-dementia/facts-stats.

Alzheimer's Society. "End of Life Care." Online. https://www.alzheimers.org.uk/about-dementia/symptoms-and-diagnosis/how-dementia-progresses/progression-alzheimers-disease.

———. "The Progression of Alzheimer's Disease." Online. https://alzheimers.org. uk/about-dementia/symptoms-and-diagnosis/how-dementia-progresses/progression-alzheimers-disease.

———. "Types of Dementia." Online. https://www.alzheimers.org.uk/info/20007/types_of_dementia.

Allen, F. Brian, and Peter G. Coleman. "Spiritual Perspectives on the Person with Dementia: Identity and Personhood." In *Dementia: Mind, Meaning, and the Person*, edited by Julian C. Hughes et al., 205–21. Oxford: Oxford University Press, 2006.

Anderson, Ray S. *On Being Human: Essays in Theological Anthropology*. Grand Rapids, MI: Eerdmans, 1982.

———. *Spiritual Caregiving as Secular Sacrament: A Practical Theology for Professional Caregivers*. London: Jessica Kingsley, 2003.

Aquinas, Thomas. *Summa Theologica*. Translated by Fathers of the English Dominican Province. 2nd rev. ed. London: Burns, Oates and Washbourne, 1922.Online. http://oll.libertyfund.org/titles/1982.

Ashworth, Peter. "Presuppose Nothing! The Suspension of Assumptions in Phenomenological Psychological Methodology." *Journal of Phenomenological Psychology* 27 (1996) 1–25. https://doi.org/10.1163/156916296X00014.

Augustine. *The City of God*. Documenta Catholica Omnia. Online. https://www. documentacatholicaomnia.eu/03d/0354-0430,_Augustinus,_De_Civitate_Dei_Contra_Paganos,_EN.pdf.

———. *Confessions*. Translated by Henry Chadwick. London: Oxford University Press, 2008.

————. *Enchiridion: On Faith, Hope, and Love*. Translated by Albert C. Outler. Philadelphia: Westminster, 1955. Online. http://www.tertullian.org/fathers/augustine_enchiridion_02_trans.htm.

————. *On Genesis: Two Books on Genesis: Against the Manichees and on the Literal Interpretation of Genesis: An Unfinished Book*. Translated by Roland J. Teske. Washington, DC: Catholic University of America Press, 2001.

Barclay, Aileen. "Psalm 88: Living with Alzheimer's." *Journal of Religion, Disability & Health* 16.1 (2012) 88–101. https://doi.org//10.1080/15228967.2012.645607.

Barrier, Roger. "Five Things You Have to Believe to Be a Christian." *Crosswalk*, April 27, 2017. Online. https://www.crosswalk.com/church/pastors-or-leadership/ask-roger/5-things-you-have-to-believe-to-be-a-christian.html.

Barth, Karl. *Church Dogmatics*. Edited by G. W. Bromiley and T. F. Torrance. Translated by G. W. Bromiley et al. Edinburgh: T&T Clark, 1936–1962.

————. "The New World in the Bible." In *The Word of God and Theology*, by Karl Barth, 15–30. Translated by Amy Marga. London: Bloomsbury, 2011.

Bartlett, Helen, and Wendy Martin. "Ethical Issues in Dementia Care Research." In *The Perspectives of People with Dementia: Research Methods and Motivations*, edited by Heather Wilkinson, 47–61. London: Jessica Kingsley, 2002.

Bayley, John. *Iris: A Memoir of Iris Murdoch*. London: Duckworth, 1998.

Bebbington, David W. "Evangelical Trends, 1959–2009." *Anvil* 26.2 (2009) 93–106.

————. *Evangelicalism in Modern Britain: A History from the 1730s to the 1930s*. London: Routledge, 1988.

Beuscher, Linda, and Cornelia Beck. "A Literature Review of Spirituality in Coping with Early-Stage Alzheimer's Disease." *Journal of Clinical Nursing* 17.5A (2008) 88–97. https://doi.org/10.1111/j.1365-2702.2007.02126.x.

Beuscher, Linda, and Victoria E. Grando. "Using Spirituality to Cope With Early-Stage Alzheimer's Disease." *Western Journal of Nursing Research* 31.5 (2009) 583–98. https://doi.org/10.1177/0193945909332776.

Boell, Sebastian K., and Dubravka Cecez-Kecmanovic. "A Hermeneutic Approach for Conducting Literature Reviews and Literature Searches." *Communications of the Association for Information Systems* 34.12 (2014) 257–87.

Bollnow, Otto Friedrich. "The Objectivity of the Humanities and the Essence of Truth." *Philosophy Today* 18.1 (1974) 3–18. https://doi.org/10.5840/philtoday197418124.

Bonhoeffer, Dietrich. *The Cost of Discipleship*. London: SCM, 1959.

Bosch, David J. *Transforming Mission: Paradigm Shifts in Theology of Mission*. Maryknoll, NY: Orbis,1991.

Bourdieu, Pierre. *Outline of a Theory of Practice*. Translated by Richard Nice. Cambridge: Cambridge University Press, 1977.

Briggs, Richard S. "The Bible Before Us: Evangelical Possibilities for Taking Scripture Seriously." In *New Perspectives for Evangelical Theology: Engaging with God, Scripture and the World*, edited by Tom Greggs, 14–28. London: Routledge, 2010.

Brock, Brian, and John Swinton. *Disability and the Christian Tradition: A Reader*. Grand Rapids, MI: Eerdmanns, 2012.

Brockmeier, Jens. *Beyond the Archive: Memory, Narrative, and the Autobiographical Process*. Oxford: Oxford University Press, 2015.

————. "Questions of Meaning: Memory, Dementia, and the Postautobiographical Perspective." In *Beyond Loss: Dementia, Identity, and Personhood*, edited by Lars C. Hydén et al., 69–90. Oxford: Oxford University Press, 2014.

Browning, Don. "Pastoral Theology in a Pluralistic Age." In *The Blackwell Reader in Pastoral and Practical Theology*, edited by James Woodward and Stephen Pattison, 89–103. Oxford: Blackwell, 2000.

Brueggemann, Walter. *Praying the Psalms: Engaging Scripture and the Life of the Spirit.* 2nd ed. Eugene, OR: Cascade, 2007.

———. *Redescribing Reality: What We Do When We Read the Bible.* London: SCM, 2009.

———. *Spirituality of the Psalms.* Minneapolis, MN: Augsburg Fortress, 2002.

———. "Suffering Produces Hope." *Biblical Theology Bulletin: Journal of Bible and Culture* 28.3 (1998) 95–103. https://doi.org/10.1177/014610799802800302.

———. *Texts Under Negotiation: The Bible and Postmodern Imagination.* Minneapolis, MN: Fortress,1993.

———. *An Unsettling God: The Heart of the Hebrew Bible.* Minneapolis, MN: Fortress, 2009.

Bryden, Christine. *Dancing with Dementia: My Story of Living Positively with Dementia.* London: Jessica Kingsley, 2005.

———. "A Spiritual Journey into the I-Thou Relationship: A Personal Reflection on Living with Dementia." *Journal of Religion, Spirituality & Aging* 28.1–2 (2016) 7–14. https://doi.org/10.1080/15528030.2015.1047294.

Bryden [Boden], Christine. *Who Will I Be When I Die?* London: Jessica Kingsley, 2012.

Bryden, Christine, and Elizabeth MacKinlay. "Dementia: A Journey Inwards to a Spiritual Self." In *Ageing, Disability and Spirituality*, edited by Elizabeth MacKinlay, 134–44. London: Jessica Kingsley, 2008.

———. "Dementia: A Spiritual Journey Towards the Divine: A Personal View of Dementia." *Journal of Religious Gerontology* 13.3–4 (2003) 69–75. https://doi.org/10.1300/J078v13n03_05.

Buber, Martin. *I and Thou.* Edinburgh: T&T Clark, 1958.

Bute, Jennifer. "My Glorious Opportunity: How My Dementia Has Been a Gift." *Journal of Religion, Spirituality and Aging* 28 (2016) 15–23. https://doi.org:10.1080/1552 8030.2015.1047295.

Caring.com. "What You Should Know about Alzheimer's Disease." Online. https://www.caring.com/articles/stages-of-alzheimers.

Childs, Brevard S. *Memory and Tradition in Israel.* London: SCM, 1962.

Chrétien, Jean-Louis. *The Ark of Speech.* Translated by Andrew Brown. Abingdon, Oxon: Routledge, 2004.

Clarke, Charlotte L., and John Keady. "Getting Down to Brass Tacks: A Discussion of Data Collection with People with Dementia." In *The Perspectives of People with Dementia: Research Methods and Motivations*, edited by Heather Wilkinson, 25–46. London: Jessica Kingsley, 2002.

Collicutt, Joanna. *Thinking of You: A Resource for the Spiritual Care of People with Dementia.* Abingdon, Oxon: Bible Reading Fellowship, 2017.

Congdon, David W., and Travis W. McMaken. "Ten Reasons Why Theology Matters." *Christianity Today*, October 27, 2016. Online. https://www.christianitytoday.com/ct/2016/october-web-only/ten-reasons-why-theology-matters.html.

Cotrell, Victoria, and Richard Schulz. "The Perspective of the Patient with Alzheimer's Disease: A Neglected Dimension of Dementia Research." *Gerontologist* 33.2 (1993) 205–11. https://doi.org/10.1093/geront/33.2.205.

Cranfield, C. E. B. *Romans: A Shorter Commentary.* Edinburgh: T&T Clark, 1985.

Crowther, Dianne. *Sustaining Persons, Grieving Losses: A Fresh Pastoral Approach for the Challenges of the Dementia Journey.* Eugene, OR: Cascade, 2017.

Crowther, Susan A. "Sacred Joy at Birth: A Hermeneutic Phenomenology Study." PhD diss., Aberdeen University, 2014.

Dalby, Padmaprabha, et al. "The Lived Experience of Spirituality and Dementia in Older People Living with Mild to Moderate Dementia." *Dementia* 11 (2012) 75–94. https://doi.org/10.1177/1471301211416608.

Davis, Robert. *My Journey into Alzheimer's Disease: Helpful Insights for Family and Friends.* Carol Stream, IL: Tyndale, 1989.

Denscombe, Martyn. *The Good Research Guide: for Small-Scale Social Research Projects.* Buckingham: Open University Press, 1998.

Denzin, Norman K., and Yvonna S. Lincoln. "Introduction: The Discipline and Practice of Qualitative Research." In *The Sage Handbook of Qualitative Research*, edited by Norman K. and Yvonna S. Lincoln, 1–32. 3rd ed. London: Sage, 2005.

Department of Health and Social Care (DHSC). "Equality Impact Assessment." February 3, 2009. Online. https://www.gov.uk/government/uploads/system/uploads/attachment_data/file/168222/dh_094054.pdf.

———. "Joint Declaration on Post-Diagnostic Dementia Care and Support." January 8, 2016. Online. https://www.gov.uk/government/publications/dementia-post-diagnostic-care-and-support.

———. "Living Well with Dementia: A National Dementia Strategy." February 3, 2009. Online. https://assets.publishing.service.gov.uk/government/uploads/system/uploads/attachment_data/file/168220/dh_094051.pdf.

Deusen-Hunsinger, Deborah van. *Theology and Pastoral Counselling: A New Interdisciplinary Approach.* Grand Rapids, MI: Eerdmans, 1995.

Dreyer, Jaco S. "Knowledge, Subjectivity, (De)Coloniality, and the Conundrum of Reflexivity." In *Conundrums in Practical Theology*, edited by Bonnie J. Miller-McLemore and Joyce Ann Mercer, 90–109. Leiden: Brill, 2016. https://doi.org/10.1163/9789004324244_006.

Dunlop, John. *Finding Grace in the Face of Dementia.* Wheaton, IL: Crossway, 2017.

Dunn, James D. G. *Romans 1–8.* Word Biblical Commentary 38A. Nashville, TN: Thomas Nelson, 1988.

Eastman, Susan. "Double Participation and the Responsible Self in Romans 5–8." In *Apocalyptic Paul: Cosmos and Anthropos in Romans 5–8*, edited by Beverly Roberts Gaventa, 93–110. Waco, TX: Baylor University Press, 2013.

Economic and Social Research Council (ESRC). "Framework for Research Ethics (FRE) (2010), Updated September 2012." Online. http://www.esrc.ac.uk/files/funding/guidance-for-applicants/esrc-framework-for-research-ethics-2010.

Erikson, Erik. *The Life Cycle Completed: Extended Version.* New York: Norton, 1997.

Finlay, Linda. "A Dance between the Reduction and Reflexivity: Explicating the 'Phenomenological Psychological Attitude.'" *Journal of Phenomenological Psychology* 39 (2008) 1–32.

———. *Phenomenology for Therapists: Researching the Lived World.* Hoboken, NJ: Wiley and Sons, 2011.

Finlay, Linda, and Ken Evans. *Relational-Centered Research for Psychotherapists: Exploring Meanings and Experience.* Chichester: Wiley-Blackwell, 2009.

Fitzmyer, Joseph. *Romans: A New Translation with Introduction and Commentary.* New Haven, CT: Yale University Press, 1993.

Fowler James W. *Stages of Faith: The Psychology of Human Development and the Quest for Meaning*. San Francisco: Harper, 1981.

Frankl, Viktor E. *Man's Search for Meaning*. New York: Washington Square, 1984.

Gadamer, Hans-Georg. *Truth and Method*. Translated by Joel Weinsheimer and Donald Marshal. 2nd. rev. ed. London: Continuum, 2004.

Gaventa, Beverley R. *Apocalyptic Paul: Cosmos and Anthropos in Romans 5–8*. Waco, TX: Baylor University Press, 2013.

———. "Which Human? What Response? A Reflection on Pauline Theology." *Ex Auditu: An International Journal of Theological Interpretation of Scripture* 30 (2014) 50–64.

Genova, Lisa. *Still Alice*. London: Simon & Schuster, 2009.

Giddens, Anthony. *Modernity and Self Identity: Self and Society in the Late Modern Age*. Cambridge: Polity, 1991.

Goffman, Erving. *Stigma: Notes on the Management of Spoiled Identity*. New York; London: Simon & Schuster, 1963.

Goldsmith, Malcolm. "Dementia: A Challenge to Christian Theology and Pastoral Care." In *Spirituality and Ageing*, edited by Albert Jewell, 125–35. London: Jessica Kingsley, 1998.

———. *Hearing the Voice of People with Dementia: Opportunities and Obstacles*. London: Jessica Kingsley, 1996.

———. *In a Strange Land . . . People with Dementia and the Local Church*. Southwell, Notts: 4M, 2004.

———. "Through a Glass Darkly." *Journal of Religious Gerontology* 12.3–4 (2002) 123–38. https://doi.org/10.1300/J078v12n03_10.

———. "Tracing Rainbows through the Rain: Addressing the Challenge of Dementia in Later Life." In *Ageing, Disability and Spirituality: Addressing the Challenge of Disability*, edited by Elizabeth MacKinlay, 118–33. London: Jessica Kingsley, 2008.

Gooder, Paula. *Body: Biblical Spirituality for the Whole Person*. London: SPCK, 2016.

Greggs, Tom. "Beyond the Binary: Forming Evangelical Eschatology." In *New Perspectives for Evangelical Theology: Engaging with God, Scripture and the World*, edited by Tom Greggs, 153–67. Abingdon, Oxon: Routledge, 2010.

———. "Introduction—Opening Evangelicalism: Towards a Post-Critical and Formative Theology." In *New Perspectives for Evangelical Theology: Engaging with God, Scripture and the World*, edited by Tom Greggs, 1–13. Abingdon, Oxon: Routledge, 2010.

———. *New Perspectives for Evangelical Theology: Engaging with God, Scripture and the World*. Abingdon, Oxon: Routledge, 2010.

Grenz, Stanley J. "The Social God and the Relational Self." In *Personal Identity in Theological Perspective*, edited by Richard Lints et al., 70–92. Grand Rapids, MI: Eerdmans, 2006.

Guba, Egon G., and Yvonna S. Lincoln. "Paradigmatic Controversies, Contradictions, and Emerging Confluences." In *The Sage Handbook of Qualitative Research*, edited by Norman Denzin and Yvonna S. Lincoln, 191–215. 3rd ed. London: Sage, 2005.

Gutiérrez, Gustavo. *A Theology of Liberation*. British ed. London: SCM, 1985.

Harris, Brian. "Beyond Bebbington: The Quest for Evangelical Identity in a Postmodern Era." *Churchman* 122.3 (2008) 201–19.

Hattam, Joy. "Mind the Gap." Unpublished paper, Ruskin College, 2007.

Hauerwas, Stanley. *A Community of Character: Toward a Constructive Christian Social Ethic*. Notre Dame, IN: University of Notre Dame Press, 1991.

————. *Cross-Shattered Christ: Meditations on the Seven Last Words.* Grand Rapids, MI: Brazos, 2011.

————. *Naming the Silences: God, Medicine, and the Problem of Suffering.* London: T&T Clark, 2004.

————. *The Peaceable Kingdom: A Primer in Christian Ethics.* Notre Dame, IN: University of Notre Dame Press, 1983.

————. "Seeing Darkness, Hearing Silence: Augustine's Account of Evil." In *Naming Evil, Judging Evil,* edited by Ruth W. Grant, 35–52. Chicago: University of Chicago Press, 2006.

Heidegger, Martin. *Being and Time.* Translated by John Macquarrie and Edward Robinson. Oxford: Blackwell, 1962.

————. *Introduction to Metaphysics.* Translated by G. Fried and R. Polt. New Haven, CT: Yale University Press, 2000.

Hellström, Ingrid. "'I'm His Wife Not His Carer!'—Dignity and Couplehood in Dementia." In *Beyond Loss: Dementia, Identity and Personhood,* edited by Lars C. Hydén et al., 53–66. Oxford: Oxford University Press, 2014.

Herth, Kaye. "Fostering Hope in Terminally-Ill People." *Journal of Advanced Nursing* 15 (1990) 1250–59.

Heuser, Stefan. "The Human Condition as Seen from the Cross: Luther and Disability." In *Disability and the Christian Tradition,* edited by Brian Brock and John Swinton, 184–215. Grand Rapids, MI: Eerdmans, 2012.

Higgins, Patricia. "The Spiritual and Religious Needs of People with Dementia." *Catholic Medical Quarterly* 61.4 (2011) 24–29.

Hoggarth, Pauline. *The Seed and the Soil: Engaging with the Word of God.* Carlisle, Cumbria: Langham Global Library, 2011.

Hudson, Rosalie. "God's Faithfulness and Dementia: Christian Theology in Context." *Journal of Religion, Spirituality and Aging* 28 (2016) 50–67. https://doi.org/10.1080/15528030.2015.1041669.

Hughes, Julian C. "A Situated Embodied View of the Person with Dementia." In *Spirituality and Personhood in Dementia,* edited by Albert Jewell, 198–206. London: Jessica Kingsley, 2011.

Hughes, Julian C., et al. *Dementia: Mind, Meaning, and the Person.* Oxford: Oxford University Press, 2006.

Hull, John. "Spiritual Development: Interpretations and Applications." *British Journal of Religious Education* 24.3 (2002) 171–82. https://doi.org/10.1080/0141620020240302.

Hunsinger, George. *How to Read Karl Barth: The Shape of His Theology.* Oxford: Oxford University Press, 1993.

Husserl, Edmund. *Ideas Pertaining to Pure Phenomenology and to a Phenomenological Philosophy.* Translated by F. Kersten. The Hague: Kluwer Academic, 1983.

————. *Logical Investigations.* Vol. 1. Translated by J. N. Findlay. London: Routledge, 2001.

Iacono, Valeria Lo, et al. "Skype as a Tool for Qualitative Research Interviews." *Sociological Research Online* 21.2 (2016) 1–15. https://doi.org/10.5153/sro.3952.

Jenson, Robert. "Nihilism: Sin, Death, and the Devil." *Newsletter: Report from the Center for Catholic and Evangelical Theology,* Summer 1998, 4.

Jewell, Albert. *Ageing, Spirituality and Well-Being.* London: Jessica Kingsley, 2004.

————. *Spirituality and Ageing.* London: Jessica Kingsley, 1998.

————. *Spirituality and Personhood in Dementia*. London: Jessica Kingsley, 2011.

Jolley, David, et al. "Spirituality and Faith in Dementia." *Dementia* 9.3 (2010) 311–25. https://doi.org./10.1177/1471301210370645.

Katsuno, Towako. "Personal Spirituality of Persons with Dementia: Is It Related to Perceived Quality of Life?" *Dementia* 2.3 (2003) 315–35. https://doi.org/10.1177/14713012030023003.

Keck, David. *Forgetting Whose We Are: Alzheimer's Disease and the Love of God*. Nashville: Abingdon, 1996.

Kent, Elizabeth. "Embodied Evangelicalism: The Body of Christ and the Christian Body." In *New Perspectives for Evangelical Theology: Engaging with God, Scripture and the World*, edited by Tom Greggs, 108–37. Abingdon, Oxon: Routledge, 2010.

Kevern, Peter. "Alzheimer's and the Dementia of God." *International Journal of Public Theology* 4 (2010) 237–53. https://doi.org/10.1163/156973210X491895.

————. "Dementia and Spirituality: The Current State of Research and its Implications." *Royal College of Psychiatrists* 6 (2013). Online. https://www.rcpsych.ac.uk/pdf/Peter%20Kevern%20Dementia%20and%20Spirituality.pdf.

————. "I Pray that I Will Not Fall over the Edge." *Practical Theology* 4.3 (2011) 283–94. https://doi.org/10.1558/prth.v4i3.283.

————. "In Search of a Theoretical Basis for Understanding Religious Coping: Initial Testing of an Explanatory Model." *Mental Health, Religion & Culture* 15.1 (2012). Online. https://doi.org/10.1080/13674676.2010.550278.

————. "Sharing the Mind of Christ: Preliminary Thoughts on Dementia and the Cross." *New Blackfriars* 91.1034 (2010) 408–22. https://doi.org/10.1111/j.1741-2005.2009.01317.x.

————. "The Spirituality of People with Late-Stage Dementia: a Review of the Research Literature, a Critical Analysis and Some Implications for Person-Centered Spirituality and Dementia Care." *Mental Health, Religion & Culture* 18.9 (2015) 765–76. https://doi.org/10.1080/13674676.2015.1094781.

————. "What Sort of a God Is to Be Found in Dementia? A Survey of Theological Responses and an Agenda for Their Development." *Theology* 113.873 (2010) 174–82. https://doi.org/10.1177/0040571X1011300303.

Kilby, Karen. "Perichoresis and Projection: Problems with Social Doctrines of the Trinity." *New Blackfriars* 81.956 (2000) 432–45. https://doi.org/10.1111/j.1741-2005.2000.tb06456.x.

Kitwood, Tom. *Dementia Reconsidered: The Person Comes First*. Maidenhead: Open University Press, 1997.

Koch, Tina. "Story Telling: Is It Really Research?" *Journal of Advanced Nursing* 28:6 (1998) 1182–90.

Kontos, Pia C. "Alzheimer Expressions or Expressions Despite Alzheimer's? Philosophical Reflections on Selfhood and Embodiment." *Occasion: Interdisciplinary Studies in the Humanities* 4 (2012) 1–12.

Kontos, Pia C., and Gary Naglie. "Expressions of Personhood in Alzheimer's Disease: An Evaluation of Research-Based Theatre as a Pedagogical Tool." *Qualitative Health Research* 17.6 (2007) 799–811. https://doi.org/10.1177/1049732307302838.

————. "Tacit Knowledge of Caring and Embodied Selfhood." *Sociology of Health & Illness* 31.5 (2009) 688–704. https://doi.org/10.1111/j.1467-9566.2009.01158.x/full.

Kuhse, Helga, and Peter Singer. *Should the Baby Live?: The Problem of Handicapped Infants*. Oxford: Oxford University Press, 1985.

Lange, Frits de. "Deterritoralizing Dementia: A Review Essay of John Swinton's *Dementia: Living in the Memories of God.*" *Health and Social Care Chaplaincy* 4.2 (2016) 168–79. https://doi.org/10.1558/hscc.v4i2.31325.

Lartey, Emmanuel. "Practical Theology as a Theological Form." In *The Blackwell Reader in Pastoral and Practical Theology*, edited by James Woodward and Stephen Pattison, 128–34.Oxford: Blackwell, 2000.

Leadbeater, Charles. "The Disremembered." *Aeon*, March 26, 2015. Online. https://aeon.co/essays/if-your-memory-fails-are-you-still-the-same-person.

Leininger, Madeleine. "Evaluation Criteria and Critique of Qualitative Research Studies." In *Critical Issues in Qualitative Research*, edited by Janice Morse, 95–116. Thousand Oaks, CA: Sage, 1994.

Locke, John. *Essay Concerning Human Understanding.* 1689. N.p.: Jonathan Bennett, 2017. Online. http://www.earlymoderntexts.com/assets/pdfs/locke1690book2.pdf.

Macadam, Jackie. "Interview with Mary Warnock: 'A Duty to Die?'" *Life and Work*, October 2008. 23–25.

MacKinlay, Elizabeth. *Ageing, Disability and Spirituality: Addressing the Challenge of Disability in Later Life.* London: Jessica Kingsley, 2008.

———. "The Spiritual Dimension of Ageing." In *Ageing, Spirituality and Well-Being*, edited by Albert Jewell, 72–85. London: Jessica Kingsley, 2004.

———. *The Spiritual Dimension of Ageing.* 2nd ed. London: Jessica Kingsley, 2017.

———. "Walking with a Person into Dementia: Creating Care Together." In *Spirituality, Personhood and Dementia*, edited by Albert Jewell, 42–51. London: Jessica Kingsley, 2011.

MacKinlay, Elizabeth, and Corinne Trevitt. *Finding Meaning in the Experience of Dementia: The Place of Spiritual Reminiscence Work.* London: Jessica Kingsley, 2012.

MacKinlay, Karen. "Listening to People with Dementia: A Pastoral Care Perspective." *Journal of Religious Gerontology* 13.3–4 (2003) 91–106. https://doi.org/10.1300/J078v13n03_07.

MacQuarrie, Colleen R. "Experiences in Early Alzheimer's Disease: Understanding the Paradox of Acceptance and Denial." *Aging & Mental Health* 9.5 (2005) 430–41. https://doi.org/10.1080/13607860500142853.

Magnusson, Sally. *Where Memories Go: Why Dementia Changes Everything.* London: Hodder & Stoughton, 2014.

Manen, Max van. *Phenomenology of Practice: Meaning-Giving Methods in Phenomenological Research and Writing.* Walnut Creek, CA: Left Coast, 2014.

———. *Researching Lived Experience: Human Science for an Action Sensitive Pedagogy.* Albany, NY: State University of New York, 1990.

Mast, Benjamin. *Second Forgetting: Remembering the Power of the Gospel during Alzheimer's Disease.* Grand Rapids, MI: Zondervan, 2014.

Matthews, Eric. "Dementia and the Identity of the Person." In *Dementia: Mind, Meaning, and the Person*, edited by Julian C. Hughes et al., 163–77. Oxford: Oxford University Press, 2006.

McFadden, Susan, et al. "Actions, Feelings, and Values: Foundations of Meaning and Personhood in Dementia." *Journal of Religious Gerontology* 11.3–4 (2001) 67–86. https://doi.org /10.1300/J078v11n03_0.

McFadyen, Donald. "Embodied Christianity." In *New Perspectives for Evangelical Theology: Engaging with God, Scripture and the World*, edited by Tom Greggs, 123–37. Abingdon, Oxon: Routledge, 2010.

McGrath, Alister. *Evangelicalism and the Future of Christianity.* London: Hodder & Stoughton, 1995.

McLeod, John. *Qualitative Research in Counselling and Psychotherapy.* 1st ed. London: Sage, 2001.

Merleau-Ponty, Maurice. *Phenomenology of Perception.* Translated by Colin Smith. London; New York: Routledge; Kegan Paul, 1962.

Moltmann, Jürgen. *The Crucified God.* London: SCM, 1974.

———. *The Trinity and the Kingdom of God.* London: SCM, 1981.

Moran, Dermot. *Introduction to Phenomenology.* Abingdon, Oxon: Routledge, 2000.

Moreland, James P., and Stan Wallace. "Aquinas versus Locke and Descartes on the Human Person and End-of-Life Ethics." *International Philosophical Quarterly* 35.3 (1995) 139.

Morse, Janice M. *Critical Issues in Qualitative Research.* Thousand Oaks, CA: Sage, 1994.

Osmer, Richard R. *Practical Theology: An Introduction.* Grand Rapids, MI: Eerdmans, 2008.

Paley, John. "Phenomenology as Rhetoric." *Nursing Inquiry* 12.2 (2005) 106–16. https://doi.org/10.1111/j.1440-1800.2005.00263.x.

Park, Hee-Kyu Heidi. "Towards a Pastoral Theological Phenomenology: Constructing a Reflexive and Relational Phenomenological Method from a Postcolonial Perspective." *Journal of Pastoral Theology* 24.1 (2014) 1–21. https://doi.org/10.1179/jpt.2014.24.1.003.

Pattison, Stephen. *A Critique of Pastoral Care.* 2nd ed. London: SCM, 1993.

———. "Some Straw for the Bricks: A Basic Introduction to Theological Reflection." In *The Blackwell Reader in Pastoral and Practical Theology,* edited by James Woodward and Stephen Pattison, 139–40. Oxford: Blackwell, 2000.

Patton, Michael Q. *Qualitative Research & Evaluation Methods.* 3rd ed. Thousand Oaks, CA: Sage, 2002.

Peace, Richard. *Conversion in the New Testament: Paul and the Twelve.* Grand Rapids, MI: Eerdmans, 1999.

Pippo, Alexander Ferrari di. "The Concept of Poiesis in Heidegger's *An Introduction to Metaphysics.*" *IWM Junior Visiting Fellows Conferences* 9.3 (2000) 1–33.

Post, Stephen G. "The Fear of Forgetfulness: A Grassroots Approach to an Ethics of Alzheimer's Disease." *Journal of Clinical Ethics* 9 (1997) 71–80.

———. *The Moral Challenge of Alzheimer Disease: Ethical Issues from Diagnosis to Dying.* 2nd ed. Baltimore: John Hopkins University Press, 2000.

———. "*Respectare*: Moral Respect for the Lives of the Deeply Forgetful." In *Dementia: Mind, Meaning, and the Person,* edited by Julian C. Hughes et al., 223–34. Oxford: Oxford University Press, 2006.

Pratt, Rebekah. "Nobody's Ever Asked How I Felt." In *The Perspectives of People with Dementia: Research Methods and Motivations,* edited by Heather Wilkinson, 165–82. London: Jessica Kingsley, 2002.

Psychology Ethics Committee (PEC), School of Psychology, University of Aberdeen. "Guidelines for Completion of Applications for Ethical Review of Research Projects." January 25, 2013. Online. www.abdn.ac.uk/psychology/documents/ethics/PEC5.00_notes.docx.

Ray, Marilyn. "The Richness of Phenomenology: Philosophic, Theoretic, and Methodologic Concerns." In *Critical Issues in Qualitative Research Methods,* edited by Janice Morse, 117–35. Thousand Oaks, CA: Sage, 1994.

Reinders, Hans S. *Disability, Providence, and Ethics: Bridging Gaps, Transforming Lives.* Waco, TX: Baylor University Press, 2014.

———. *Receiving the Gift of Friendship: Profound Disability, Theological Anthropology, and Ethics.* Grand Rapids, MI: Eerdmans, 2008.

Robinson, Elaine. "Should People with Alzheimer's Disease Take Part in Research?" In *The Perspectives of People with Dementia: Research Methods and Motivations*, edited by Heather Wilkinson, 101–7. London: Jessica Kingsley, 2002.

Root, Andrew. *Christopraxis: A Practical Theology of the Cross.* Minneapolis, MN: Fortress, 2014.

Sabat, Steven R. *The Experience of Alzheimer's Disease: Life through a Tangled Veil.* Oxford: Blackwell, 2001.

———. "Mind, Meaning, and Personhood in Dementia: The Effects of Positioning." In *Dementia: Mind, Meaning, and the Person*, edited by Julian C. Hughes et al., 287–302. Oxford: Oxford University Press, 2006.

Saga. "Dementia More Feared Than Cancer." May 14, 2016. Online. https://newsroom. saga.co.uk/news/dementia-more-feared-than-cancer-new-saga-survey-reveals.

Sandelowski, Margarete. "The Problem of Rigour in Qualitative Research." *Advances in Nursing Science* 8.3 (1986) 27–37.

Sapp, Stephen. "Living with Alzheimer's: Body, Soul and the Remembering Community." *Christian Century*, January 21, 1998. 54–60.

———. "Spiritual Care of People with Dementia and their Carers." In *Supportive Care for the Person with Dementia*, edited by Julian C. Hughes et al., 199–206. Oxford: Oxford University Press, 2010.

Saunders, James. *Dementia: Pastoral Theology and Pastoral Care.* Cambridge: Grove, 2002.

Schacter, Daniel. *Searching for Memory: The Brain, the Mind, and the Past.* New York: Basic, 1996.

Schleiermacher, Friedrich, D. E. *Christian Caring: Selections from Practical Theology.* Minneapolis, MN: Fortress, 1988.

Schultz, Phyllis R., and Affaf I. Meleis. "Nursing Epistemology: Traditions, Insights, Questions." *Image: Journal of Nursing Scholarship* 20.4 (1998) 217–21. https://doi. org/10.1111/j.1547-5069.1988.tb00080.x.

Scripture4All. "2Corinthians." Greek Interlinear Bible. Online. https://www. scripture4all.org/OnlineInterlinear/NTpdf/2co1.pdf.

———. "Romans 5." Greek Interlinear Bible. Online. https://www.scripture4all.org/ OnlineInterlinear/NTpdf/rom5.pdf.

Scripture Union International Council (SUIC). "Aims, Beliefs and Working Principles of Scripture Union." January 12, 2011. Online. https://issuu.com/scripture_ union_australia/docs/aims__beliefs__working_principles.

Shamy, Eileen. *A Guide to the Spiritual Dimension of Care for People with Alzheimer's Disease and Related Dementia: More than Body, Brain and Breath.* London: Jessica Kingsley, 2003.

Singer, Peter. *Practical Ethics.* 2nd ed. Cambridge: Cambridge University Press, 1993.

Smythe, Elizabeth, and Deborah Spence. "Re-Viewing Literature in Hermeneutic Research." *International Journal of Qualitative Methods* 11.1 (2012) 12–25. https:// doi.org/10.1177/160940691201100102.

Snyder, Lisa. "Satisfactions and Challenges in Spiritual Faith and Practice for Persons with Dementia." *Dementia* 2 (2003) 299–313. https://doi. org/10.1177/14713012030023002.

————. *Speaking Our Minds: What It's Like to Have Alzheimer's*. Rev. ed. Baltimore: Health Professions, 2009.

Spaemann, Robert. *Persons: The Difference between "Someone" and "Something."* Translated by Oliver O'Donovan. Oxford: Oxford University Press, 2017.

Stanley, Brian. *The Global Diffusion of Evangelicalism: The Age of Billy Graham and John Stott*. Nottingham: IVP, 2013.

Stott, John. "The Age of Dependence." *Christianity Magazine*, January 2010. Online. https://www.premierchristianity.com/Past-Issues/2010/January-2010/The-age-of-dependence.

————. *The Bible Speaks Today: The Message of Romans*. Nottingham: IVP, 1994.

Strong, James. "3820 *Leb*." In *Strong's Exhaustive Concordance of the Bible*. Nashville: Abingdon, 1890. Online. https://biblehub.com/hebrew/3820.htm.

Stuckey, Jon C. "Blessed Assurance: The Role of Religion and Spirituality in Alzheimer's Disease Caregiving and Other Significant Life Events." *Journal of Aging Studies* 15.1 (2001) 69–84. https://doi.org/10.1016/S0890-4065(00)00017-17.

Stuckey, Jon C., and Lisa P. Gwyther. "Dementia, Religion, and Spirituality." *Dementia* 2.3 (2003) 291–97. https://doi.org/10.1177/14713012030023001.

Summa, Michela, and Thomas Fuchs. "Self-Experience in Dementia." *Rivista Internazionale di Filosofia e Psicologia* 6.2 (2015) 387–405. https://doi.org/10.4453/rifp.2015.0038.

Swinton, John. *Becoming Friends of Time: Disability, Timefullness and Gentle Discipleship*. London: SCM, 2017.

————. *Dementia: Living in the Memories of God*. Grand Rapids, MI: Eerdmans, 2012.

————. *Raging with Compassion: Pastoral Responses to the Problem of Evil*. Grand Rapids, MI: Eerdmans, 2007.

————. "Reforming, Revisionist, Refounding: Practical Theology as Disciplined Seeing." *Reforming Practical Theology: The Politics of Body and Space, International Academy of Practical Theology Conference Series* 1 (2019) 5–12. Online. https://doi.org/10.25785/iapt.cs.v1io.46.

————. *Spirituality and Mental Health Care: Rediscovering a Forgotten Dimension*. London: Jessica Kingsley, 2001.

————. "What the Body Remembers: Theological Reflections on Dementia." *ABC Religion and Ethics*, June 26, 2013. Online. http://www.abc.net.au/religion/articles/2013/06/26/3790480.htm.2013.

————. "What's in a Name?: Why People with Dementia Might Be Better Off without the Language of Personhood." *International Journal of Practical Theology* 18.2 (2014) 234–47. https://doi.org/10.1515/ijpt-2014-0017.

Swinton, John, and Harriet Mowat. *Practical Theology and Qualitative Research*. London: SCM, 2006.

Tallis, Raymond. *Aping Mankind: Neuromania, Darwinitis and the Misrepresentation of Humanity*. London: Routledge, 2014.

Tornstam, Lars. *Gerotranscendence: Developmental Theory of Positive Aging*. New York: Springer, 2005.

Vanhoozer, Kevin J. *Is There a Meaning in This Text?* Grand Rapids, MI: Zondervan, 1998.

Volpe, Medi A. "Living the Mystery: Doctrine, Intellectual Disability, and Christian Imagination." *Journal of Moral Theology* 6.2 (2017) 87–102. Online. https://jmt.scholasticahq.com/article/11362.

Wallace, Daphne. "Maintaining a Sense of Personhood." In *Spirituality and Personhood in Dementia*, edited by Albert Jewell, 24–30. London: Jessica Kingsley, 2011.

Weil, Simone. *Waiting on God.* London: Routledge and Kegan Paul, 1951.

Westminster Assembly. "Westminster Shorter Catechism." July 28, 1648. *Centre for Reformed Theology and Apologetics.* Online. https://www.reformed.org/documents/wsc/index.html.

Whitman, Lucy. *People with Dementia Speak Out.* London: Jessica Kingsley, 2016.

Wilkinson, Heather. *The Perspectives of People with Dementia: Research Methods and Motivations.* London: Jessica Kingsley, 2002.

Williams, Patricia S. "Knowing God in Dementia: What Happens to Faith When You Can No Longer Remember?" *Journal of Health and Social Care Chaplaincy* 4.2 (2016) 1–16. https://doi.org/10.1558/hscc.v4i2.30960.

———. "What Happens to Faith When Christians Get Dementia? A Critical Exploration of How Dementia Affects the Faith Experience and Practice of Christians from the Evangelical Tradition Living with Mild to Moderate Symptoms of Dementia." PhD diss., University of Aberdeen, 2018.

Williams, Rowan. *Being Disciples: Essentials of Christian Life.* London: SPCK, 2016.

———. "The Person and the Individual: Human Dignity, Human Relationships and Human Limits." Fifth Annual Theos Lecture delivered at Methodist Central Hall, London, October 1, 2012. Online. https://www.theosthinktank.co.uk/research/2012/10/01/the-person-and-the-individual-human-dignity-human-relationships-and-human-limits.

Williams, Tricia. *Words of Faith.* Being with God: A Bible and Prayer Guide for People with Dementia. Milton Keynes: Scripture Union, 2010.

———. *Words of Hope.* Being with God: A Bible and Prayer Guide for People with Dementia. Milton Keynes: Scripture Union, 2010.

———. *Words of Peace.* Being with God: A Bible and Prayer Guide for People with Dementia. Milton Keynes: Scripture Union, 2010.

Williamson, Toby. *My Name Is Not Dementia.* London: Alzheimer's Society, 2010. Online. https://www.cardi.ie/userfiles/My_name_is_not_dementia_report%5B1%5D.pdf.

Wolverson (Radbourne), Emma L., et al. "Remaining Hopeful in Early-Stage Dementia: A Qualitative Study." *Aging & Mental Health* 14.4 (2010) 450–60. https://doi.org/10.1080/13607860903483110.

Woodward, James, and Stephen Pattison. *The Blackwell Reader in Pastoral and Practical Theology.* Oxford: Blackwell, 2000.

Wright, N. T. "Mind, Spirit, Soul and Body: All for One and One for All: Reflections on Paul's Anthropology in his Complex Contexts." Paper presented at the Society of Christian Philosophers, Fordham University, New York, March 18, 2011. Online. https://ntwrightpage.com/2016/07/12/mind-spirit-soul-and-body.

Wright, Tom. *Surprised by Hope.* London: SPCK, 2007.

Zahl, Simeon. "Reformation Pessimism or Pietist Personalism?: The Problem of the Holy Spirit in Evangelical Theology." In *New Perspectives for Evangelical Theology: Engaging with God, Scripture and the World,* edited by Tom Greggs, 78–92. Abingdon, Oxon: Routledge, 2010.

Zizioulas, John D. *Being as Communion: Studies in Personhood and the Church.* New York: St Vladimir's Seminary, 1985.

———. *Communion and Otherness: Further Studies in Personhood and the Church.* London: T&T Clark, 2006.

Index